D0838427

Asian Literature
in English

AMERICAN LITERATURE, ENGLISH LITERATURE, AND WORLD LITERATURES IN ENGLISH: AN INFORMATION GUIDE SERIES

Series Editor: Theodore Grieder, Curator, Division of Special Collections, Fales Library, New York University

Associate Editor: Duane DeVries, Associate Professor, Polytechnic Institute of New York, Brooklyn

Other books on world literatures in this series:

BLACK AFRICAN LITERATURE IN ENGLISH—*Edited by Bernth Lindfors*

AUSTRALIAN LITERATURE TO 1900—*Edited by Barry G. Andrews and William H. Wilde*

MODERN AUSTRALIAN POETRY, 1920-1970—*Edited by Herbert C. Jaffa*

MODERN AUSTRALIAN PROSE, 1901-1975—*Edited by A. Grove Day*

ENGLISH-CANADIAN LITERATURE TO 1900—*Edited by R.G. Moyles*

MODERN ENGLISH-CANADIAN POETRY—*Edited by Peter Stevens*

MODERN ENGLISH-CANADIAN PROSE—*Edited by Helen Hoy**

INDIAN LITERATURE IN ENGLISH, 1827-1979—*Edited by Amritjit Singh, Rajiva Verma, and Irene Joshi**

IRISH LITERATURE, 1800-1875—*Edited by Brian McKenna*

NEW ZEALAND LITERATURE TO 1977—*Edited by John Thomson*

SCOTTISH LITERATURE IN ENGLISH—*Edited by William Aitken**

AUTHOR NEWSLETTERS AND JOURNALS—*Edited by Margaret Patterson*

*in preparation

The above series is part of the
GALE INFORMATION GUIDE LIBRARY

The Library consists of a number of separate series of guides covering major areas in the social sciences, humanities, and current affairs.

General Editor: Paul Wasserman, Professor and former Dean, School of Library and Information Services, University of Maryland

Managing Editor: Denise Allard Adzigian, Gale Research Company

Ref.
SS

Asian Literature in English

A GUIDE TO INFORMATION SOURCES

*Volume 31 in the American Literature, English
Literature, and World Literatures in English
Information Guide Series*

G.L. Anderson

*Professor of English
University of Hawaii
Honolulu*

Universitas
BIBLIOTHECA
ttaviensis

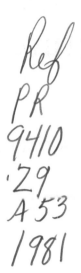

Ref
PR
9410
.Z9
A 53
1981

572294

Library of Congress Cataloging in Publication Data

Anderson, George Lincoln, 1920-
    Asian Literature in English.

    (American literature, English literature, and world
literatures in English ; v. 31) (Gale information guide
library)
    Includes index.
    1. Oriental literature (English)—Bibliography.
I. Title.
Z30001.A655 [PR9410]   016.895   80-23981
ISBN 0-8103-1362-6

Copyright © 1981 by
G.L. Anderson

No part of this book may be reproduced in any form without permission in
writing from the publisher, except by a reviewer who wishes to quote brief
passages or entries in connection with a review written for inclusion in a
magazine or newspaper. Manufactured in the United States of America.

For Kristin and Kristen
East and West

VITA

G.L. Anderson is professor of English at the University of Hawaii. He received his A.B., A.M., and Ph.D. at the University of Pennsylvania. He founded the Modern Language Association Conference on Oriental-Western Literary Relations and its newsletter, LITERATURE EAST & WEST, and has edited MASTERPIECES OF THE ORIENT (New York: W.W. Norton, 1977) and GENIUS OF THE ORIENTAL THEATER (New York: New American Library, 1966). His interests also include eighteenth-century English literature.

CONTENTS

Contents

Contents

Contents

Contents

INTRODUCTION

This volume is a guide to translations into English and to major scholarship and criticism in English of the literatures of East Asia. With the two much-studied and -translated literatures, Chinese and Japanese, the emphasis is on books, though a number of significant articles are included. With the other literatures, there has been more reliance on periodical material. Indian literature in English is treated in a separate volume in this Gale series (Singh, Verma, and Joshi, vol. 36, 1981).

In the last three decades there has been a renaissance of studies and translations of Far Eastern literature. Translations have appeared which combine scholarly exactness with grace and style, and modern technique of criticism have been brought to bear on Asian literature, so that a wealth of material is now available for the reader in English. Despite this, the material is encompassable. The number of specialists engaged in Asian studies is still few, and the total production of books and articles in a given year--in English--is not much greater than for Shakespeare alone in English literature. There is still much to be done, but the excellence of what has been achieved is apparent in the listings following.

Certain special problems in dealing with Asian literatures need explanation:

TRANSLITERATION. Over the years, systems of transliterating Asian languages written in characters into the Latin alphabet have been devised. The system called "Wade-Giles" has been used for many years for transliterating Chinese. This is a scientific system which works well enough, but it is not an adequate guide to the pronunciation of Chinese for the nonspecialist. Chou En-Lai, the late premier of China, is closer to being "Mr. Joe" than "Mr. Choo," and the true Tao rhymes more or less with "dow" as in "Dow-Jones." Readers who wish to discuss Chinese literature will be well advised to cultivate a civilized English version of Chinese pronunciation by consulting with a Chinese friend, and will find Chinese dictionaries unusable. Happily this bibliography appears at a time when almost all of the material to be listed follows the Wade-Giles system, which is also the system used for indexing Chinese names and titles used by the Library of Congress, and used below. A new, somewhat more scientific system has been devised, pin-yin. This is likely to be the system of the future, and is being adopted rapidly in most areas of Chinese studies, with literature perhaps last to change. A Chinese word or name in this new system may not be recognizable to the reader who does not read Chinese for its equivalent in Wade-Giles. (For an example of this see entry no. 549.) Further, there are variant systems of transliteration used in Europe. Examples of these have been noted where they are useful. The other languages either present few difficulties (like Japanese) or a single transliteration system has been agreed upon. Japanese long vowels are indicated by a macron. The chief popular variant which will be encountered is the use of oh for o, as in NO play or Noh play. I follow the Library of Congress systems of transliteration, since this is the system which the reader will encounter in most libraries, and where it is clearer, the usage of Jenner (see entry no. 1648) for Southeast Asia.

Literary works are listed under the original title in transliteration. This is necessary because the translator quite properly often uses an imaginative rendering of the title of the original, one calculated to catch the spirit of the work rather than to be a literal rendition. Thus the same work may be called, in English, WATER MARGIN or ALL MEN ARE BROTHERS.

PROPER NAMES. Many Asian writers adopt pen names. These are the names that appear in literary history and criticism and the names that I use for the main entry. Thus, Lu Hsun, whose "real" name was Chou Shu-Jen, is listed under "Lu." Variants of the pen name follow the main entry in brackets, and the "real" name follows in parentheses, as "Lu Hsun [Lu Xun] (Chou Shu-Jan)." The name and all the variants are included in the index. The reader is warned that the Library of Congress will put Lu Hsun under "Chou." Chinese names commonly contain two or three monosyllables, with the order reversed from the Western. Lu Hsun is Mr. Lu, and Lin Yutang is Mr. Lin, whether spelled Lin Yutang, Lin Yu Tang, or Lin Yu-Tang. Japanese names do not present similar difficulties, though it must be noted that library cataloging systems and literary history are at variance again. Soseki Natsume is discussed in literary history as Soseki; in the library catalog he will be found under "Natsume." The order of names for earlier Japanese writers is the same as for modern, but a comma has been inserted with the modern names. No general principles can be set down for names from Korea or Southeast and Central Asia. I follow the Library of Congress or Jenner. With Southeast Asian names, it is sometimes useful to give the writer's honorary title to identify him. Thus, with the two Burmese personages best known to the Western world, U Nu and U Win, the U is a title, and titles are indicated by underlining.

PERIODICALS. A list of periodicals devoted to more than one area of Asia is included at the end of section 1. Periodicals devoted to one area are listed at the end of the appropriate section. However, many nonspecialized periodicals (the ATLANTIC MONTHLY is an example) occasionally publish valuable criticism and translations of Asian literature. These articles are noted in their proper place but the journals are not listed. The periodicals lists are confined to journals where the reader may expect to find, regularly, studies and translations of literature.

THE INDEX. The main entry for each author is, as has been explained, under his pen name. Variants of this are indexed, as is his name at birth. The names of Western scholars, critics, and translators are indexed. The titles of Asian works in transliteration are indexed where this is important, and all of the various distinctive English titles of such works are indexed. Titles such as "The Poems of. . ." are indexed, but titles of scholarly and critical works are not unless they are by an author who is a main entry.

Though this work is dependent on a great many scholarly bibliographies, I must acknowledge a special debt to a colleague and to a former colleague at the University of Hawaii. The work of Philip Jenner, professor of Indo-Pacific languages at the University of Hawaii, on the bibliography of Southeast Asian literature is indispensible and remains unique for any worker in the field. I am also indebted to Norman Thorpe, formerly with the Asian Studies Program of the University of Hawaii and my former student, for much help with the Korean bibliography.

Chapter 1

FAR EAST

A. BIBLIOGRAPHY AND REFERENCE

1　Association for Asian Studies. BIBLIOGRAPHY OF ASIAN STUDIES.
1936--. Annual.

First published by the Far Eastern Association as BULLETIN OF
FAR EASTERN BIBLIOGRAPHY, ed. Earl Pritchard (Washington, D.C.: American Council of Learned Societies, 1936-
40); as BULLETIN OF FAR EASTERN BIBLIOGRAPHY, 1941-
45, and FAR EASTERN BIBLIOGRAPHY, 1946-55, in FAR
EASTERN QUARTERLY; and as BIBLIOGRAPHY OF ASIAN
STUDIES, 1956-- , by the Association of Asian Studies in
JOURNAL OF ASIAN STUDIES. Indispensable annual bibliog-
raphy of entire Far East, excluding South Asia, in all fields.
Divided by countries, and in later issues by subjects. Liter-
ary material may be found under "Philosophy" as well as
"Literature." Drama is usually included separately under the
"Fine Arts."

2　Beasley, W[illiam] G., and E.G. Pulleybank, eds. HISTORIANS OF
CHINA AND JAPAN. Oxford: Oxford Univ. Press, 1961.

Essays on Chinese and Japanese history and on historians.

3　Besterman, Theodore, ed. A WORLD BIBLIOGRAPHY OF ORIENTAL
BIBLIOGRAPHIES. Rev. by J.D. Pierson. New York: Rowman and
Littlefield, 1975.

Revised with additions from his WORLD BIBLIOGRAPHY OF
BIBLIOGRAPHIES, 1965. Very useful.

4　California, University of. Berkeley. East Asiatic Library. AUTHOR-
TITLE CATALOGUE. 13 vols. Boston: G.K. Hall, 1968; SUBJECT
CATALOGUE. 6 vols. Boston: G.K. Hall, 1968.

Guides to one of the nation's major collections.

5   Cressey, George B. ASIA'S LANDS AND PEOPLES. New York: McGraw-Hill Book Co., 1944.

    Standard account of the geographical bases for the cultures.

6   Gillian, Donald G., et al. EAST ASIA: A BIBLIOGRAPHY FOR UNDERGRADUATE LIBRARIES. Williamsport, Pa.: Bro-Dart, 1970.

7   Harvard University. Library. CHINA, JAPAN AND KOREA. Cambridge, Mass.: Harvard Univ. Press, 1968.

    Shelflist of the Widener Library holdings.

8   Hinton, Harold C., and Marius B. Jansen. MAJOR TOPICS ON CHINA AND JAPAN: A HANDBOOK FOR TEACHERS. [New York:] Institute of Pacific Relations, 1957.

    Good outline of the cultures, ancient and modern.

9   Kerner, Robert J., comp. NORTHEASTERN ASIA, A BIBLIOGRAPHY. Berkeley: Univ. of California Press, 1939.

10   Komroff, Manuel, ed. CONTEMPORARIES OF MARCO POLO. New York: Liveright, 1928.

    Accounts by medieval European travelers to Asia.

11   Lach, Donald F. ASIA IN THE MAKING OF EUROPE. 2 vols in 5. Chicago: Univ. of Chicago Press, 1965-77.

    Detailed scholarly history of the contacts between all of Asia and all of Europe from the Renaissance. "Literary Arts," vol. II, part 3. Vol. I is in 2 vols.; vol. II in 3 vols.

12   Moore, Charles A., ed. PHILOSOPHY EAST AND WEST. Princeton: Princeton Univ. Press, 1944.

    Essays on Asian and Western ways of thinking.

13   Northrup, F.S.C. THE MEETING OF EAST AND WEST: AN INQUIRY CONCERNING WORLD UNDERSTANDING. New York: Macmillan, 1960.

    Influential, controversial work contrasting Asian and Western ways of thinking.

14   Nunn, G[odfrey] Raymond, comp. ASIA, A SELECTED AND UNANOTATED GUIDE TO REFERENCE WORKS. Cambridge: MIT Press, 1971.

    Especially good annotations.

15   Olschki, Leonardo. MARCO POLO'S PREDECESSORS. Baltimore:
      Johns Hopkins Univ. Press, 1943.

      Brief survey by an eminent medievalist of the knowledge of
      Asia in medieval Europe.

16   Philips, C.H., ed. HANDBOOK OF ORIENTAL HISTORY. London:
      Royal Historial Society, 1951.

      Much useful background material for Asian history.

17   Reischauer, Edwin O., and John K. Fairbank. EAST ASIA: THE
      GREAT TRADITION. Vol. I of A HISTORY OF EAST ASIAN CIVILIZA-
      TION. Boston: Houghton Mifflin Co., 1960.

      Best available history of the area. Includes China, Japan,
      and Korea.

18   Silberman, Bernard S., comp. JAPAN AND KOREA: A CRITICAL
      BIBLIOGRAPHY. Tucson: Univ. of Arizona Press, 1962.

      Good introductory material and annotations. A most useful
      guide for beginners.

19   Spencer, Joseph. ASIA EAST BY SOUTH: A CULTURAL GEOGRAPHY.
      New York: John Wiley, 1954.

      Especially good on racial and linguistic distribution of the
      peoples of Asia.

B. LITERATURE—ANTHOLOGIES

20   Anderson, G[eorge] L., ed. GENIUS OF THE ORIENTAL THEATER.
      New York: New American Library, 1966.

      Translations of two Sanskrit plays, five Japanese no plays, and
      two kabuki plays. Full annotations.

21   _____. MASTERPIECES OF THE ORIENT, EXPANDED EDITION. New
      York: W.W. Norton and Co., 1977.

      Large anthology of selections in conservative translations of
      Islamic, Indic, Chinese, and Japanese literature, prose, and
      poetry. Introductions and notes. Shorter version published
      as MASTERPIECES OF THE ORIENT, 1961.

22   Brandon, James R., ed. TRADITIONAL ASIAN PLAYS. New York:
      Hill and Wang, 1972.

      Indian, Japanese, Chinese, and Thai plays in careful translations designed for Western production. Good introduction and notes.

23 Chin, Frank, et al., eds. AIIIEEEEE! AN ANTHOLOGY OF ASIAN-AMERICAN WRITINGS. Garden City, N.Y.: Doubleday, 1974.

Good collection of "ethnic" writers.

24 Courlander, Harold, ed. THE TIGER'S WHISKER AND OTHER TALES AND LEGENDS FROM ASIA AND THE PACIFIC. New York: Harcourt, Brace and Co., 1959.

25 Cultural and Social Centre for the Asian and Pacific Region, Asian and Pacific Council [Seoul]. ASIAN AND PACIFIC SHORT STORIES. Rutland, Vt.: Charles E. Tuttle Co., 1974.

Contains selections from Asia, the Pacific area, and from Australia and New Zealand.

26 Feinberg, Leonard, ed. ASIAN LAUGHTER: AN ANTHOLOGY OF ORIENTAL SATIRE AND HUMOR. New York: Weatherhill, 1971.

Large collection of a little-studied area of literature.

27 French, Joseph Lewis, ed. LOTUS AND CHRYSANTHEMUM: AN ANTHOLOGY OF CHINESE AND JAPANESE POETRY. New York: Boni and Liveright, 1934.

Important collection for its time (first published 1928). Much of it has been superseded by more modern translations.

28 Garnett, Wilma Leslie, ed. LITERATURE OF OTHER LANDS: ASIA. Evanston, Ill.: Harper and Row, 1965.

A good collection aimed at the high-school level.

29 Hanrahan, Gene Z., ed. 50 GREAT ORIENTAL STORIES. New York: Bantam Books, 1965.

Very useful. Includes material from Southeast Asia.

30 Irwin, Vera R., ed. FOUR CLASSICAL ASIAN PLAYS. Baltimore: Penguin Books, 1972.

An Indian, a Chinese, and two Japanese plays. Good translations and notes.

31 José, F. Sionil, ed. ASIAN P. E. N. ANTHOLOGY. New York: Taplinger, 1966.

Excellent collection of writers from all over Asia.

32   Liu Wu-Chi, et al., eds. K'UEI HSING: A REPOSITORY OF ASIAN
LITERATURE IN TRANSLATION. Bloomington: Indiana Univ. Press,
1974.

Prose and poetry. Large, useful collection from Chinese,
Japanese, Mongolian, and Tibetan.

33   Miller, James E., Robert O'Neal, and Helen M. McDonnell, eds.
LITERATURE OF THE EASTERN WORLD. Glenview, Ill.: Scott,
Foresman Co., 1970.

Prose and poetry. Ranges from the Ancient Near East to
China and Japan. Designed for high school use.

34   Milton, Daniel, and William Clifford, eds. TREASURY OF MODERN
ASIAN STORIES. New York: New American Library, 1961.

Good selection. Includes material from Southeast Asia.

35   Shimer, Dorothy Blair, ed. THE MENTOR BOOK OF MODERN ASIAN
LITERATURE. New York: New American Library, 1969.

Prose and poetry. A superior collection with good notes.

36   _____. VOICES OF MODERN ASIA. New York: New American
Library, 1973.

Stories, poems, and essays. A good survey. Includes India,
Pakistan, and Vietnam.

37   Stryk, Lucien, Ikemoto Takashi, and Takayama Taigan, trans. ZEN
POEMS OF CHINA AND JAPAN. Garden City, N.Y.: Doubleday,
1973.

Unusual selection. Good introduction on Zen in poetry.

38   Wells, Henry Willis, comp. ANCIENT POETRY FROM CHINA,
JAPAN, AND INDIA. Columbia: Univ. of South Carolina Press,
1968.

Large selection in very readable translations.

39   Wigmore, Lionel, ed. SPAN: AN ADVENTURE IN ASIAN AND
AUSTRALIAN WRITING. Melbourne: F.W. Cheshire, 1958.

Prose and poetry. A good modern selection.

40   Yohannan, John D., ed. A TREASURY OF ASIAN LITERATURE. New
York: John Day, 1956.

Poetry and prose from the Near East, China, and Japan.
Mostly sacred material.

C. LITERARY HISTORY AND CRITICISM

41   Blyth, R.H. ORIENTAL HUMOUR. Tokyo: Hokuseido Press, 1959.

Entertaining discussion of humor in China, Japan, and Korea. Many poetical examples.

42   _____. ZEN IN ENGLISH LITERATURE AND ORIENTAL CLASSICS. Tokyo: Hokuseido Press, 1942.

Much valuable material. The connections with English examples are often subjective.

43   Bowers, Faubion. THEATRE IN THE EAST: A SURVEY OF ASIAN DANCE AND DRAMA. New York: Grove Press, 1960.

A report on theatrical activities in almost every Asian country, including Hong Kong and Okinawa.

44   Brandon, James R. BRANDON'S GUIDE TO THEATER IN ASIA. Honolulu: Univ. of Hawaii Press, 1976.

Very useful. By a professor of drama who is also a theater director and actor.

45   Campbell, Joseph. THE MASKS OF GOD: ORIENTAL MYTHOLOGY. New York: Viking Press, 1971.

Analysis of Oriental mythology by the leading expert in the field.

46   Ceadel, Eric B., ed. LITERATURES OF THE EAST, A SURVEY. New York: Grove Press, 1959.

Excellent brief surveys of the literatures of the Near East, China, and Japan.

47   Christy, Arthur, ed. THE ASIAN LEGACY AND AMERICAN LIFE. New York: John Day, 1945.

Essays on all aspects of cultural relations.

48   _____. THE ORIENT IN AMERICAN TRANSCENDENTALISM. New York: Columbia Univ. Press, 1932.

Mostly on Indian influences, but some Far Eastern references.

49   Davis, A.R. SEARCH FOR IDENTITY: MODERN LITERATURE AND THE CREATIVE ARTS IN ASIA. Sydney: Angus and Robertson, 1974.

Critical study of the problems of modern literature and art in Asia.

50   DeBary, William T., ed. APPROACHES TO THE ORIENTAL CLAS-
      SICS: ASIAN LITERATURE AND THOUGHT IN GENERAL EDUCATION.
      New York: Columbia Univ. Press, 1959.

> Essays on the problem of interpreting Asian works for West-
> erners.

51   DeBary, William T., and Ainslie T. Embree, eds. A GUIDE TO THE
      ORIENTAL CLASSICS. 2d ed. New York: Columbia Univ. Press,
      1975.

> Critical and bibliographical material on some seventy-five
> major works of Islamic, Indic, Chinese, and Japanese litera-
> ture.

52   Frenz, Horst, ed. ASIA AND THE HUMANITIES. Bloomington:
      Indiana Univ. Press, 1959.

> Useful collection of papers on Asian literature, mostly Far
> East.

53   Frenz, Horst, and G.L. Anderson, eds. PAPERS OF THE INDIANA
      CONFERENCE ON ORIENTAL-WESTERN LITERARY RELATIONS. Univ.
      of North Carolina Studies in Comparative Literature, no. 18. Chapel
      Hill: Univ. of North Carolina, 1954.

> Contains a series of papers on poetics and on modern litera-
> ture, as well as comparative studies.

54   Hatto, Arthur T. EOS: AN ENQUIRY INTO THE THEME OF LOVERS'
      MEETINGS AND PARTINGS AT DAWN IN POETRY. London and Paris:
      Mouton, 1965.

> Although Western in orientation, includes Asian material.

55   Keene, Donald. "The Hippolytus Triangle, East and West." YEAR-
      BOOK OF COMPARATIVE AND GENERAL LITERATURE, 11 (1962),
      162-71.

> The Phaedra and Hippolytus theme in India, China, and Japan.

56   Kramer, Samuel Noah, ed. MYTHOLOGIES OF THE ANCIENT
      WORLD. Chicago: Quadrangle Books, 1961.

> Brief but authoritative surveys of myth, including China.

57   Lang, David M., ed. GUIDE TO THE EASTERN LITERATURES. New
      York: Praeger, 1971.

> The relevant material in this work is noted in the appropriate
> sections below.

58   Laufer, Berthold. ORIENTAL THEATRICALS. Chicago: Field Museum
      of Natural History, 1923.

      A pioneering work on the Asian shadow play.

59   Preminger, Alexander, ed. ENCYCLOPEDIA OF POETRY AND POETICS.
      Princeton: Princeton Univ. Press, 1965.

      Includes articles on prosodic systems of Asian literatures.

60   Pronko, Leonard C. THEATRE EAST AND WEST: PERSPECTIVES
      TOWARD A TOTAL THEATRE. Berkeley: Univ. of California Press,
      1967.

      Study of the theater of China, Japan, and Bali with refer-
      ence to techniques that might be used in the West.

61   Prušek, Jaroslav, ed. DICTIONARY OF ORIENTAL LITERATURES. 3
      vols. New York: Basic Books, 1974.

      Valuable entries on many authors, including modern writers:
      vol. I, East Asia; vol. II, South and Southeast Asia; vol. III,
      West Asia and North Africa.

62   Shipley, Joseph T., ed. DICTIONARY OF WORLD LITERARY TERMS.
      Rev. ed. Boston: Writer, 1970.

      Includes brief articles on poetic systems of Asia.

63   Thompson, Stith. MOTIF-INDEX OF FOLK LITERATURE. 6 vols.
      Bloomington: Indiana Univ. Press, 1955–58.

      The standard classification system for motifs in folktales and
      traditional story collections. Used in many studies of Asian
      material.

64   Wells, Henry Willis. THE CLASSICAL DRAMA OF THE ORIENT. New
      York: Asia Publishing House, 1965.

      Contains good studies of Chinese and Japanese drama.

65   Wimsatt, W[illiam] K., ed. VERSIFICATION: MAJOR LANGUAGE
      TYPES. SIXTEEN ESSAYS. New York: Modern Language Association
      of America, 1972.

      Contains excellent essays on Chinese and Japanese poetics.

D. PERIODICALS

All of the periodicals listed here, unless otherwise indicated, are scholarly
journals devoted to history, philology, and literature.

66 ACTA ASIATICA: BULLETIN OF THE INSTITUTE OF EASTERN CULTURE. Tokyo: Institute of Eastern Culture, 1960-- .

67 ARCHIV ORIENTÁLNÍ. Prague: Orientální Ústav, 1929-- .

68 ASIAN AND AFRICAN STUDIES [BRATISLAVA]. Bratislava: Slovak Academy of Sciences, 1965-- .

69 ASIAN AND AFRICAN STUDIES [JERUSALEM]. Jerusalem: Israel Oriental Society, 1965-- .

70 ASIAN HORIZONS. London: Asian Publications, 1948-- .

A high level journal of general culture.

71 ASIAN REVIEW. London: East and West [and various other publishers], 1886-- .

For the general reader. On all aspects of Asian culture.

72 ASIATISCHE STUDIEN. Bern: 1947-- .

Journal of the Schweizerische Gesellschaft fur Asienkunde. Some articles in English.

73 BULLETIN OF THE MUSEUM OF FAR EASTERN ANTIQUITIES. Stockholm: Ostaisatisk Samlinggarna, 1929-- .

Mostly archaeology, but contains significant material on literature.

74 BULLETIN OF THE SCHOOL OF ORIENTAL AND AFRICAN STUDIES. London: Univ. of London, 1917-- .

75 EASTERN HORIZON. Hong Kong: N.p., 1960-- .

76 EASTERN WORLD. London: Eastern World, 1947-- .

77 EAST-WEST REVIEW. Kyoto: Doshisha Univ., 1964-- .

78 FAR EASTERN QUARTERLY. See JOURNAL OF ASIAN STUDIES.

79 HARVARD JOURNAL OF ASIATIC STUDIES. Cambridge, Mass.: Havard-Yenching Institute, 1936-- .

80 JOURNAL OF ASIAN STUDIES. Ann Arbor, Mich.: Association for Asian Studies, 1941-- .

Begun as FAR EASTERN QUARTERLY by the Far Eastern Association for Asian Studies. Much political and sociological
material, but regularly prints important articles on literature.

81   JOURNAL OF ASIATIC STUDIES. Manila: Univ. of Manila, 1951-- .

82   JOURNAL OF ORIENTAL LITERATURE. Honolulu: Univ. of Hawaii,
1947-68.

83   JOURNAL OF THE AMERICAN ORIENTAL SOCIETY. New Haven:
American Oriental Society, 1843--.

Journal of the oldest of the American Oriental societies. Early
years mostly devoted to Near East and Indic studies; later years
include more Far Eastern material.

84   JOURNAL OF THE ORIENTAL SOCIETY OF AUSTRALIA. Sydney:
Univ. of Sydney, 1962-- .

85   JOURNAL OF THE ROYAL ASIATIC SOCIETY. London: Royal Asiatic
Society, 1834-- .

86   LITERATURE EAST & WEST. New Paltz, N.Y.: Conference on Oriental-
Western Literary Relations of the Modern Language Association of America,
1954-- .

A high-level critical journal devoted to the literature of the
entire area from the Arab world to the Far East. Also pub-
lishes translations.

87   ORIENS EXTREMUS: ZEITSCHIRFT FÜR SPRACHE, KUNST UND KULTUR
DES LANDES DES FERNEN OSTENS. Wiesbaden: Harrasowitz, 1954-- .

Occasional articles in English.

88   ORIENT/WEST. Tokyo: N.p., 1956-- .

On all aspects of Asian culture for the general reader. Title
varies.

Chapter 2

CHINA

A. BIBLIOGRAPHY

89   Bailey, Roger B. A GUIDE TO CHINESE POETRY AND DRAMA.
Boston: G.K. Hall, 1973.

> Especially useful because of lengthy annotations. Over one
> hundred works.

90   Chan Wing-Tsit. AN OUTLINE AND ANNOTATED BIBLIOGRAPHY
OF CHINESE PHILOSOPHY. New Haven: Far Eastern Publications,
Yale Univ., 1969.

> Essential work by a leading authority in the field.

91   Cordier, Henri, comp. BIBLIOTHECA SINICA. 2d ed. rev. 4 vols.
Paris: E. Guilmoto, 1904-08. SUPPLEMENT ET INDEX. 4 vols. in
1. Paris: E. Geuthner, 1922-24. AUTHOR INDEX. New York:
East Asiatic Library, Columbia Univ., 1953.

> The great pioneering bibliography of China, but of little use
> today except to the specialist.

92   Davidson, Martha, comp. A LIST OF PUBLISHED TRANSLATIONS
FROM CHINESE INTO ENGLISH, FRENCH, AND GERMAN. 2 vols.
New Haven: Far Eastern Publications, Yale Univ., 1952-57.

> Very thorough list. Vol. 2 includes poetry, vol. 1 other
> forms.

93   Hucker, Charles O., comp. CHINA: A CRITICAL BIBLIOGRAPHY.
Tucson: Univ. of Arizona Press, 1962.

> Valuable introduction and annotations. Especially useful for
> the beginner.

94   _____. CHINESE HISTORY: A BIBLIOGRAPHICAL REVIEW. Washington, D.C.: American Historical Association, 1958.

A lengthy essay on the materials of and studies of Chinese history, with bibliographical references.

95 Leslie, Donald, and Jeremy Davidson. AUTHOR CATALOGUES OF WESTERN SINOLOGISTS. Canberra: Department of Far Eastern History, Australia National Univ., 1966.

Alphabetical list of some five hundred Western writers and scholars on China, with references to their works.

96 Li Tien-Yi, comp. THE HISTORY OF CHINESE LITERATURE: A SELECTED BIBLIOGRAPHY. New Haven: Far Eastern Publications, Yale Univ., 1970.

Useful brief bibliography.

97 Lowe, C.H., comp. NOTABLE BOOKS ON CHINESE STUDIES. Taipei: China Printing, 1978.

Up-to-date list of books on all fields of Chinese culture, with useful background essays.

98 Lust, John, comp. INDEX SINICUS: A CATALOGUE OF ARTICLES RELATING TO CHINA IN PERIODICALS AND OTHER COLLECTIVE PUBLICATIONS, 1920-1955. Cambridge, Engl.: W. Heffer and Sons, 1964.

Almost twenty thousand entries. Author and subject indexes.

99 Paper, Jordan D. GUIDE TO CHINESE PROSE. Boston: G.K. Hall, 1973.

Lengthy critical and historical notes on about 140 works in translation.

100 RÉVUE BIBLIOGRAPHIE DE SINOLOGIE. Paris: Mouton, 1957-- .

Reviews selected books and articles, including works in English. First year covers 1955.

101 Yang, Winston L.Y., and Teresa S. Yan, comps. A BIBLIOGRAPHY OF THE CHINESE LANGUAGE. New York: American Association of Teachers of Chinese Language and Culture, 1966.

Covers about fifteen hundred books and articles. No annotations.

102 Yuan Tung-Li, comp. CHINA IN WESTERN LITERATURE, A CONTINUATION OF CORDIER'S BIBLIOTHECA SINICA. New Haven: Far Eastern Publications, Yale Univ., 1958.

The basic bibliography for Chinese civilization. Few users
will need to refer to Cordier.

B. REFERENCE

103 Bauer, Wolfgang. CHINA AND THE SEARCH FOR HAPPINESS: RE-
CURRING THEMES IN FOUR THOUSAND YEARS OF CHINESE CUL-
TURAL HISTORY. Trans. Michael Shaw. New York: Seabury, 1976.

Learned and lengthy intellectual history. Not easy for
readers unfamiliar with general Chinese history.

104 Bodde, Derk. CHINA'S CULTURAL TRADITION: WHAT AND
WHITHER? New York: Rinehart, 1957.

Briefly touches on some major historical problems.

105 Cotterell, Arthur, and David Morgan. CHINA'S CIVILIZATION:
SURVEY OF ITS HISTORY, ARTS AND TECHNOLOGY. New York:
Praeger, 1975.

Superior synthetic history that includes cultural material but
also references to economics and politics and makes comparisons with the West.

106 Creel, Herrlee G. THE BIRTH OF CHINA: A STUDY OF THE
FORMATIVE PERIOD OF CHINESE CIVILIZATION. New York: John
Day, 1937.

Best general introduction to the earliest period, to about 600
B.C.

107 _____. CHINESE THOUGHT FROM CONFUCIUS TO MAO TSE-TUNG.
Chicago: Univ. of Chicago Press, 1953.

Stimulating survey of Chinese thought.

108 Cressey, George B. LAND OF THE 500 MILLION. New York:
McGraw-Hill Book Co., 1955.

Most complete study of the geographical and economic nature
of China.

109 Dawson, Raymond S., ed. THE LEGACY OF CHINA. Oxford:
Clarendon Press, 1964.

Essays on most aspects of traditional Chinese culture by major
authorities.

110   Eberhard, Wolfgang. A HISTORY OF CHINA. Trans. E.W. Dickes. 4th rev. ed. Berkeley: Univ. of California Press, 1977.

       Valuable, if controversial history, of China from a sociological point of view.

111   Eichhorn, Werner. CHINESE CIVILIZATION, AN INTRODUCTION. Trans. Janet Seligman. New York: Praeger, 1969.

       A well-rounded cultural history.

112   Fairbank, John K., ed. CHINESE THOUGHT AND INSTITUTIONS. Chicago: Univ. of Chicago Press, 1957.

       Studies by specialists on various aspects of Chinese thought.

113   Fitzgerald, Charles P. CHINA, A SHORT CULTURAL HISTORY. New York: Praeger, 1961.

       Not short, but a good cultural history of the early period.

114   Forest, R[obert] A.D. THE CHINESE LANGUAGE. 3d ed. London: Faber and Faber, 1973.

       Authoritative and technical discussion of the language and the dialects.

115   Fung Yu-Lan. A HISTORY OF CHINESE PHILOTOPHY. Trans. Derk Bodde. 2 vols. Princeton: Princeton Univ. Press, 1952-53.

       The standard history. Somewhat technical for the user whose interests are purely literary.

116   _____. A SHORT HISTORY OF CHINESE PHILOSOPHY. Trans. Derk Bodde. New York: Macmillan, 1948.

       Authoritative and adequate for the general reader without recourse to the two-volume history.

117   Goodrich, L. Carrington. A SHORT HISTORY OF THE CHINESE PEOPLE. 4th ref. ed. New York: Harper, 1969.

       Perhaps the best short history. Mostly political history.

118   Goodrich, L. Carrington, and Henry C. Fenn. A SYLLABUS OF THE HISTORY OF CHINESE CIVILIZATION AND CULTURE. 6th ed. New York: China Society of America, 1958.

       Maps and useful bibliographical material.

119   Granet, Marcel. CHINESE CIVILIZATION. London: Kegan Paul, 1930.

120   Grentzler, J[ennings] Mason. A SYLLABUS OF CHINESE CIVILIZA-
TION. New York: Columbia Univ. Press, 1968.

Intended for teachers. Good sketch of the entire field and
guide to illustrated materials.

121   Grousset, René. CHINESE ART AND CULTURE. Trans. Haakon
Chevalier. New York: Grove Press, 1959.

Lively cultural history, focusing mostly on art.

122   _____. RISE AND SPLENDOUR OF THE CHINESE EMPIRE. Trans.
Anthony Watson-Gandy and Terence Gordon. Berkeley: Univ. of
California Press, 1953.

Very original treatment with emphasis on major cultural events.

123   Hu Chang-Tu, et al. CHINA: ITS PEOPLE, ITS SOCIETY, ITS CUL-
TURE. New Haven: Human Relations Area Files, 1960.

Sociologically oriented history. Especially good on recent
developments.

124   Hucker, Charles O. CHINA'S IMPERIAL PAST: AN INTRODUCTION
TO CHINESE HISTORY AND CULTURE. Stanford: Stanford Univ.
Press, 1975.

Perhaps the best introduction to history of traditional China.

125   Karlgren, Bernhard. THE CHINESE LANGUAGE. New York: Ronald
Press, 1949.

Excellent study of the features of the language and its historical development.

126   _____. "Legends and Cults in Ancient China." BULLETIN OF THE
MUSEUM OF FAR EASTERN ANTIQUITIES, 18 (1946): 199-365.

Very thorough treatment of the earliest period.

127   _____. PHILOLOGY AND ANCIENT CHINA. Cambridge, Mass.:
Harvard Univ. Press, 1926.

On the nature of the language and historical study of it.

128   _____. SOUND AND SYMBOL IN CHINESE. London: Oxford Univ.
Press, 1923.

Studies the development of the writing system.

129   Latourette, Kenneth Scott. THE CHINESE, THEIR HISTORY AND
      CULTURE. 2 vols. in 1. 4th ed. New York: Macmillan, 1964.

      An important cultural history, now in need of updating.

130   Levenson, Joseph, and Franz Schurmann. CHINA: AN INTERPRETA-
      TIVE HISTORY FROM THE BEGINNINGS TO THE FALL OF HAN.
      Berkeley: Univ. of California Press, 1969.

      Brief useful introduction to early Chinese history.

131   Li Dun-Jen. THE AGELESS CHINESE, A HISTORY. 2d rev. ed.
      New York: Charles Scribner's Sons, 1974.

      Good modern history. Includes cultural material.

132   MacNair, Harley Farnsworth, ed. CHINA. Berkeley: Univ. of
      California Press, 1946; rpt. 1951.

      Essays on various aspects of Chinese civilization.

133   Moule, Arthur C. THE RULERS OF CHINA, 221 B.C.-A.D. 1949.
      New York: Praeger, 1957.

      Useful handbook of historical facts.

134   Scharfstein, Ben-Ami. THE MIND OF CHINA. New York: Basic
      Books, 1974.

      Excellent study of the role of intellectuals, especially writers
      and artists, in Chinese government. Illustrated.

135   Wright, Arthur F., ed. STUDIES IN CHINESE THOUGHT. Chicago:
      Univ. of Chicago Press, 1953.

      Essays by nine specialists on intellectual history.

136   Yang Lien-Sheng. TOPICS IN CHINESE HISTORY. Cambridge, Mass.:
      Harvard Univ. Press, 1950.

      A syllabus for a course in Chinese history and a useful outline
      with bibliography.

C. ANTHOLOGIES

137   Birch, Cyril, ed. ANTHOLOGY OF CHINESE LITERATURE. 2 vols.
      New York: Grove Press, 1952-72.

      Extensive collection in superior translations, from earliest
      times to the modern period.

138　Chai Ch'u, and Winberg Chai, eds. and trans. A TREASURY OF CHINESE LITERATURE: A NEW PROSE ANTHOLOGY, INCLUDING FICTION AND DRAMA. New York: Appleton-Century-Crofts, 1965.

　　Extensive selection from earliest to modern times.

139　Chang H[sin]-C[hang], ed. CHINESE LITERATURE: POPULAR FICTION AND DRAMA. Edinburgh: Edinburgh Press, 1973.

　　Large anthology covering various periods and types.

140　DeBary, William T., Chan Wing-Tsit, and Burton Watson, eds. SOURCES OF CHINESE TRADITION. New York: Columbia Univ. Press, 1960.

　　Philosophy and history rather than literature, but excellent large collection of background material from the earliest to modern times.

141　Giles, Herbert A., trans. GEMS OF CHINESE LITERATURE. 2 vols. Shanghai: Kelly and Walsh, 1923; rpt. 2 vols. in 1, New York: Paragon Books, 1965.

　　Somewhat obsolete today. Includes prose and poetry.

142　Hughes, E[rnest] R., trans. CHINESE PHILOSOPHY IN CLASSICAL TIMES. Everyman's Library. New York: E.P. Dutton, 1942.

　　Generous selection in good translations. Historical introduction.

143　Kao, George [Kao K'o-I], ed. and trans. CHINESE WIT AND HUMOR. New York: Coward-McCann, 1946.

　　Substantial collection of little-studied material.

144　Legge, James, trans. THE SACRED BOOKS OF CHINA: THE TEXTS OF TAOISM. 1891; rpt. New York: Dover Books, 1962.

　　The separate texts are noted in the appropriate sections, below.

145　Li Dun Jen, ed. and trans. THE CIVILIZATION OF CHINA, FROM THE FORMATIVE PERIOD TO THE COMING OF THE WEST. New York: Charles Scribner's Sons, 1975.

　　Useful collection of texts chronologically arranged. Material not available elsewhere.

146　_____. THE ESSENCE OF CHINESE CIVILIZATION. Princeton: Van Nostrand-Reinhold, 1967.

Brief excerpts from writers of all periods arranged by topics.

147   Lin Yutang, ed. and trans. THE IMPORTANCE OF UNDERSTANDING. Cleveland: World Publishing Co., 1960.

Mostly short stories and anecdotes arranged topically.

148   _____. THE WISDOM OF CHINA AND INDIA. New York: Modern Library, 1942.

Large selection from China in good translations. The critical material is weak. Covers to the end of the classical period.

149   McNaughton, William, ed. CHINESE LITERATURE: AN ANTHOLOGY FROM THE EARLIEST TIMES TO THE PRESENT DAY. Rutland, Vt.: Charles E. Tuttle Co., 1974.

Large, well-balanced selection in modern translations.

150   Morris, Ivan, ed. MADLY SINGING IN THE MOUNTAINS: AN APPRECIATION AND ANTHOLOGY OF ARTHUR WALEY. London: Allen and Unwin, 1970.

Essays on the life and career of the great sinologist-translator and about fifty selections of prose and poetry translated by him.

151   Waley, Arthur, trans. THREE WAYS OF THOUGHT IN ANCIENT CHINA. New York: Doubleday, 1956.

Translations from Chuang Tzu, Mencius, and Han Fei Tzu. Noted below under the three authors.

152   Watson, Burton, trans. JAPANESE LITERATURE IN CHINESE. 2 vols. New York: Columbia Univ. Press, 1975-78.

Excellent translations of court poetry written in Chinese by Japanese writers, an area otherwise neglected in translations.

D. LITERARY HISTORY AND CRITICISM

153   Birch, Cyril, ed. STUDIES IN CHINESE LITERARY GENRES. Berkeley: Univ. of California Press, 1974.

An essential collection of studies on the types by specialists.

154   Bishop, John L., ed. STUDIES IN CHINESE LITERATURE. Cambridge, Mass.: Harvard Univ. Press, 1965.

Important collection of studies, mostly reprinted from HARVARD JOURNAL OF ASIATIC STUDIES.

155   Ch'ên Shou-Yi. CHINESE LITERATURE: A HISTORICAL INTRODUC-
       TION. New York: Ronald Press, 1961.

       A detailed history, but difficult to use and not always based
       on the most recent scholarship.

156   Egerod, Søren, ed. STUDIA SERICA BERNHARD KARLGREN DEDICATA:
       SINOLOGICAL STUDIES DEDICATED TO BERNHARD KARLGREN.
       Copenhagen: Ejnar Munksgaard, [1959].

       Varied collection of studies on literature and culture.

157   Fêng Yüan-Chün [Fêng Shu-Lan]. A SHORT HISTORY OF CLASSICAL
       CHINESE LITERATURE. Trans. Yang Hsien-Yi and Gladys Yang.
       Peking: Foreign Languages Press, 1958.

       Covers period to 1919. A brief Marxist interpretation.

158   Giles, Herbert A. A HISTORY OF CHINESE LITERATURE. New York:
       Appleton, 1901; rpt. New York: F. Ungar, [1967].

       Important for its day, but now obsolete. The reprint contains
       a supplement for the modern period by Liu Wu-Chi.

159   Hightower, James Robert. "Individualism in Chinese Literature."
       JOURNAL OF THE HISTORY OF IDEAS, 22 (1961), 159-68.

       Important discussion of a much-debated topic.

160   _____. TOPICS IN CHINESE LITERATURE. Rev. ed. Cambridge,
       Mass.: Harvard Univ. Press, 1953.

       Valuable. Actually a brief, accurate history of the literature
       with bibliographical references.

161   Kaltenmark, Odile. CHINESE LITERATURE. Trans. Anne-Marie
       Geoghegar. New York: Walker and Co., 1964.

       A brief sketch.

162   Lai Ming. A HISTORY OF CHINESE LITERATURE. New York: John
       Day, 1964.

       Unfortunately contains many errors of fact and interpretation.

163   Liu, James J.Y. CHINESE THEORIES OF LITERATURE. Chicago:
       Univ. of Chicago Press, [1975].

Valuable survey of Chinese ideas about the nature of literature.

164   Liu Wu-Chi. AN INTRODUCTION TO CHINESE LITERATURE.
Bloomington: Indiana Univ. Press, 1966.

Excellent history, intelligible to the beginner. Down to the
early modern period.

165   Mayers, William Frederick. THE CHINESE READER'S MANUAL: A
HANDBOOK OF BIOGRAPHICAL, MYTHOLOGICAL, AND GENERAL
LITERARY REFERENCE. London: Probsthain, 1910; rpt. Detroit:
Gale Research Co., 1968.

In need of revision but includes material not available elsewhere. The 1910 edition is a reprint of the 1874 Shanghai
edition.

166   Průsek, Jaroslav. CHINESE HISTORY AND LITERATURE: COLLECTION
OF STUDIES. Dordrecht: Reidel Publishing Co., 1970.

Studies by an eminent Czech sinologist, mostly reprinted from
journals. Important especially for fiction and the study of
popular literature.

167   _____. "The Importance of Tradition in Chinese Literature." ARCHIV
ORIENTÁLNÍ, 26 (1958), 212-23.

168   _____. "Reality and Art in Chinese Literature." ARCHIV ORIENTÁLNÍ,
32 (1964), 605-18.

169   Rickett, Adele Austin, ed. CHINESE APPROACHES TO LITERATURE
FROM CONFUCIUS TO LIANG CHI-I-CH'AO. Princeton: Princeton
Univ. Press, 1977.

Important collection on literary theory in China.

170   Schafer, Edward H. THE DIVINE WOMAN: DRAGON LADIES AND
RAIN MAIDENS IN T'ANG LITERATURE. Berkeley: Univ. of California Press, 1973.

Learned study of an important topic.

171   Teele, Roy E. THROUGH A GLASS DARKLY: A STUDY OF ENGLISH
TRANSLATIONS OF CHINESE POETRY. Ann Arbor, Mich: Privately
printed, 1949.

Perceptive study of the difficulties of translating and the fail-
ures in (mostly) twentieth-century translations. Still useful.

172　Tjan Tjoe Som [Tjan Tju Som]. PO HU T'UNG: THE COMPREHEN-
　　　SIVE DISCUSSIONS IN THE WHITE-TIGER HALL. 2 vols. Leiden:
　　　E. Brill, 1949-52.

　　　　Translation of a report on an imperial conference on the clas-
　　　　sics in 79 A.D. A major scholarly work.

173　Tsien Tsuen-Hsuin. WRITTEN ON BAMBOO AND SILK: THE BEGIN-
　　　NINGS OF CHINESE BOOKS AND INSCRIPTIONS. Chicago: Univ.
　　　of Chicago Press, [1962].

　　　　Well-illustrated study of the writing system and early books.

174　Wang Chi-Chen. "Traditional Literature: Nature and Limitations."
　　　In CHINA, pp. 386-96. See entry 132.

　　　　On the historical development of literary forms.

175　Watson, Burton. EARLY CHINESE LITERATURE. New York: Columbia
　　　Univ. Press, 1962.

　　　　Covers period to about 100 A.D. Well-written and authorita-
　　　　tive study of early poetry, philosophy, and history in China.

176　Wells, Henry Willis. TRADITIONAL CHINESE HUMOR: A STUDY IN
　　　ART AND LITERATURE. Bloomington: Indiana Univ. Press, [1971].

　　　　Good treatment of material not often studied or translated.

177　Werner, E[dward] T.C. DICTIONARY OF CHINESE MYTHOLOGY.
　　　1932; rpt. New York: Julian Press, 1961.

178　_____. MYTHS AND LEGENDS OF CHINA. New York: Brentano,
　　　1922.

　　　　Both of Werner's works are somewhat outdated but are still
　　　　valuable for reference.

179　Wylie, Alexander. NOTES ON CHINESE LITERATURE. 1867; rpt.
　　　New York: Paragon Book Corp., 1964.

　　　　A major pioneering work, now largely superseded.

E. POETRY—ANTHOLOGIES

180　Alley, Rewi, trans. PEACE THROUGH THE AGES: TRANSLATIONS
　　　FROM THE POETS OF CHINA. Peking: 1954.

181　_____. THE PEOPLE SPEAK OUT: TRANSLATIONS OF POETRY AND

SONGS OF THE PEOPLE OF CHINA. Peking: [1954].

Poems of protest from earliest times to modern in good but somewhat literal translations.

182   Ayscough, Florence, and Amy Lowell, trans. FIR-FLOWER TABLETS: POEMS TRANSLATED FROM THE CHINESE. Boston: Houghton Mifflin Co., 1921.

An influential work, but based on erroneous notions of Chinese poetry.

183   Budd, Charles, trans. CHINESE POEMS. Oxford: Oxford Univ. Press, 1912.

Expansive rhymed translations. Somewhat dated.

184   Bynner, Witter, and Kiang Kang-Hu, trans. THE JADE MOUNTAIN: A CHINESE ANTHOLOGY. New York: Alfred A. Knopf, 1929; rpt. Garden City, N.Y.: Anchor Books, 1964; New York: Vintage Books, 1972.

Good translations of a major Chinese (eighteenth-century) collection. Includes a study of technique.

185   Chandlin, Clara M., trans. THE HERALD WIND: TRANSLATIONS OF SUNG POEMS, LYRICS, AND SONGS. London: John Murray, [1931].

Rather free translation but important for its time.

186   Ch'en, Jerome, and Michael Bullock, trans. POEMS OF SOLITUDE. London: Abelard-Schuman, 1960; rpt. Rutland, Vt.: Charles E. Tuttle Co., 1970.

Selections from six poets in good translations.

187   Christy, Arthur, trans. IMAGES IN JADE: TRANSLATIONS FROM CLASSICAL AND MODERN CHINESE POETRY. New York: E.P. Dutton Co., 1929.

An important early effort, now outmoded.

188   Ch'u Ta-Kao, trans. CHINESE LYRICS. Cambridge, Engl.: Cambridge Univ. Press, 1937.

Good translations of early poets.

189   Cranmer-Byng, L., trans. A FEAST OF LANTERNS. London: John Murray, 1916.

190   _____. A LUTE OF JADE: SELECTIONS FROM THE CLASSICAL

POETS OF CHINA. London: John Murray, 1909.

Both of these volumes contain very free translations and un-
reliable notes.

191   Davis, A[lbert] R., ed. PENGUIN BOOK OF CHINESE VERSE.
Baltimore: Penguin Books, 1962.

Over one hundred poets are represented in this excellent collection of translations by Robert Kotewell and Norman L. Smith.

192   Fletcher, William J.B., trans. GEMS OF CHINESE POETRY, TRANS-
LATED INTO ENGLISH VERSE. Shanghai: Commercial Press, 1919.

193   _____. MORE GEMS OF CHINESE POETRY, TRANSLATED INTO
ENGLISH VERSE. Shanghai: Commercial Press, 1933. This and the
preceding entry rept. as 2 vols. in 1. New York: Paragon Book Co.,
1966.

A large selection of classical poetry with parallel Chinese
texts.

194   Frankel, Hans H., trans. THE FLOWERING PLUM AND THE PALACE
LADY: INTERPRETATIONS OF CHINESE POETRY. New Haven: Yale
Univ. Press, 1976.

About one hundred poems, with Chinese and English, pre-
cisely translated and with full annotations and discussion.

195   Frodsham, J.D., trans. AN ANTHOLOGY OF CHINESE VERSE:
HAN, WEI, CHIN AND THE NORTHERN AND SOUTHERN DYNASTIES.
London: Oxford Univ. Press, 1967.

Lyrics, folksongs, and ballads chosen to be historically representative. Excellent translations with annotations.

196   Gordon, David, trans. EQUINOX: A GATHERING OF T'ANG
POEMS, TRANSLATIONS AND ADAPTATIONS. Athens: Ohio Univ.
Press, 1975.

Attractive but very free adaptations.

197   Graham, A.C., trans. POEMS OF THE LATE T'ANG. Baltimore:
Penguin Books, [1965].

Seven poets, including Tu Fu, in accurate translations.
Valuable discussion of translations in the introduction.

198   Hart, Henry H., trans. THE CHARCOAL BURNER AND OTHER
POEMS: ORIGINAL TRANSLATIONS FROM THE POETRY

OF THE CHINESE. Norman: Univ. of Oklahoma Press, [1974].

199 _____. A CHINESE MARKET: LYRICS FROM THE CHINESE IN ENGLISH VERSE. Peking: French Bookstore, [1931].

200 _____. A GARDEN OF PEONIES: TRANSLATIONS OF CHINESE POEMS INTO ENGLISH VERSE. Stanford: Stanford Univ. Press, [1938].

201 _____. POEMS OF THE HUNDRED NAMES: A SHORT INTRODUC-TION TO CHINESE POETRY TOGETHER WITH 209 ORIGINAL TRANS-LATIONS. 3d ed. New York: Greenwood Press, 1968.

> Published in 1933 as THE HUNDRED NAMES. In this and the three preceding entries, Hart translates a great body of verse from all periods. Free, occasionally inaccurate, renderings.

202 Holbrook, David, comp. PLUCKING THE RUSHES: AN ANTHOLOGY OF CHINESE POETRY IN TRANSLATIONS BY ARTHUR WALEY, EZRA POUND, HELEN WADDELL. London: Heinemann, 1968.

> Waley's translations are both literary and accurate; Waddell's are freer and elegant; Pound has his usual flashes of brilliance.

203 Jenyns, Soame. FURTHER SELECTIONS FROM THE THREE HUNDRED POEMS OF THE T'ANG DYNASTY. London: John Murray, 1944.

204 _____. SELECTIONS FROM THE THREE HUNDRED POEMS OF THE T'ANG DYNASTY. London: John Murray, 1940.

> Quite adequate translations with good notes.

205 Kwock, C.H., and Vincent McHugh, trans. WHY I LIVE ON THE MOUNTAIN: 30 CHINESE POEMS WITH THE GREAT DYNASTIES. San Francisco: Golden Mountain Press, 1958.

> Slender volume of free translations by an American poet and a Chinese-American critic.

206 Lai, T.C., and Y.T. Kwong, trans. CHINESE POETRY. Kowloon, Hong Kong: Swindon Book Co., 1972.

> Brief collection of attractive translations.

207 Liu, James J.Y., trans. MAJOR LYRICISTS OF THE NORTHERN SUNG (A.D. 60-1126). Princeton: Princeton Univ. Press, [1974].

> Study and translations of twenty-eight lyric poems with Chinese texts and full notes.

208   Liu Shih-Shun, trans. ONE HUNDRED AND ONE CHINESE POEMS. London: Oxford Univ. Press, [1968].

> Literal translations with Chinese text and valuable comments on other translations.

209   Liu Wu-Chi, and Irving Yucheng Lo, trans. SUNFLOWER SPLENDOR: THREE THOUSAND YEARS OF CHINESE POETRY. Garden City, N.Y.: Doubleday, 1975.

> Comprehensive anthology covering the whole field of Chinese poetry. Superior translations.

210   MacIntosh, Duncan, trans. A COLLECTION OF CHINESE LYRICS. London: Routledge and Kegan Paul, 1965.

211   _____. A FURTHER COLLECTION OF CHINESE LYRICS, AND OTHER POEMS. London: Routledge and Kegan, Paul, 1969.

> Two volumes of verse translations. Table of metrical patterns.

212   Payne, Robert, ed. THE WHITE PONY: AN ANTHOLOGY OF CHINESE POETRY FROM THE EARLIEST TIMES TO THE PRESENT DAY. New York: John Day Co., [1947].

> Good collection is competent translations.

213   Rexroth, Kenneth, trans. LOVE AND THE TURNING YEAR: ONE HUNDRED MORE POEMS FROM THE CHINESE. New York: New Directions, 1970.

214   _____. ONE HUNDRED POEMS FROM THE CHINESE. New York: New Directions, [1956].

215   _____. THE ORCHID BOAT: WOMEN POETS OF CHINA. New York: McGraw-Hill Book Co., [1972].

> This and the two preceding entries are volumes of highly interpretative translations by an American poet and essayist.

216   Robins, Richard, trans. CHINESE BUDDHIST VERSE. London: John Murray, 1954.

217   Scott, John, ed. and trans. LOVE AND PROTEST: CHINESE POEMS FROM THE SIXTH CENTURY B.C. TO THE SEVENTEENTH CENTURY A.D. New York: Harper and Row, 1972.

> Competent translations with biographical sketches and notes.

218   Tang Zi-Chang, trans. POEMS OF T'ANG: 600 POEMS WRITTEN IN T'ANG STYLE BY T'ANG POETS. San Rafael, Calif.; T.C. Press, [1969].

      Large selection, uneven translations.

219   Ts'ai T'ing-Kan, trans. CHINESE POEMS IN ENGLISH RHYME. Chicago: Univ. of Chicago Press, [1972].

      Over a hundred poems with the Chinese text. The English rhyme makes for rather free translations.

220   Turner, John A., comp. A GOLDEN TREASURY OF CHINESE POETRY. Ed. John J. Deeney and Kenneth K.B. Li. Hong Kong: Chinese Univ. of Honk Kong, 1976.

      From early times to the end of the nineteenth century. Good selection of quite adequate translations.

221   Waddell, Helen, trans. LYRICS FROM THE CHINESE. New York: Henry Holt and Co., [1935].

      First published 1913. About thirty poems from the SHIH CHING in free but attractive translations.

222   Waley, Arthur, trans. BALLADS AND SONGS FROM TUN-HUANG. New York: Macmillan, 1960.

      Ancient popular ballads and songs, A.D. 406-996, by the greatest translator of Chinese poetry in our century.

223   _____. CHINESE POEMS: SELECTIONS FROM "170 CHINESE POEMS," "MORE TRANSLATIONS FROM THE CHINESE," "THE TEMPLE," AND "THE BOOK OF SONGS." London: Allen and Unwin, 1946.

      Good selections from Waley's earlier volumes. Good notes.

224   _____. A HUNDRED AND SEVENTY CHINESE POEMS. New York: Alfred A. Knopf, 1922; rpt. London: Constable, 1932.

      Contains an excellent essay on the translating of Chinese poetry and a historical survey.

225   _____. MORE TRANSLATIONS FROM THE CHINESE. London: Allen and Unwin, 1919.

      About half of this volume is devoted to Po Chu-I.

226   _____. THE NINE SONGS: A STUDY OF SHAMANISM IN AN-

CIENT CHINA. London: Allen and Unwin, [1956].

Translations and detailed study of nine early religious poems, ca. 343-277 B.C.

227 _____. THE TEMPLE AND OTHER POEMS. New York: Alfred A. Knopf, 1923.

Translations and a study of early poetic genres. Appendix of verse forms.

228 _____. TRANSLATIONS FROM THE CHINESE. New York: Alfred A. Knopf, 1941.

Handsome reprint of selections from previous volumes, with some new poems and two prose T'ang stories. About two hundred poems.

229 Watson, Burton, trans. CHINESE LYRICISM: SHIH POETRY FROM THE SECOND TO THE TWELFTH CENTURY. New York: Columbia Univ. Press, 1971.

230 _____. CHINESE RHYME PROSE: POEMS IN THE FU FORM FROM THE HAN AND SIX DYNASTIES PERIOD. New York: Columbia Univ. Press, 1971.

This and the preceding entry contain accurate and very readable translations with historical notes.

231 Yang, Richard F.S., and Charles R. Metzgar, trans. FIFTY SONGS OF THE YUAN: POEMS OF THIRTEENTH-CENTURY CHINA. London: Allen and Unwin, 1967.

Contains careful literary and also literal translations and full notes.

232 Yip, Wai-Lim, trans. CHINESE POETRY: MAJOR MODES AND GENRES. Berkeley: University of California Press, 1977.

Translates about 150 poems into free verse, occasionally providing word-for-word versions for comparison. Argues for a new approach to translation.

F. POETRY—HISTORY AND CRITICISM

233 Baxter, Glen W. SONGS OF TENTH-CENTURY CHINA: A STUDY OF THE FIRST TZ'U ANTHOLOGY. Cambridge, Mass.: Harvard Univ. Press, 1952.

Excellent scholarly study of an early court anthology.

234   Bishop, John L.   "Prosodic Elements in T'ang Poetry."   In PAPERS OF THE INDIANA CONFERENCE, pp. 49–63.   See entry no. 53.

235   Dobson, W[illiam] A.C.H.   THE LANGUAGE OF THE BOOK OF SONGS.   Toronto: Univ. of Toronto Press, 1968.

236   _____.   "The Origin and Development of Prosody in Early Chinese Poetry."   T'OUNG PAO, 54 (1968):   231–50.

       The first Dobson entry studies the SHIH CHING, the oldest of the major anthologies.   The second considers early poetry in general.

237   Downer, G.B., and A.C. Graham.   "Tone Patterns in Chinese Poetry." BULLETIN OF THE SCHOOL OF ORIENTAL AND AFRICAN STUDIES, 26 (1963), 145–48.

238   Fenollosa, Ernest.   THE CHINESE WRITTEN CHARACTER AS A MEDIUM FOR POETRY.   New York: Arrow Editions, 1936.

       Contains a preface and notes by Ezra Pound.   An important early work by a major interpreter of Chinese and Japanese culture to the West.   A major influence on Pound's work.

239   Frodsham, J.D.   "The Origins of Chinese Nature Poetry."   ASIA MAJOR 8 (1960), 68–104.

       Early landscape poetry and its relation to Buddhist and Taoist thought.

240   Hawkes, David.   "The Quest of the Goddess."   In STUDIES IN CHI- NESE LITERARY GENRES, pp. 42–68.   See entry no. 153.

241   _____.   "The Supernatural in Chinese Poetry."   UNIVERSITY OF TORONTO QUARTERLY 30 (1961):   311–24.

       Study of origins of the T'ZU and FU with translated examples.

242   Liu, James J.Y.   THE ART OF CHINESE POETRY.   Chicago: Univ. of Chicago Press, [1962].

       A major study of the nature of Chinese poetry.

243   _____.   MAJOR LYRICISTS OF THE NORTHERN SUNG (A.D. 960– 1126).   Princeton: Princeton Univ. Press, 1974.

       Study of six major poets of the period.

244   Lo, Irving Yucheng.   "Problems in Translating and in Teaching Chinese Poetry."   LITERATURE EAST & WEST, 7 (1963), 29–58.

       Useful also in understanding the nature of the poetry.

245 _____. "Style and Vision in Chinese Poetry: An Inquiry into Apollonian and Dionysian Dimensions." TSING HUA JOURNAL OF CHINESE STUDIES, 7 (1968), 99-113.

246 Watson, Burton. "Chinese Protest Poetry from the Earliest Times through the Sung Dynasty." ASIA, 17 (1969-70), 76-91.

An objective treatment of this subject.

247 Wu, John C.H. [Wu Ching-Hsiung]. THE FOUR SEASONS OF T'ANG POETRY. Rutland, Vt.: Charles E. Tuttle Co., 1972.

Critical study of a major period in Chinese poetry.

248 Yip Wai-Lim. "The Chinese Poem, a Different Mode of Representation." DELOS, No. 3 (1969), pp. 62-79.

Useful reminder of major differences in attitude towards poetry betwen China and the West.

249 Yoshikawa, Kōjirō. AN INTRODUCTION TO SUNG POETRY. Trans. Burton Watson. Cambridge, Mass.: Harvard Univ. Press, [1967].

An important study by an eminent Japanese sinologist.

G. DRAMA—ANTHOLOGIES

250 Arlington, L[ewis] C., and Harold Acton, trans. FAMOUS CHINESE PLAYS. Peiping: H. Vetch, 1937; rpt. New York: Russell and Russell, 1963.

Synopses of more than thirty plays from the Peking theater as they were played in modern times. Good introduction.

251 Hung, Josephine Huang, trans. CHILDREN OF THE PEAR GARDEN. Taipei: Heritage Press, [1961].

Five plays translated and adapted. Introduction and notes.

252 _____. CLASSICAL CHINESE PLAYS. Taipei: Mei Ya Publications, [1972].

Translations of a large number of plays from the repertoire.

253 Liu Jung-En, trans. SIX YÜAN PLAYS. Baltimore: Penguin Books, [1972].

Excellent translations. Includes the famous ORPHAN OF CHAO.

254   Scott, A[dolphe] C., trans. TRADITIONAL CHINESE PLAYS. 3 vols.
       Madison: Univ. of Wisconsin Press, 1969-75.

       Perhaps the best modern collection of plays in translation.
       Good introductions, including a study of the staging.

255   Yang, Richard Fu-Sen, comp. FOUR PLAYS OF THE YÜAN DRAMA.
       Taipei: China Post, [1972].

       Readable translations of plays from this important period.

H. DRAMA—HISTORY AND CRITICISM

256   Arlington, L[ewis] C. THE CHINESE DRAMA FROM THE EARLIEST
       TIMES UNTIL TODAY. Shanghai: Kelly and Walsh, 1930; rpt. New
       York: Benjamin Blom, 1966.

       Valuable plates showing costumes, make-up, musical instru-
       ments. Down to the 1920s.

257   Bailey, Roger B. A GUIDE TO CHINESE POETRY AND DRAMA.
       See entry no. 89.

258   Buss, Kate. STUDIES IN THE CHINESE DRAMA. Boston: Four Seas
       Co., 1922; rpt. New York: Jonathan Cape and Harrison Smith, [1930].

       General factual survey of the theatrical elements.

259   Chen, Jack. THE CHINESE THEATRE. London: Dennis Dobson, 1948.

       Brief discussion of three types: the classical "opera," Western
       type plays from about 1915, and the ancient folk drama now
       being revised by the Revolution.

260   Chu Chia-Chien. THE CHINESE THEATRE. Trans. by James A. Graham.
       London: John Lane, 1922.

       Mostly useful for illustrations.

261   Crump, James I. "The Elements of Yüan Opera." JOURNAL OF
       ASIAN STUDIES, 27 (1957-58), 417-34.

       Valuable analysis by an expert.

262   Delza, Sophia. "The Classic Chinese Theater." JOURNAL OF AES-
       THETICS AND ART CRITICISM, 15 (1956): 181-97.

       An excellent introduction to the form.

263 Dolby, William. A HISTORY OF CHINESE DRAMA. New York: Harper and Row, 1976.

Best available history. From the beginnings to the present.

264 Hsiun Shih-I. "Drama." In CHINA, pp. 372-85. See entry no. 132.

Excellent brief survey of the Peking opera.

265 Hung, Josephine Huang. MING DRAMA. Taipei: Heritage Press, 1966.

Good survey of the later drama.

266 Johnston, Reginald Fleming. THE CHINESE DRAMA. Shanghai: Kelly and Walsh, 1921.

Brief account important for its time but now superseded.

267 Leung, George Kin [Liang Shè-Ch'ien]. MEI LANG-FANG, FORE-MOST ACTOR OF CHINA. Shanghai: Commercial Press, 1929.

In the early years of the century the great actor Mei Lang-Fang gave performances in the West and instructed many Westerners in the art of traditional Chinese drama. This account is well-illustrated.

268 _____. SPECIAL PLAYS AND SCENES TO BE PRESENTED BY MEI LAN-FANG ON HIS AMERICAN TOUR. Peking: 1929.

269 Mackerras, Colin. THE RISE OF THE PEKING OPERA, 1770-1870: SOCIAL ASPECTS OF THE THEATRE IN MANCHU CHINA. Oxford: Clarendon Press, 1972.

Good study of a neglected area--the classical drama before any Western influences came to China.

270 Schlepp, Wayne. SAN-CH'Ü: ITS TECHNIQUE AND IMAGERY. Madison: Univ. of Wisconsin Press, [1970].

271 Scott, A[dolphe] C. THE CLASSICAL THEATRE OF CHINA. London: Allen and Unwin, 1957.

An excellent introduction to the subject.

272 _____. AN INTRODUCTION TO THE CHINESE THEATRE. New York: Theatre Arts Books, 1959.

Valuable. Includes comments on some twenty well-known plays.

273 _____. MEI LAN-FANG: LEADER OF THE PEAR GARDEN. Hong Kong: Hong Kong Univ. Press, 1959.

> Most up-to-date account of the famous actor.

274 Shih Chung-Wen. THE GOLDEN AGE OF CHINESE DRAMA. Princeton: Princeton Univ. Press, 1976.

> Thorough scholarly account of Yuan dynasty drama, 1260-1368.

275 Wells, Henry W. "Chinese Drama in English." YEARBOOK OF COMPARATIVE AND GENERAL LITERATURE, 13 (1964), 13-27.

276 _____. THE CLASSICAL DRAMA OF THE ORIENT. New York: Asia Publishing House, 1965.

> Part 1 surveys Chinese drama.

277 Wimsatt, Genevieve B. CHINESE SHADOW PLAYS. Cambridge, Mass.: Harvard Univ. Press, 1936.

> Study of the Chinese form of the shadow play, a type of drama popular throughout Asia. Good illustrations.

278 Yang, Daniel Shih-P'êng, comp. AN ANNOTATED BIBLIOGRAPHY OF MATERIALS FOR THE STUDY OF THE PEKING THEATRE. Madison: Univ. of Wisconsin Press, 1967.

> Some 162 titles from the A.C. Scott Collection. Nearly all in Chinese.

279 Zucker, Adoph E. THE CHINESE THEATER. Boston: Little, Brown and Co., 1925.

> Still useful. Considerable material on Mei Lan-Fang, and comparisons of Chinese and Western drama by a specialist in German.

280 Zung, Cecilia S.L. [Ch'eng Hsiu-Ling]. SECRETS OF THE CHINESE DRAMA. Shanghai: Kelly and Walsh, 1937; rpt. New York: Benjamin Blom, [1964].

> Summaries of many popular plays. Good plates.

I. FICTION—ANTHOLOGIES

281 Bauer, Wolfgang, and Herbert Franke, trans. THE GOLDEN CASKET: CHINESE NOVELLAS OF TWO MILLENIA. Trans. from German by Christopher Levenson. New York: Harcourt, Brace and Co., 1964.

282 Birch, Cyril. CHINESE MYTHS AND FANTASIES RETOLD. London: Oxford Univ. Press, 1961.

Superior retellings by a major scholar.

283 _____. STORIES FROM A MING COLLECTION. London: Bodley Head, 1958.

Six colloquial stories of the seventeenth century, well-translated.

284 Bodde, Derk. "Some Chinese Tales of the Supernatural: Kan Pao and his Sou-shen chi." HARVARD JOURNAL OF ASIATIC STUDIES, 6 (1942), 338-44.

Translations from a fourth-century collection with commentary.

285 Chang H[sin]-C[hang], ed. CHINESE LITERATURE. See entry no. 139.

286 Edwards, E[vangeline] D., trans. CHINESE PROSE LITERATURE OF THE T'ANG PERIOD, A.D. 618-906. 2 vols. London: Arthur Probsthain, 1937-38.

Very thorough coverage of the period in accurate translations. Vol. 2 is devoted to fiction.

287 _____. THE DRAGON BOOK. London: William Hodge, [1938].

Short tales and anecdotes, and miscellaneous verse and prose.

288 Fêng Mêng-Lung (1547?-1645?), supposed comp. FOUR CAUTIONARY TALES. Trans. Harold Acton and Lee Yi-Hsieh. London: John Lehmann, 1947. Issued earlier as GLUE AND LACQUER, 1941.

Rewritings of storytellers' prompt books. Good introduction by Arthur Waley and good translations.

289 _____. THE PERFECT LADY BY MISTAKE AND OTHER STORIES. Trans. William Dolby. St. Lawrence, Mass.: Paul Elek, 1976.

Six stories with valuable introduction on the development of vernacular literature.

290 _____. STORIES FROM A MING COLLECTION: THE ART OF THE CHINESE STORY-TELLER. Trans. Cyril Birch. New York: Grove Press, 1968.

Excellent translations with full commentary.

291 Levy, Harold S., trans. THE ILLUSORY FLAME: TEN TRANSLATIONS

OF CHINESE LOVE STORIES. Tokyo: Kenkyusha, 1962.

Good translations from a very popular genre.

292 Lin Yutang, trans. FAMOUS CHINESE SHORT STORIES. New York: John Day Co., 1952.

T'ang and Sung stories attractively retold.

293 _____. WIDOW, NUN, AND COURTESAN. New York: John Day Co., [1951].

Three short novels.

294 Liu I-Ch'ing, supposed comp. A NEW ACCOUNT OF TALES OF THE WORLD. Trans. Richard Mather. Minneapolis: Univ. of Minnesota Press, 1976.

Large collection of anecdotes and conversations, dating from ca. 430 B.C. Excellent scholarly translation with valuable introduction.

295 P'u Sung-Ling (1640-1715), supposed comp. CHINESE GHOST AND LOVE STORIES. Trans. Rose Quong. New York: Pantheon, 1946.

296 _____. STRANGE STORIES FROM A CHINESE STUDIO. Trans. Herbert A. Giles. New York: Boni and Liveright, 1925.

First published 1880. From the LIAO CHAI CHIH I collection. Quong's translation (preceding entry) is more modern. Giles includes more material, and notes.

297 Soulié de Morant, Charles, trans. CHINESE LOVE TALES. Garden City, N.Y.: Halycon House, 1935.

Charming love stories from the seventeenth century. Free translations.

298 Wang Chi-Chen, trans. TRADITIONAL CHINESE TALES. New York: Columbia Univ. Press, 1944; rpt. New York: Greenwood Press, 1968.

Twenty short stories from the sixth to the sixteenth centuries.

299 Wang, Elizabeth Tê Chên, trans. LADIES OF THE T'ANG: 22 CLASSICAL CHINESE STORIES. Taipei: Heritage Press, [1966].

Large collection in somewhat literal translations. Introduction and notes.

300 Yang Hsien-Yi, and Gladys Yang, trans. THE COURTESAN'S JEWEL

BOX: CHINESE STORIES OF THE XTH–XVIITH CENTURIES. Peking: Foreign Languages Press, 1957.

301 _____. THE DRAGON KING'S DAUGHTER: TEN T'ANG DYNASTY STORIES. 2d rev. ed. Peking: Foreign Languages Press, 1962.

302 _____. THE MAN WHO SOLD A GHOST: CHINESE TALES OF THE 3RD–6TH CENTURIES. Peking: Foreign Languages Press, 1958.

> This and the two preceding entries are valuable collections. The first is the largest in English. The last deals with the earliest stories, derived from oral tradition.

303 Yen, W.W., trans. STORIES OF OLD CHINA. Peking: Foreign Languages Press, 1938.

> Good collection from earliest times to the Ch'ing dynasty.

J. FICTION—HISTORY AND CRITICISM

304 Bishop, John Lyman. THE COLOQUIAL SHORT STORY IN CHINA: A STUDY OF THE "SAN YEN" COLLECTIONS. Cambridge, Mass.: Harvard Univ. Press, 1956.

> Excellent scholarly study of three important seventeenth-century collections, with translations.

305 _____. "Some Limitations of Chinese Fiction." FAR EASTERN QUARTERLY, 15 (1955-56), 239-47.

> Important article on the characteristics of early fiction.

306 Buck, Pearl S. EAST AND WEST AND THE NOVEL: SOURCES OF THE EARLY CHINESE NOVEL. Peiping: North China Union Language School, 1932.

> On the popular aspects of tradition fiction. Nobel Prize Lecture for 1938.

307 Feuerwerker, Yi-Tse Mei. "The Chinese Novel." In APPROACHES TO THE ORIENTAL CLASSICS, pp. 171-85. See entry no. 50.

> An excellent brief analysis of the form.

308 Frankel, Hans. "The Chinese Novel: A Confrontation of Critical Approaches to Chinese and Western Novels." LITERATURE EAST & WEST, 8 (1964), 2-5.

> Problems of definition of fiction East and West.

309 Hanan, Patrick. THE CHINESE SHORT STORY: STUDIES IN DATING, AUTHORSHIP, AND COMPOSITION. Cambridge, Mass.: Harvard Univ. Press, 1973.

A scholarly study. Parts of this require a knowledge of Chinese.

310 Hsia, Chih-Tsing. THE CLASSIC CHINESE NOVEL: A CRITICAL INTRODUCTION. New York: Columbia Univ. Press, 1968.

The best general survey. Lengthy analysis of the most important novels.

311 _____. "'To What Fyn Lyve I Thus?'--Society and Self in the Chinese Short Story." KENYON REVIEW, 24 (1962), 519-41.

312 Li Tien-Yi. CHINESE FICTION: A BIBLIOGRAPHY OF BOOKS AND ARTICLES IN CHINESE AND ENGLISH. New Haven: Far Eastern Publications, Yale Univ., 1968.

313 Liu, James J.Y. THE CHINESE KNIGHT ERRANT. Chicago: Univ. of Chicago Press, 1967.

The origins of the legendary warrior who is a popular subject in Chinese literature.

314 Průšek, Jaroslav. "The Realistic and Lyric Elements in the Chinese Mediaeval Story." ARCHIV ORIENTÁLNÍ, 32 (1964), 4-15.

315 _____. "Researches into the Beginning of the Chinese Popular Novel." ARCHIV ORIENTÁLNÍ, 9 (1939), 91-132.

Detailed treatment of the forms of Sung dynasty fiction out of which the later novel emerged.

316 Ruhlman, Robert. "Traditional Heroes in Chinese Popular Fiction." In THE CONFUCIAN PERSUASION, pp. 141-76. See entry no. 386.

A comparison between the heroes of popular and classical literature. A perceptive essay.

317 Schurmann, H.F. "On Social Themes in Sung Tales." HARVARD JOURNAL OF ASIATIC STUDIES, 20 (1957), 239-61.

318 Schyns, Joseph, et al. 1500 MODERN CHINESE NOVELS AND PLAYS. Peiping: Catholic Univ. Press, Scheut Editions, 1948; rpt. Hong Kong: Lungman Bookstore, 1966.

Useful summaries of many works analyzed for their moral acceptability. Uncritical.

K. MISCELLANEOUS WRITINGS—ANTHOLOGIES

319   Edwards, E[vangeline] D., trans. CHINESE PROSE LITERATURE OF THE
      T'ANG PERIOD. Vol. I. See entry no. 286.

320   Giles, Herbert A., trans. GEMS OF CHINESE LITERATURE. See
      entry no. 141.

321   Scarborough, William, ed. A COLLECTION OF CHINESE PROVERBS.
      Rev. and enl. by C. Wilfrid Allan. New York: Paragon Book Co.,
      1964.

      Useful collection, with Chinese characters, transliterations,
      and translations.

L. MISCELLANEOUS WRITINGS—HISTORY AND CRITICISM

322   Dawson, Raymond. "The Writing of History in China." HISTORY
      TODAY, 2 (1952), 281-86.

      Good brief sketch of the field.

323   Frankel, Hans H. CATALOGUE OF TRANSLATIONS FROM THE
      CHINESE DYNASTIC HISTORIES FOR THE PERIOD 220-960. Berkeley:
      Univ. of California Press, 1957.

324   Gardiner, Charles S. TRADITIONAL CHINESE HISTORIOGRAPHY.
      Rev. ed. Cambridge, Mass.: Harvard Univ. Press, 1961.

      Major study of the tradition.

325   Hightower, James Robert. "Some Characteristics of Parallel Prose."
      In STUDIA SERICA BERNHARD KARLGREN DEDICATA, pp. 60-91.
      See entry no. 156.

      Important article on the elaborate metrical prose form called
      parallel prose. Includes translations.

M. COMPARATIVE STUDIES

326   Appleton, William W. A CYCLE OF CATHAY. New York: Columbia
      Univ. Press, 1951.

      An excellent summary of the relatively minor influence of
      China on English literature.

327 Bagchi, Prabdoh Chandra. INDIA AND CHINA; A THOUSAND YEARS OF CULTURAL RELATIONS. 2d ed. New York: Philosophical Library, 1951.

Includes all aspects of cultural exchange.

328 Blunden, Edmund. "China in English Literature." EASTERN HORIZON, No. 1 (August 1960), pp. 27-33.

By an English poet long resident in the Far East.

329 Bridgewater, Patrick. "Arthur Waley and Brecht." GERMAN LIFE AND LETTERS, 17 (1964), 216-32.

330 Chang Hsin-Hai. "American Cultural Influence on China." CHINESE CULTURE, 4 (1962), 128-33.

331 Duyvendak, J.J.L. A CHINESE "DIVINA COMMEDIA." Leiden: E. Brill, 1952.

Moslem, Chinese, and Buddhist ideas of hell.

332 Eber, Irene. "Translations Literature in Modern China: The Yiddish Author and his Tale." ASIAN AND AFRICAN STUDIES [Jerusalem], 8 (1972), 291-314.

333 _____. "Yiddish Literature and the Literary Revolution in China." JUDAISM, 16 (1967), 42-59.

334 Frankel, Hans H. "Poetry and Painting: Chinese and Western Views of their Convertibility." COMPARATIVE LITERATURE, 9 (1957), 289-307.

335 Frodsham, J.D. "Reluctant Muse: Chinese Poetry in the West." ORIENT/WEST, 9, No. 5 (September-October 1964), 21-30.

336 Gálik, Marián. "On the Influence of Foreign Ideas on Chinese Literary Criticism, 1898-1904." ASIAN AND AFRICAN STUDIES [Bratislava], 2 (1966), 38-48.

337 Hightower, James Robert. "Chinese Literature in the Context of World Literature." COMPARATIVE LITERATURE, 5 (1953), 117-24.

338 Hou Chien. "Irving Babbitt and Chinese Thought." TAMKANG REVIEW, 5 (1974), 135-85.

339 Hudson, Geoffrey F. EUROPE AND CHINA: A SURVEY OF THEIR RELATIONS FROM EARLIEST TIMES TO 1800. London: Edward Arnold, 1931.

Excellent survey of all aspects of cultural exchange.

340 Jennings, Lane Eaton. CHINESE LITERATURE AND THOUGHT IN THE POETRY AND PROSE OF BERTOLT BRECHT. Cambridge, Mass.: Harvard Univ. Press, 1970.

Good assessment of Brecht's interest in China and its influence on his work.

341 Lach, Donald F. "China and the Era of the Enlightenment." JOURNAL OF MODERN HISTORY, 14 (1942), 209-23.

342 _____. "Leibnitz and China." JOURNAL OF THE HISTORY OF IDEAS, 14 (1953), 437-55.

343 McDougall, Bonnie S. "'The Importance of Being Earnest' in China: Early Chinese Attitudes towards Oscar Wilde." JOURNAL OF THE ORIENTAL SOCIETY OF AUSTRALIA, 9 (1972-73), 84-98.

344 _____. THE INTRODUCTION OF WESTERN LITERARY THEORIES INTO CHINA, 1919-1925. Tokyo: Centre for East Asian Cultural Studies, 1971.

Extensive study of this critical period of influence.

345 North, William Roberts. CHINESE THEMES IN AMERICAN VERSE. Philadelphia: The Author, 1937.

Useful study of a minor, exotic movement. Published thesis from the University of Pennsylvania.

346 Průšek, Jaroslav. "A Confrontation of Traditional Oriental Literature with Modern European Literature in the Context of the Chinese Literary Revolution." ARCHIV ORIENTALNI, 32 (1964), 365-75.

347 Wang Chi-Chen. "Traditional Literature: Nature and Limitations." In CHINA, pp. 386-96. See entry no. 132.

Useful contrasts between Western and Chinese attitudes to literature.

348 Wang Yang-Lo. "Chinese Translations of Latin-American Literature." CHINESE LITERATURE, No. 7 (1963), pp. 109-13.

349   Yip Wai-Lim. EZRA POUND'S "CATHAY." Princeton: Princeton Univ. Press, 1969.

> Learned analysis of Chinese borrowings and of the influence of Chinese ideas on Pound.

350   Yule, Henry, ed. CATHAY AND THE WAY THITHER, BEING A COLLECTION OF MEDIEVAL NOTICES OF CHINA. Rev. by Henri Cordier. London: Hakluyt Society, 1931.

> Western travellers to China and Western writers on China in the Middle Ages.

N. EARLIER AUTHORS AND WORKS

Chan-Kuo Ts'e (Intrigues of the Warring States) (ca. 80 B.C.)

351   Crump, James I., trans. CHAN KUO-TS'E. Oxford: Clarendon Press, 1970.

> Documents, anecdotes, dialogues from the period 403-22 B.C. A thorough, scholarly translation with full apparatus. Incorporates much of Crump's INTRIGUES: STUDIES OF THE CHAN KUO-TS'E (Ann Arbor: Univ. of Michigan Press, [1964]).

Chang Hêng (78-139)

352   Hughes, E[rnest] R., trans. TWO CHINESE POETS: VIGNETTES OF HAN LIFE AND THOUGHT. Princeton: Princeton Univ. Press, 1960.

> Translations of poems in the fu form, with commentary.

Chang Wen-Ch'eng (ca. 657-730)

353   Levy, Harold S., trans. THE DWELLING OF PLAYFUL GODDESSES: CHINA'S FIRST NOVELETTE. Tokyo: Dai Nippon Instasu, 1965.

> A journey to the land of the fairies, this early work of fiction blends poetry with prose. Good notes and introduction.

Chao-Shih Ku-Erh (The Orphan of Chao)

TRANSLATIONS

354   Liu Jung-En, trans. FIVE YÜAN PLAYS. See entry no. 253.

355   MacLachlan, Ian, and Stephen Wang, trans. "The Orphan Chao."

EASTERN HORIZON, 3 (January 1964), 46-65; (February 1964), 40-53; (March 1964), 48-57.

Two good modern translations of a famous operatic drama.

356   Liu Wu-Chi. "The Original Orphan of Chao." COMPARATIVE LITERA-TURE, 5 (1953), 193-212.

Study of the play which had, in adaptation, a European vogue.

Chia I (201-169 B.C.)

357   Knechtges, David R. TWO STUDIES ON THE HAN "FU." Seattle: Univ. of Washington Press, 1968.

Brief study of this almost legendary early poet.

Chin-Ku Ch-I-Kuan (seventeenth century)

358   Howell, E.B., trans. THE INCONSTANCY OF MADAME CHUANG AND OTHER STORIES FROM THE CHINESE. London: T.W. Laurie, 1924.

359   _____ . THE RESTITUTION OF THE BRIDE AND OTHER STORIES FROM THE CHINESE. London: T.W. Laurie, [1926].

360   Hundhausen, Vincenz, trans. THE OIL-VENDER AND THE SING-SONG GIRL, A CHINESE TALE IN FIVE CANTOS. Trans. from German by Fritz Ruesch. 3 vols. New York: F. Ruesch, 1938.

An important seventeenth-century collection of fiction. Howell (entry nos. 358-59, above) translates six stories each in his two volumes and Hundhausen a long novel in his three volumes.

Chin P'ing Mei (early sixteenth century)

TRANSLATIONS

361   Egerton, Clement, trans. THE GOLDEN LOTUS. 4 vols. London: Routledge and Kegan Paul, 1939.

Famous novel of social intrigue and sexual excess. A good translation with the erotic passages in Latin.

362   [Kuhn, Fritz, trans.] CHIN P'ING MEI: THE ADVENTUROUS HIS-TORY OF HSI MEN AND HIS SIX WIVES. Trans. from German by

Bernard Miall. 2 vols. New York: G.P. Putnam, 1940; rpt. 2 vols. in 1, 1947.

Both translations abridged and expurgated. Waley contributes a useful introduction to Kuhn's translation.

STUDIES

363   Hanan, Patrick D. "Sources of the CHIN P'ING MEI." ASIA MAJOR, 10 (1963), 23–67.

Important study of the background of the work.

364   Ono, Shinobu. "CHIN P'ING MEI: A Critical Study." ACTA ASIATICA, 5 (1963), 76–89.

Ching Sheng-T'an (1610-61)

365   Wang, John Ching-Yu. CHING SHENG-T'AN. New York: Twayne, 1972.

Biographical study of a pioneer in the advocating of literature in the vernacular.

Chu Yüan (ca. 343-277 B.C.)

TRANSLATIONS

366   Hawkes, David, trans. CH'U TZ'U: SONGS OF THE SOUTH, AN ANCIENT CHINESE ANTHOLOGY. Oxford: Oxford Univ. Press, 1959.

A major anthology of Chinese poetry, most of which has been attributed to Chu Yüan. Accurate, somewhat literal translations, with an early biography of the poet and an introduction to his poetic technique.

367   Lim Boon Keng, trans. THE LI SAO: AN ELEGY ON ENCOUNTERING SORROWS, BY CHU YÜAN. Shanghai: Commercial Press, 1929.

A rather free translation. Chinese text included.

368   Yang Hsien-Yi, and Gladys Yang, trans. LI SAO, AND OTHER POEMS BY CHU YÜAN. Peking: Foreign Languages Press, 1953.

Good translation in English verse. Contains a sketch of the poet by the twentieth-century critic Kuo Mo-Jo.

STUDIES

369   Hightower, James Robert. "Ch'u Yüan Studies." In SILVER JUBILEE
       VOLUME OF THE ZINBUM-KAGAKU-KENKYUSYO. Kyoto: Kyoto
       Univ., 1954.

       An important study of the poet and the collection.

Chuang-Tzǔ (fourth century B.C.)

It is difficult to decide whether this is the name of the author or the work.
He is treated here as an author.

TRANSLATIONS

370   Feng, Gia-Fu, and Jane English, trans. INNER CHAPTERS, A NEW
       TRANSLATION. New York: Alfred A. Knopf, 1974.

       An interpretive translation with the Chinese text and symbolic
       photographs.

371   Fung Yu-Lan, trans. CHUANG TZǓ: A NEW SELECTED TRANSLA-
       TION. Shanghai: Commercial Press, 1931; rpt. New York: Paragon
       Book Co., 1964.

       A good selection. Contains an ancient commentary.

372   Giles, Herbert A., trans. CHUANG TZǓ: MYSTIC, MORALIST AND
       SOCIAL REFORMER. London: B. Quaritch, 1926; rpt. London: Allen
       and Unwin, [1961], as CHUANG TZǓ, TAOIST PHILOSOPHER AND
       MYSTIC.

       Excellent, complete translation. This and Waley's below, are
       the preferred ones.

373   Legge, James, trans. THE SACRED BOOKS OF CHINA; THE TEXTS
       OF TAOISM. See entry no. 144.

       Old but still valuable translation, frequently cited.

374   Lin Yutang, trans. THE WISDOM OF CHINA AND INDIA. See entry
       no. 148.

       A readable, improved version of Giles, above.

375   Waley, Arthur, trans. THREE WAYS OF THOUGHT IN ANCIENT
       CHINA. See entry no. 151.

       Excellent translation with valuable introduction.

376   Ware, James R., trans. THE SAYINGS OF CHUANG CHOU, A NEW
       TRANSLATION. New York: New American Library, 1968.

       Good modern translation--somewhat free--by a philosopher.

377   Watson, Burton, trans. THE COMPLETE WORKS OF CHUANG TZǓ.
       New York: Columbia Univ. Press, 1968.

       Modern, excellent translation. Selections from this are in
       CHUANG TZǓ: BASIC WRITINGS (New York: Columbia
       Univ. Press, 1968).

STUDIES

378   Giles, Lionel, ed. MUSINGS OF A CHINESE MYSTIC. London:
       John Murray, [1927].

       A good brief introduction. Includes selections translated by
       Herbert A. Giles.

Confucius [Kung Fu-Tsi] (sixth-fifth centuries B.C.)

The collection of ancient classics known as the Confucian canon consists of
works attributed to Confucius, works supposedly edited by him, and works as-
cribed to his early disciples. These classics (ching) have been much revered
in China and have for centuries formed the basis for a liberal education.
The oldest or "great" classics are (1) I CHING (BOOK OF DIVINATION),
(2) SHU CHING (BOOK OF DOCUMENTS), (3) SHIH CHING (BOOK OF
SONGS OR ODES), (4) CH'UN CH'IU (SPRING AND AUTUMN ANNALS),
(5) LI CHING BOOK OF RITUAL), and (6) YÜEH CHING (BOOK OF MUSIC).
Of these, the most important literary work is the SHIH CHING, the ancient
anthology of poetry. To these works were added four other classics: (7) LUN
YÜ (ANALECTS), which may best represent the actual sayings of Confucius as
a philosopher; (8) MENG TZU, the work of Mencius, who is considered separately
below; (9) three commentaries on the SPRING AND AUTUMN ANNALS; and
(10) ERH YA, a lexical work. Finally, later orthodox Confucianism set aside
two parts of the ritual collection as of special worthiness. These are (11) TA
HSEUH (GREAT LEARNING) and (12) CHUNG YUNG (GOLDEN MEAN,
DOCTRINE OF THE MEAN, HAPPY MEAN). Of these the ANALECTS,
Mencius, and the last two have the most literary interest.

ANTHOLOGIES

379   Chai Ch'u, and Winberg Chai, eds. and trans. THE SACRED BOOKS
       OF CONFUCIUS AND OTHER CONFUCIAN CLASSICS. New Hyde
       Park, N.Y.: University Books, [1965].

       A good selection of essential texts, well translated.

380   Legge, James, trans. THE CHINESE CLASSICS. 6 vols. Hong Kong:

Hong Kong Univ. Press, 1960.

First published 1892–95. The 1960 reprint corrects the first
five volumes and contains a sixth, supplementary volume.

381 _____. THE SACRED BOOKS OF CHINA: THE TEXTS OF CONFU-
CIANISM. 4 vols. Oxford: Clarendon Press, 1879–95.

Despite its age and somewhat old-fashioned translations,
Legge's work is still the major Confucian collection and is
often referred to. The Chinese texts are included.

382 Ware, James R., trans. THE BEST OF CONFUCIUS. Garden City,
N.Y.: Halcyon House, [1950].

A good brief selection, well translated.

STUDIES

383 Creel, Herrlee G. CONFUCIUS, THE MAN AND THE MYTH. New
York: John Day Co., 1949.

Valuable study by an eminent authority. Reissued as CONFU-
CIUS AND THE CHINESE WAY. (New York: Harper, 1949).

384 Liu Wu-Chi. A SHORT HISTORY OF CONFUCIAN PHILOSOPHY.
New York: Dell Publishing Co., 1964.

An enthusiatic and learned study, somewhat controversial in
its conclusions.

385 Nivison, David S., and Arthur F. Wright, eds. CONFUCIANISM IN
ACTION. Stanford: Stanford Univ. Press, 1959.

386 Wright, Arthur F., ed. THE CONFUCIAN PERSUASION. Stanford:
Stanford Univ. Press, 1960; rpt. as CONFUCIANISM AND CHINESE
CIVILIZATION, New York: Atheneum, [1964].

387 Wright, Arthur F., and Denis Twitchett, eds. CONFUCIAN PERSON-
ALITIES. Stanford: Stanford Univ. Press, 1962.

These three volumes (entry nos. 385–87) are collections of
papers by specialists on all aspects of Confucian thought.

INDIVIDUAL WORKS

Ch'un Ch'iu (Spring and Autumn Annals)

388 Legge, James, trans. "Ch'un Ts'ew with the Tso Chuen." In THE
CHINESE CLASSICS, V, 1–835. See entry no. 380.

An interpretation of the history of the state of Lu, Confucius's native state, from 722 to 481 B.C. An obscure text.

Chung Yung (Doctrine of the Mean)

389 Hughes, E[rnest] R., trans. THE GREAT LEARNING AND THE MEAN IN ACTION. New York: E.P. Dutton, 1943.

Good translation with commentary.

390 Legge, James, trans. "The Doctrine of the Mean." In THE CHINESE CLASSICS, I, 382–434. See entry no. 380.

391 Lin Yutang, trans. "The Golden Mean." In THE WISDOM OF CHINA AND INDIA, pp. 843–66. See entry no. 148.

392 Pound, Ezra, trans. CONFUCIUS: THE GREAT DIGEST AND THE UNWOBBLING PIVOT. New York: New Directions, [1951].

A highly interpretative translation. Illustrated with the stone-rubbing text, with a commentary on that by Achilles Fang.

I Ching (Book of Divination)

TRANSLATIONS

393 Blofeld, John, trans. I CHING (THE BOOK OF CHANGES). New York: E.P. Dutton, 1968.

Translation and detailed instructions about how the book is to be used for divination.

394 Legge, James, trans. "Yi King." In THE SACRED BOOKS OF CHINA: THE TEXTS OF CONFUCIANISM II, 57–210. Rpt. as I CHING. New York: Dover Books, [1963]. See entry no. 381.

395 Wilhelm, Richard, trans. THE I CHING OR BOOK OF CHANGES. Trans. into English by Cary F. Baynes. Princeton: Princeton Univ. Press, 1967.

A good translation with extensive commentary. Foreword by Karl Jung and another by Helmut Wilhelm.

STUDIES

396 Siu, R[alph] G.R. THE MAN OF MANY QUALITIES: A LEGACY OF THE I CHING. Cambridge, Mass.: Harvard Univ. Press, [1968].

Lengthy scholarly study of the work with a new translation.

397   Waley, Arthur. "The Book of Changes." BULLETIN OF THE MUSEUM OF FAR EASTERN ANTIQUITIES, 5 (1933), 121–42.

How the work was used in divination. Scholarly.

398   Wilhelm, Helmut. CHANGE: EIGHT LECTURES ON THE I CHING. Trans. Cary F. Baynes. New York: Pantheon Books, 1960.

399   _____. HEAVEN, EARTH, AND MAN IN THE BOOK OF CHANGES. Seattle: Univ. of Washington Press, 1977.

400   _____. "The Interplay of Image and Concept in the Book of Changes." ERANOS JAHRBUCH, 36 (1967), 31–57.

Wilhelm's are valuable studies. The first, entry no. 398, is perhaps the best introduction to the work.

Li Ching (book of Ritual)

Though listed as a single classic, this is actually a collection of ritual texts which includes the CHUNG YUNG (DOCTRINE OF THE MEAN) and the TA HSUEH (GREAT LEARNING), which are listed separately, above and below.

401   Legge, James, trans. "Li Ki." In THE SACRED BOOKS OF CHINA: THE TEXTS OF CONFUCIANISM, III, GI–479; IV, I–470. See entry no. 381.

402   Steele, John, trans. The I-LI OR BOOK OF ETIQUETTE AND CEREMONIAL. 2 vols. London: Arthur Probsthain, 1917.

This part of the LI CHING is the basis for ritual in public and religious life. An authoritative translation.

Lun-Yü (Analects)

TRANSLATIONS

403   Giles, Lionel, trans. THE SAYINGS OF CONFUCIUS. London: John Murray, 1907.

A generous selection arranged by topics.

404   Legge, James, trans. "The Confucian Analects." In THE CHINESE CLASSICS, I, 137–349. See entry no. 380.

405   Lin Yutang, trans. THE WIDOM OF CONFUCIUS. New York: Modern Library, [1938].

Complete with long introduction. Partly reprinted in his
THE WISDOM OF CHINA AND INDIA, pp. 811-42. See
entry no. 148.

406 Pound, Ezra. THE CONFUCIAN ANALECTS. London: Peter Owen,
[1956].

A free translation done with Pound's usual verve and imagination.

407 Soothill, William E., trans. THE ANALECTS OR CONVERSATIONS
OF CONFUCIUS. Oxford: Oxford Univ. Press, 1937.

An authoritative translation. The style may determine
whether the reader prefers this or Waley's, immediately below.

408 Waley, Arthur, trans. THE ANALECTS OF CONFUCIUS. New York:
Ramdom House, 1938.

Excellent, accurate translation with useful introduction and
a discussion of the technical terms.

409 Ware, James R., trans. THE SAYINGS OF CONFUCIUS. New York:
New American Library, [1955].

Another accurate translation, directed more at the general
American reader.

STUDIES

410 Leslie, D. "Notes on the ANALECTS. Appendixed by a Select Bibliography for the ANALECTS." T'OUNG PAO, 49 (1961), 1-63.

Useful, if somewhat technical.

411 Sinaiko, Herman L. "The ANALECTS of Confucious." In APPROACHES
TO THE ORIENTAL CLASSICS, pp. 142-52. See entry no. 50.

A good introduction for the nonspecialist.

Shih Ching (Book of Songs)

TRANSLATIONS

412 Karlgren, Bernhard, trans. THE BOOK OF ODES. Stockholm: Museum
of Far Eastern Antiquities, 1950.

Chinese text, transcription, and a quite literal translation by
an eminent sinologist. Valuable in conjunction with all other
translations.

413 Legge, James, trans. "She King." In THE CHINESE CLASSICS, IV, 1–647. See entry no. 380.

414 Pound, Ezra, trans. THE CLASSIC ANTHOLOGY AS DEFINED BY CONFUCIUS. Cambridge, Mass.: Harvard Univ. Press, 1954.

Brilliant interpretation with occasional errors. Perhaps Pound's masterpiece in his recreation of Chinese literature.

415 Waley, Arthur, trans. THE BOOK OF SONGS. New York: Grove Press, 1960.

An accurate, elegant literary translation. Poems rearranged according to subject matter, but an index of the original numbers enables one to consult Legge and Karlgren.

STUDIES

416 Dembo, L.S. THE CONFUCIAN ODES OF EZRA POUND: A CRITICAL APPRAISAL. Berkeley: Univ. of California Press, 1963.

An essential study of Pound's theory and practice.

417 Hightower, James Robert. HAN SHI WAI CHUAN: HAN YING'S ILLUSTRATIONS OF THE DIDACTIC APPLICATION OF THE CLASSIC OF SONGS. Cambridge, Mass.: Harvard Univ. Press, 1952.

The SHIH CHING was believed to contain great wisdom, as Confucius notes. This well-translated Han dynasty commentary illustrates the traditional moralistic interpretation. Thorough annotations.

418 McNaughton, William. THE BOOK OF SONGS. New York: Twayne, [1971].

A very useful "handbook" covering all aspects of the work.

Shu Ching (Book of Documents)

419 Karlgren, Bernhard, trans. THE BOOK OF DOCUMENTS. Stockholm: Museum of Far Eastern Antiquities, 1950.

The oldest surviving Chinese history, from the beginnings to 626 B.C. Literal, scholarly translation with the Chinese text.

420 Legge, James, trans. "Shoo King." In THE CHINESE CLASSICS, III, 1–620. See entry no. 380. Also in THE SACRED BOOKS OF CHINA: THE TEXTS OF CONFUCIANISM, I, 275–446. See entry no. 381.

421   Waltham, Clae, ed. SSU CHING: BOOK OF HISTORY. Chicago: Regnery, 1971.

A reworking and modernization of Legge's two translations.

Ta Hsüeh (The Great Learning)

422   Hughes, E[rnest] R., trans. THE GREAT LEARNING AND THE MEAN IN ACTION. See entry no. 389.

A standard translation and study.

423   Legge, James. "The Great Learning." In THE CHINESE CLASSICS, I, 355-381. See entry no. 381.

Fa Hsien (fl. 399-444)

424   Beal, Samuel, trans. TRAVELS OF FAH-HIAN AND SUNG-YUN, BUDDHIST PILGRIMS, FROM CHINA TO INDIA (400 A.D. and 518 A.D.) London: Susil Gupta, [1964].

Pilgrim-mediators who brought back basic books of Buddhism. Good translation with notes.

425   Giles, Herbert A., trans. THE TRAVELS OF FA-HSIEN (399-414 A.D.) OR RECORD OF THE BUDDHIST KINGDOMS. London: Routledge and Kegan Paul, 1959.

Good translation, no commentary.

Han Fei Tzu (d. 233 B.C.)

426   Liao, W.K., trans. THE COMPLETE WORKS OF HAN FEI TZU. 2 vols. London: Arthur Probsthain, 1939.

Scholarly translation with commentary.

427   Waley, Arthur, trans. THREE WAYS OF THOUGHT IN ANCIENT CHINA. See entry no. 151.

428   Watson, Burton, trans. HAN FEI TZU: BASIC WRITINGS. New York: Columbia Univ. Press, 1964.

Both Waley's above, and Watson's translations are accurate and highly readable. Watson translates more of the argumentative prose of this political philosopher and has an excellent intro-duction.

Han Shan (fl. 627-49)

TRANSLATIONS

429   Fackler, Herbert V., trans. "Three English Versions of Han-Shan's Cold Mountain Poems." LITERATURE EAST & WEST, 15 (1972), 269-78.

430   Watson, Burton, trans. COLD MOUNTAIN: 100 POEMS BY THE TANG POEM HAN-SHAN. New York: Columbia Univ. Press, [1962].

A scholarly study with translations. Fackler's article provides a different perspective.

Han Yü (768-824)

431   Owen, Stephen. THE POETRY OF MENG CHIAO AND HAN YÜ. New Haven: Yale Univ. Press, 1975.

A good study of an important poet. The only complete translation of the works is in German in Edwin von Zach's POETISCHE WERKE (Cambridge, Mass.: Harvard Univ. Press, 1952). James Robert Hightower's introduction to this, in English, is recommended.

Hsi Hsiang Chi (The West Chamber) (thirteenth century)

432   Hart, Henry H., trans. THE WEST CHAMBER: A MEDIEVAL DRAMA. Stanford: Stanford Univ. Press, [1936].

433   Hsiung, S.I., trans. THE ROMANCE OF THE WESTERN CHAMBER (HSI HSIANG CHI), A CHINESE PLAY WRITTEN IN THE THIRTEENTH CENTURY. London: Methuen, [1935]; New York: Columbia Univ. Press, 1968.

Often attributed to Wang Shih-Fu (fl. 1295-1307). Both this and the preceding translations are adequate and both have introductions.

Hsi K'ang [Chi K'ang] (223-62)

434   Gulik, R.H. Van, trans. HSI K'ANG AND HIS POETICAL ESSAY ON THE LUTE. Tokyo: Sophia Univ.; Rutland, Vt.: Charles E. Tuttle Co., [1969].

Literary and philosophical rhapsody on lute playing by a sage. Full annotations on the poem, the CHIN-FU.

Hsieh Ling-Yün (385-433)

435   Frodsham, J.D. "Hsieh Ling-Yün: China's First Nature Poet." ORIENT/WEST, 8 (May-June 1964), 52-61.

Provides a brief introduction to the poet.

436   _____. THE MURMURING STREAM: THE LIFE AND WORKS OF THE CHINESE NATURE POET HSIEH LING-YÜN (385-433), DUKE OF K'ANG-LO. 2 vols. London: Oxford Univ. Press, 1967.

Detailed study with translations.

437   Mather, Richard. "The Landscape Buddhism of the Fifth-Century Poet Hsieh Ling-Yün." JOURNAL OF ASIAN STUDIES, 18 (1958-59), 67-79.

Useful article with some translations.

Hsin Ch'i (1140-1207)

438   Lo, Irving Yucheng. HSIN CH'I-CHI. New York: Twayne, [1971].

Biography of the poet with detailed discussion of the poetry.

Hsiu Ou-Yang (1007-72)

439   Liu, James T.C. OU-YANG HSIU: AN ELEVENTH CENTURY NEO-CONFUCIANIST. Stanford: Stanford Univ. Press, 1967.

A major poet who was also a philosopher and political thinker. Detailed study.

Hsüan Tsang (ca. 596-664)

440   Beal, Samuel, trans. SI-YU-KI: BUDDHIST RECORDS OF THE WESTERN REGION. 2 vols. London: Kegan Paul, Trench, Trubner, [1906].

A rather old-fashioned translation of the HSI YU-CHI [SI YU-KI], an account of a pilgrimage to India begun in 629. Important for Chinese Buddhism and the basis for the novel MONKEY (see Wu Ch'eng-En, below).

441   Waley, Arthur, trans. THE REAL TRIPITAKA AND OTHER PIECES. London: Allen and Unwin, [1952].

Includes an abridged version of the travels in an excellent translation.

Hsueh-Tou Chung-Hsien (ca. 980-1052)

442   Shaw, R.D.M., trans. THE BLUE-CLIFF RECORDS: THE HEKIGAN ROKU. London: Michael Joseph, 1961.

> The HEKIGAN ROKU is the Japanese title for the PI YEN LU, a collection of stories and sayings of the Buddha in verse and prose, a scripture of the Zen (Chan) tradition. Full commentary.

Hsün Tzu (340-245 B.C.)

TRANSLATIONS

443   Dubs, Homer H., trans. THE WORKS OF HSÜNTZE. London: Arthur Probsthain, 1928.

444   Watson, Burton, trans. HSÜN TZU: BASIC WRITINGS. New York: Columbia Univ. Press, 1963.

> An important later Confucian writer. Watson's introduction is excellent and his translation is preferable, but there is a more generous selection in Dubs (above entry).

STUDIES

445   Dubs, Homer H. HSÜNTZU, THE MOLDER OF ANCIENT CONFU-CIANISM. London: Arthur Probsthain, 1927.

> A good study which now needs to be brought up to date.

Hui Neng (638-713)

446   Chan Wing-Tsit, trans. THE PLATFORM SCRIPTURES. New York: St. John's Univ. Press, 1963.

> A collection of of the sayings of a Zen (Chan) patriarch, which became a sacred scripture. Good translation for the general reader by a specialist in Chinese philosophy.

447   Yampolsky, Philip B., trans. THE PLATFORM SUTRA OF THE SIXTH PATRIARCH. New York: Columbia Univ. Press, 1967.

> Also an authoritative translation, with good introduction.

Hung Sheng (1645-1704)

448   Yang Hsien-Yi, and Gladys Yang, trans. THE PALACE OF ETERNAL

YOUTH. Peking: Foreign Languages Press, [1955].

A romantic historical drama with commentary.

449   Bodde, Derk. "Some Chinese Tales of the Supernatural: Kan Pao and his Sou-shen Chi." HARVARD JOURNAL OF ASIATIC STUDIES, 6 (1942), 338–44.

Study of early ghost stories with some translations.

Kao Ch'i (1336-74)

450   Mote, Frederick W., trans. THE POET KAO CH'I, 1336–1374. Princeton: Princeton Univ. Press, 1962.

Translations with commentary and historical background.

Ko-Lien Hua-Ying (seventeenth century)

451   Kuhn, Fritz, trans. KO-LIEN HUA-YING. FLOWER SHADOWS BE-HIND THE CURTAIN. Trans. from German by Vladimir Kean. New York: Pantheon, 1959.

A sequel by an unknown author to the CHIN P'ING MEI (see above).

Kuan Han Ch'ing (ca. 1210-98)

452   Shih Chung-Wen, trans. INJUSTICE TO TOU O (TOU O YUAN), A STUDY AND TRANSLATION. Cambridge, Engl.: Cambridge Univ. Press, 1972.

Detailed study with translation of a play by a major dramatist.

453   Yang Hsien-Yi, and Gladys Yang, trans. SELECTED PLAYS. Peking: Foreign Languages Press, 1958.

Eight plays in satisfactory translations.

Kuei Wang-Jung (thirteenth century)

454   Gulik, R.H. van., trans. T'ANG-YIN PI-SHIH: PARALLEL CASES FROM UNDER THE PEAR TREE, A THIRTEENTH CENTURY MANUAL OF JURISPRUDENCE AND DETECTION. Leiden: E.J. Brill, 1956.

Interesting background for a popular Chinese genre, fiction on crime and detection.

K'ung Shang-Jën (1648-1718)

455   Chen Shih-Hsiang, and Harold Acton, trans. THE PEACH BLOSSOM FAN. Trans. with collaboration of Cyril Birch. Berkeley: Univ. of California Press, 1976.

Historical drama based on the overthrow of the Ming by the Manchus, with a powerful love story. Excellent translation.

Kung Tzu-Chên (1792-1841)

456   Wong, Shirleen S. KUNG TZU-CHÊN. New York: Twayne, 1975. Biography of a poet and public official.

Kuo Hsi (fl. 1020)

457   Sakanishi, Shio, trans. LIN CH'UAN KAU CHIH: ESSAY ON LAND-SCAPE PAINTING. London: John Murray, 1935.

Important because of the close relationship between poetry and landscape painting in China.

Lao Tzu (ca. third century B.C.)

The author is no more than a name, though the work seems to be by one author. An elusive, difficult work, central to the Taoist philosophy. The TAO TE CHING (WAY OF TAO) has probably been translated into English more than any other Chinese work.

TRANSLATIONS

458   Bahm, Archie J., trans. TAO TEH KING, INTERPRETED AS NATURE AND INTELLIGENCE. New York: Frederick Ungar, [1958].

Often full of insight but interpretive. Should be used in conjunction with other translations.

459   Blakney, R.B., trans. THE WAY OF LIFE: A NEW TRANSLATION OF THE TAO TE CHING. New York: New American Library, [1955].

Satisfactory modern translation with annotations. Good introduction on interpretation.

460   Bynner, Witter, trans. THE WAY OF LIFE ACCORDING TO LAOTZU, AN AMERICAN VERSION. New York: Capricorn Books, [1962].

Readable but somewhat free translation.

461   Carus, Paul, trans. THE CANON OF REASON AND VIRTUE. Chicago: Open Court Publishing Co., 1913.

Conservative translation. Still useful. Some annotations.

462   Chan Wing-Tsit, trans. THE WAY OF LAO TZU (TAO-TÊ CHING). Indianapolis: Bobbs-Merrill Co., 1963.

Superior translation with extensive commentary.

463   Ch'u Ta-Kao, trans. TAO TÊ CHING: A NEW TRANSLATION. London: Allen and Unwin, [1959].

Good translation with order to text somewhat rearranged.

464   Duyvendak, J.J.L., trans. TAO TE CHING: THE BOOK OF THE WAY AND ITS VIRTUE. London: John Murray, 1954.

Scholarly translation which attempts to recover the original order of some sections. Good notes.

465   Giles, Lionel, trans. THE SAYINGS OF LAO TZǓ. London: John Murray, [1905]; rpt. 1926.

Convenient arrangement under topics, rather than in the conventional order.

466   Lau, D.C., trans. TAO TE CHING. Baltimore: Penguin Books, [1963].

Perhaps the best modern translation. Full notes and a valuable introduction.

467   Legge, James, trans. THE SACRED BOOKS OF CHINA: THE TEXTS OF TAOISM. See entry no. 144.

468   Lin Yutang, trans. THE WISDOM OF LAOTSE. New York: Modern Library, [1948].

Complete translation with comparable passages from the CHUANG TSE. Very Chinese, antimystical translation.

469   Muller, Leone, trans. TAO-TEH-CHING: LAOTSE'S BOOK OF LIFE. Ed. K.O. Schmidt. New York: CSA Press, 1975.

An attempt to relate the work to modern ideas of psychoanalysis. The commentary does not seem to have much relationship to the text.

470   Waley, Arthur, trans. THE WAY AND ITS POWER: A STUDY OF THE

TAO TE CHING AND ITS PLACE IN CHINESE THOUGHT. Boston: Houghton Mifflin Co., [1934].

Both a study and a translation with Waley's usual authority. Useful introduction on the early stages of the tradition.

471   Wu, John C.H., trans. TAO TE CHING: Ed. Paul K.T. Sih. New York: St. John's Univ. Press, 1961.

Conservative translation. Includes the Chinese text.

STUDIES

472   Erkes, Edward, trans. HO-SHANG-KING'S COMMENTARY ON LAO-TSE. Ascona: Artibus Asiae, 1958.

An early Chinese translation and commentary on the work as it was used by believers.

473   Welch, Holmes. THE PARTING OF THE WAY: LAO TZU AND THE TAOIST MOVEMENT. Boston: Beacon Press, [1957]. Rev. and rpt. as TAOISM: THE PARTING OF THE WAY, [1966].

An essential commentary on the work, with extensive translation.

Li Ch'ing Chao (1084-ca. 1141)

474   Hsu Kai-Yu. "The Poems of Li Ch'ing Chao (1084-1141)." PMLA: PUBLICATIONS OF THE MODERN LANGUAGE ASSOCIATION OF AMERICA, 77 (1962), 521-28.

Good introduction to the poet, with some translations.

475   Hu Ping-Ching. LI CH'ING-CHAO. New York: Twayne, [1966].

Biographical and critical study.

Li Ho (791-817)

TRANSLATIONS

476   Frodsham, J.D., trans. THE POEMS OF LI HO (791-817). Oxford: Oxford Univ. Press, 1970.

Superior translations with a lengthy introduction and full notes.

STUDIES

477   South, Margaret Tudor. LI HO, A SCHOLAR OFFICIAL OF THE YUAN-

HO PERIOD. Adelaide: Libraries Board of South Australia, 1967.

Full biographical study with some explication of the poems.

478   Yu Kwang-Chung. "To the White Jade Palace: A Critical Study of Li Ho (791-817)." TAMKANG REVIEW, 7 (1968), 193-225.

Li Hou-Chu (937-78)

479   Liu Yih-Ling, and Shadid Suhrawardy, trans. POEMS OF LEE HOU-CHU. Bombay: Orient Longmans, [1948].

Overly literal but useful translations of poems by a king of the T'ang dynasty.

Li Hsing-Tao

TRANSLATIONS

480   Hume, Francis, trans. THE STORY OF THE CIRCLE OF CHALK, A DRAMA FROM THE OLD CHINESE. London: Rodale Press, [1954].

The CHALK CIRCLE [HUI LAN CHI] was one of the earliest Chinese dramas to be read in the West. This translation is from the French of Stanislas Julien.

481   Laver, James, trans. THE CIRCLE OF CHALK, A PLAY IN FIVE ACTS, ADAPTED FROM THE CHINESE BY KLABUND. London: W. Heinemann, 1929.

A retranslation from the German. Probably the best in English, but an entirely new one is needed.

482   Van de Meer, Ethel, trans. "The Chalk Circle." In WORLD DRAMA. Ed. Barrett Clark. New York: D. Appleton, 1933.

Also retranslated from the French of Julien.

STUDIES

483   Ludowyk, E.F.C. "The Chalk Circle, a Legend in Four Cultures." COMPARATIVE LITERATURE, 9 (1960), 249-56.

Good study of the vogue of the play.

Li Po [Li T'ai Po] (705?-62)

TRANSLATIONS

484   Cooper, Arthur D., trans. LI PO AND TU FU'S POEMS, SELECTED

AND TRANSLATED. Baltimore: Penguin Books, [1973].

Good selection in excellent modern translation.

485   Pound, Ezra, trans. CATHAY, TRANSLATION BY EZRA POUND, FOR
       THE MOST PART FROM THE CHINESE OF RIHAKU. London: E.
       Mathews, 1915.

       Free, imaginative translations. Rihaku is the Japanese form
       of Li Po's name.

486   Shigeyoshi, Obata, trans. THE WORKS OF LI PO, THE CHINESE
       POET. New York: E.P. Dutton, 1923; rpt. New York: Paragon Book
       Co., 1965.

       Good selection, but superseded by Cooper and Waley.

STUDIES

487   Waley, Arthur. THE POETRY AND CAREER OF LI PO, 701-762 A.D.
       London: Allen and Unwin, [1950].

       Good biography of the poet with translations and commentary
       on the poems.

Li Shang-Yin (812-58)

488   Liu, James J.Y. THE POETRY OF LI SHANG-YIN, NINTH CENTURY
       BAROQUE CHINESE POET. Chicago: Univ. of Chicago Press, [1969].

       Excellent study. Some translations.

489   Tsukimura, Reiko. "Shang-Yin's Poetry: Three Ways of Looking at
       the Inner Reality--Introspection, Recollection, and Vision." LITERA-
       TURE EAST & WEST, 11 (1967), 273-91.

Liang Chien-Wen Ti (fl. 549-51)

490   Marney, John. LIANG CHIEN-WEN TI. New York: Twayne, 1976.

       A good study of the poetic and literary career of the puppet
       emperor of Liang.

Lieh-Tzu (third century B.C.)

491   Giles, Lionel, trans. TAOIST TEACHINGS FROM THE BOOK OF
       LIEH TZU. 2nd ed. London: John Murray, 1947.

       The LIEH-TZU is the third most important book of Taoism,

after the CHUANG-TZU and LAO TZU. A standard translation.

492　Graham, A.C., trans. LIEH-TZU. THE BOOK OF LIEH-TZU. London: John Murray, 1950.

Both readable and accurate. Good introduction.

Liu Chih-Yüan (d. 848)

493　Dolezelelová-Velingerová, M., and James I. Crump., trans. BALLAD
OF THE HIDDEN DRAGON. Oxford: Clarendon Press, 1971.

Excellent translation of a poetic drama. Full introduction and
notes.

Liu Hsieh (ca. 465-ca. 522)

TRANSLATIONS

494　Shih, Vincent Yu-Chung, trans. THE LITERARY MIND AND THE
CARVING OF DRAGONS. New York: Columbia Univ. Press, 1959.

Major translation and study of an early, influential work of
literary criticism and theory.

495　Yang Hsien-Yu, and Gladys Yang, trans. "Carving a Dragon at the
Core of Things." CHINESE LITERATURE, No. 8 (August 1962), pp.
58-71.

Readable modern translation, but Shih's (above entry) is preferable.

STUDIES

496　Tökei, Ferenc. GENRE THEORY IN CHINA IN THE 3RD-6TH CEN-
TURIES (LIU HSIEH'S THEORY OF POETIC GENRES). Budapest:
Akademiai Kiado, 1971.

Valuable, somewhat technical study.

Liu Tsung-Yüan (773-819)

497　Nienhauser, William H., et al. LIU TSUNG-YÜAN. New York:
Twayne, [1973].

Study of a minor poet, essayist, and writer of miscellaneous
prose.

Lo Kuan-Chung (ca. 1330-ca.1400)

498   Brewitt-Taylor, C.H., trans. ROMANCE OF THE THREE KINGDOMS
(SAN KUO CHIH YEN-I). 2 vols. Shanghai: Kelly and Walsh,
1925; rpt. Rutland, Vt.: Charles E. Tuttle Co., 1959.

An important historical novel, dealing with the conflicts of
the post-Han period. The attribution is conventional, and
parts of the novel may have existed earlier. A serviceable
translation but superseded by Roberts, below.

499   Roberts, Moss, trans. THREE KINGDOMS: CHINA'S EPIC DRAMA.
New York: Panthon, 1976.

Condenses and abridges the 120 chapters of this novel. Good
notes. A very readable translation.

Lu Chi (261-303)

TRANSLATIONS

500   Chen Shih-Hsiang, trans. ESSAY ON LITERATURE WRITTEN BY THE
THIRD CENTURY CHINESE POET LU CHI. Portland, Maine: Athoensen
Press, 1953; rpt. in ANTHOLOGY OF CHINESE LITERATURE, pp. 203-
14. See entry no. 137.

A difficult, evocative work in verse on the nature of poetry,
the WEN FU is a major piece of criticism. Superior translation.

501   Fang, Achilles, trans. "Lu Ki's RHYMEPROSE ON LITERATURE." NEW
MEXICO QUARTERLY, 22 (1952), 269-81.

502   _____. "Rhymeprose on Literature: The WEN FU of Lu Chi." HAR-
VARD JOURNAL OF ASIATIC STUDIES, 14 (1951), 527-66.

The HJAS translation is scholarly with philological and other
notes. The NMQ version, which Fang prefers, is very readable. Fang's and Chen's translations are preferable to Hughes,
below.

503   Hughes, E[rnest] R., trans. THE ART OF LETTERS: LU CHI'S "WEN
FU" (A.D. 302). New York: Pantheon Books, [1951].

A good discussion of the work in the introduction.

STUDIES

504   Knoerle, Mary Gregory. "The Poetic Theories of Lu Chi, with a Brief

Comparison with Horace's ARS POETICA." JOURNAL OF AESTHETICS AND ART CRITICISM, 25 (1966), 137–43.

Interesting comparison of the WEN FU with the most influential of all Western poetic treatises.

Lu Hsi-Hsing, supposed author (mid-sixteenth century)

TRANSLATIONS

505   Liu Ts'un-Yan [Liu Ts'un Jên], trans. BUDDHIST AND TAOIST INFLUENCES ON CHINESE NOVELS. Vol. 1. Wiesbaden: Harassowitz, 1962.

This is really a translation and study of one work, the FÊNG-SHÊN YÊN-I, a historical novel of intrigue in high places in the twelfth century.

STUDIES

506   Brewster, Paul G. "Some Parallels between the FÊNG-SHÊN-YÊN-I and the SHAHNAMAH and the Possible Influences of the Former on the Persian Epic." ASIAN FOLKLORE STUDIES, 31 [1972], 115–22.

The SHAHNAMAH, the Persian national epic, is by Firdausī, who died ca. 1025.

Lu Yu [Lu Fang-Weng] (1125-1210)

TRANSLATIONS

507   Candlin, Clara M., trans. THE RAPIER OF LU: PATRIOT POET OF CHINA. London: John Murray, 1946.

Reasonably good translations of the more patriotic poems of this important poet. Includes biographical sketch.

508   Ho Peng Yoke, et al., trans. LU YU THE POET ALCHEMIST. Canberra: Australian National Univ. Press, 1972.

509   Watson, Burton, trans. THE OLD MAN WHO DOES AS HE PLEASES: SELECTIONS FROM THE POETRY AND PROSE OF LU YU. New York: Columbia Univ. Press, 1973.

Good translations in both Ho, above, and Watson; a fuller selection in Watson and a useful introduction.

STUDIES

510   Duke, Michael S. LU YOU. New York: Twayne, 1977.

New interpretation of his life relying heavily on the works
themselves.

Mei Yao-Ch'en (1002-60)

511 Chaves, Jonathan. MEI YAO-CH'EN AND THE DEVELOPMENT OF
EARLY SUNG POETRY. New York: Columbia Univ. Press, 1975.

Critical study of one of a group of reformist poets.

Mencius [Meng Tzu] (372-289 B.C.)

The works of this important early philosopher are considered to be among the
classics. See Confucius, above.

TRANSLATIONS

512 Dobson, W[illiam] A.C.H., trans. MENCIUS, A NEW TRANSLATION
ARRANGED AND ANNOTATED FOR THE GENERAL READER. Toronto:
Univ. of Toronto Press, [1963].

An attempt by an expert to interpret and paraphrase the work.
Not a close translation.

513 Giles, Lionel, trans. THE BOOK OF MENCIUS. London: John
Murray, 1942.

A selection in a good translation.

514 Lau, D.C., trans. MENCIUS. Baltimore: Penguin Books, [1970].

An excellent modern translation, with introduction and notes.

515 Legge, James, trans. "The Works of Mencius." In THE CHINESE
CLASSICS, II, 1-587. See entry no. 380.

516 Lin Yutang, trans. In THE WISDOM OF CHINA AND INDIA, pp. 743-
84. See entry no. 148.

517 Lyall, Leonard A., trans. MENCIUS. New York: Longmans, Green
and Co., 1932.

A complete and accurate translation.

518 Richards, I[vor] A., trans. MENCIUS ON THE MIND. London: Kegan
Paul, 1932.

Highly speculative translation by a noted semanticist.

519   Waley, Arthur, trans. "Mencius." In THREE WAYS OF THOUGHT
       IN ANCIENT CHINA, pp. 83-147. See entry no. 151.

       Mixed translation and commentary. Highly recommended.

520   Ware, James R., trans. THE SAYINGS OF MENCIUS. New York:
       New American Library, [1960].

       Complete. A good translation. No notes.

STUDIES

521   Chang, Carson. "The Significance of Mencius." PHILOSOPHY EAST
       AND WEST, 8 (1958-59), 37-48.

       A modern analysis with comparisons with Western thought.

Meng Chiao (751-814)

522   Owen, Stephen. THE POETRY OF MENG CHIAO AND HAN YÜ.
       See entry no. 431.

       Good study with valuable material on literary schools.

Mo Tzu [Mo Ti] (ca. 470-391 B.C.)

523   Mei Yi-Pao, trans. THE ETHICAL AND POLITICAL WRITINGS OF
       MOTSE. London: Arthur Probsthain, 1929.

       General selection with commentary. Mo Tzu founded the
       Mohist anti-Confucian school of Chinese philosophy.

524   Watson, Burton, trans. MO TZU; BASIC WRITINGS. New York:
       Columbia Univ. Press, 1963.

       Excellent modern translation, more selective than the Mei-Yi-
       Pao.

Pan Ku (32-92)

525   Dubs, Homer H., trans. HISTORY OF THE FORMER HAN DYNASTY.
       3 vols. New York: American Council of Learned Societies, 1938-55.

       An important historical work covering the years 209 B.C. to
       A.D. 25. Extensive commentary.

526   Hughes, E[rnest] R., trans. TWO CHINESE POETS: VIGNETTES OF
       HAN LIFE AND THOUGHT. See entry no. 352.

       Translation and commentary. A good introduction to Pan Ku.

527   Watson, Burton, trans. COURIER AND COMMONER IN ANCIENT
CHINA, SELECTIONS FROM THE HISTORY OF THE FORMER HAN.
New York: Columbia Univ. Press, 1974.

A more lively translation than Dubs's.

Pao Chao (421-65)

528   Frodsham, J.D. "The Nature of Poetry of Pao Chao." ORIENT/WEST,
8, (November-December 1963), 85-93.

Introduction to a minor early poet.

Po Chü-I [Pai Chu-I] (772-846)

529   Levy, Howard S., trans. TRANSLATIONS FROM PO CHÜ-I'S
COLLECTED WORKS. 2 vols. New York: Paragon Book Co., 1971.

Extensive selection in a modern translation of the best known
poet of his age.

530   Waley, Arthur, trans. THE LIFE AND TIMES OF PO CHÜ-I, 772-846
A.D. London: Allen and Unwin [1949].

Study of the poet with about one hundred poems elegantly translated.

Shên Fu (1763-ca. 1808)

531   Black, Shirley M., trans. CHAPTERS FROM A FLOATING LIFE: THE
AUTOBIOGRAPHY OF A CHINESE ARTIST. New York: Oxford Univ.
Press, 1960.

Colorful account of the life of a painter and writer. Includes
some translations from Li Po and Tu Fu.

532   Lin Yutang, trans. SIX CHAPTERS OF A FLOATING LIFE, RENDERED
INTO ENGLISH. Shanghai: West Wind Monthly, 1935. Rev. and
partly rpt. in THE WISDOM OF CHINA AND INDIA. See entry no.
148.

Good translation of a larger portion of the work than is in
Black, above.

Shui Hu Chuan (fourteenth century)

TRANSLATIONS

533   Buck, Pearl S., trans. ALL MEN ARE BROTHERS. New York: John
Day Co., [1933].

Very readable, generally close translation of a Chinese novel of a band of robbers in the Middle Ages. The title is usually rendered as "WATER MARGIN."

534   Jackson, J.A., trans. SHUI HU CHUAN: WATER MARGIN. 2 vols. New York: Paragon Book Co., 1968.

Another good translation. First published 1937 and somewhat freer than Buck. Index of names.

STUDIES

535   Alber, Charles J. "A Summary of English Language Criticism of the SHUI-HU CHUAN." TSING HUA JOURNAL OF CHINESE STUDIES, 7 (1969), 102-18.

Useful survey.

536   Hsia, C.T. "Comparative Approaches to WATER MARGIN." YEARBOOK OF COMPARATIVE AND GENERAL LITERATURE, 11 (1962), 121-28.

Comparisons with Western literature, especially Scandinavian.

537   Irwin, Richard Gregg. THE EVOLUTION OF A CHINESE NOVEL: SHUI-HU-CHUAN. Cambridge, Mass.: Harvard Univ. Press, 1953.

A thorough, scholarly study, including a chapter-by-chapter summary.

Ssu-Ma Ch'ien (1450?-90? B.C.)

TRANSLATIONS

538   Bodde, Derk, trans. STATESMAN, PATRIOT, AND GENERAL IN ANCIENT CHINA: THREE "SHIH CHI" BIOGRAPHIES OF THE CH'IN DYNASTY. New Haven: American Oriental Society, 1940.

Three brief biographies from the RECORDS (SHI CHI): a wealthy citizen, a criminal, and the builder of the great wall. Well translated.

539   Watson, Burton, trans. RECORDS OF THE GRAND HISTORIAN OF CHINA (SHIH CHI). 2 vols. New York: Columbia Univ. Press, 1961.

Major Chinese history covering the entire world from the beginning to author's own time. Also a literary classic. Excellent translation of the portion covering 209-100 B.C.

STUDIES

540   Watson, Burton. SSU-MA CH'IEN: GRAND HISTORIAN OF CHINA.
New York: Columbia Univ. Press, 1958.

Scholarly study of the writer and the work.

Ssu-Ma Kuang (1019-86)

541   Fang, Achilles, trans. THE CHRONICLE OF THE THREE KINGDOMS.
CHAPTERS 68-78 FROM THE TZU CHIH T'UNG CHIEN. 2 vols.
Cambridge, Mass.: Harvard Univ. Press, 1952.

The "Comprehensive Mirror for Aid in Government," completed
in 1084, a complete history of China. The part translated
here covers the period A.D. 220-65. A major work of scholarship.

Su Tung-P'o [Su Shih] (1036-1101)

TRANSLATIONS

542   Clark, Cyril D. Le Gros, trans. THE PROSE-POETRY OF SU TUNG-
P'O. London: Kegan Paul, 1935; rpt. New York: Paragon Book Co.,
1964.

A large selection of poems by a great poet of the Sung period.
Good translation.

543   Watson, Burton, trans. SU TUNG-P'O: SELECTIONS FROM A SUNG
DYNASTY POET. New York: Columbia Univ. Press, 1964.

Some eighty poems, well translated with annotations.

STUDIES

544   Lin Yutang. THE GAY GENIUS: THE LIFE AND TIMES OF SU
TUNGPO. New York: John Day, [1947].

Popular biography with Lin's own reflections on the meaning
of Su's life.

T'ao Ch'ien [T'ao Yüan-Ming] (365-427)

545   Acker, William, trans. T'AO THE HERMIT: SIXTY POEMS OF T'AO
CHI'EN. London: Thames and Hudson, [1952].

Attractive, somewhat free translations. Lengthy introduction
on the life and works.

546 Cheng, Lily Pao-Hu, and Marjorie Sinclair, trans. POEMS OF T'AO CHIEN. Honolulu: Univ. of Hawaii Press, [1953].

Contains all or nearly all the known poems in a modern translation.

547 Hightower, James Robert, trans. THE POETRY OF T'AO CH'IEN. New York: Oxford Univ. Press, 1970.

Excellent translations with historical background and full annotations.

Ts'ai Wen-Chi (fl. 195)

548 Alley, Rewi, trans. THE EIGHTEEN LAMENTS. Peking: World Press, 1963.

Poems by a Chinese woman exile among the northern barbarians.

Ts'ao Chan [Ts'ao Hsueh-Ch'in] (ca. 1717-63)

TRANSLATIONS

549 Hawkes, David, trans. THE STORY OF THE STONE. Baltimore: Penguin Books, 1973.

This is part 1 of the HUNG LOU MENG, usually translated as the DREAM OF THE FRED CHAMBER, in an accurate and readable translation which is now the best in English. Four more volumes are to come. Hawkes uses the new system of transliterating Chinese--Ts'ao becomes Cao Xueqin. A complex family novel.

550 Kuhn, Franz, trans. THE DREAM OF THE RED CHAMBER. Trans. from German by Florence and Isabel McHugh. New York: Pantheon, [1958].

Abridged version in adequate translation.

551 Wang Chi-Chen, trans. DREAM OF THE RED CHAMBER. New York: Twayne, [1958].

Also an adequate translation.

STUDIES

552 Ho Chi-Fang. "On the DREAM OF THE RED CHAMBER." CHINESE LITERATURE, 1 (1963), 65-86.

A modern Socialist interpretation.

553 Hsia, C.T. "Love and Compassion in the DREAM OF THE RED CHAMBER." CRITICISM, 5 (1963), 261-71.

A good introduction to the main theme of the novel.

554 Palandri, Angela Jung. "Women in DREAM OF THE RED CHAMBER." LITERATURE EAST & WEST, 12 (1968), 226-38.

555 Plaks, Andrew H. ARCHETYPE AND ALLEGORY IN THE "DREAM OF THE RED CHAMBER." Princeton: Princeton Univ. Press, [1976].

Learned study with valuable critical insights.

556 Wu Shih-Ch'ang. ON "THE RED CHAMBER DREAM": A CRITICAL STUDY OF TWO ANNOTATED MANUSCRIPTS OF THE XVIIITH CENTURY. Oxford: Clarendon Press, 1961.

Valuable historical study; somewhat technical.

Ts'ao Chih (192-232)

TRANSLATIONS

557 Frankel, Hans H., trans. "Fifteen Poems by Ts'ao Chih: An Attempt at a New Approach." JOURNAL OF THE AMERICAN ORIENTAL SOCIETY, 84 (1964), 1-14.

A brief but good introduction to the poet and his work.

558 Kent, George W., trans. WORLDS OF DUST AND JADE: 47 POEMS AND BALLADS OF THE THIRD CENTURY CHINESE POET TS'AO CHIH. New York: Philosophical Library, [1969].

Good selection.

STUDIES

559 Roy, David T. "The Theme of the Neglected Wife in the Poetry of Ts'ao Chih." JOURNAL OF ASIAN STUDIES, 19 (1959-60), 25-31.

Tu Fu (712-70)

TRANSLATIONS

560 Ayscough, Florence, trans. TU FU: THE AUTOBIOGRAPHY OF A CHINESE POET, A.D. 712-770. 2 vols. Boston: Houghton Mifflin Co., 1929-34.

Life of this major poet reconstructed from his poems (in prose translations). Superseded by the works below.

561   Cooper, Arthur D., trans. LI PO AND TU FU'S POEMS SELECTED AND TRANSLATED. Baltimore: Penguin Books, [1973].

  Good selection in attractive modern translation.

562   Feng Chih, comp., and Rewi Alley, trans. TU FU: SELECTED POEMS. 2d ed. Peking: Foreign Languages Press, [1964].

  About 150 poems in free translations. Illustrated.

563   Hawkes, David, trans. A LITTLE PRIMER OF TU FU. Oxford: Clarendon Press, 1967.

  Contains thirty-five poems with carefully annotated prose translations plus a literal, word-for-word translation of each poem. Valuable insights into the poems and the difficulties of translation.

564   Hung, William, ed. and trans. TU FU: CHINA'S GREATEST POET. 2 vols. Cambridge, Mass.: Harvard Univ. Press, 1929-34. Supp. vol. of notes, 1952.

  Essential scholarly study of the poems. Life, works, and prose translations, with notes, of 374 pieces.

565   Underwood, Edna Wortley, and Chu Chi Hwang, trans. TU FU: WANDERER AND MINSTREL UNDER THE MOONS OF CATHAY. Portland, Maine: Mosher Press, 1929.

  Good selection but translation now obsolete.

STUDIES

566   Davis, A.R. TU FU. New York: Twayne, [1971].

  Up-to-date brief study of the poet and his works.

567   Mei Tsu-Lin, and Lao Yu-Kung. "Tu Fu's 'Autumn Mediations': An Exercise in Linguistic Criticism." HARVARD JOURNAL OF ASIATIC STUDIES, 28 (1968), 44-80.

  Excellent if technical study of problems of interpretation.

568   Wells, Henry Willis. "Tu Fu and the Aesthetics of Poetry." LITERATURE EAST & WEST, 17 (1967), 238-49.

  Good critical introduction by a well-known translator.

569   Yoshikawa, Kōjirō. "Tu Fu's Poetic and Poetry." ACTA ASIATICA, 16 (1969), 1-26.

  Excellent essay by an eminent Japanese scholar.

Tu Pien-Pu (1645-1704)

570 Yang Hsien-Yi, and Gladys Yang, trans. THE PALACE OF ETERNAL YOUTH. Peking: Foreign Languages Press, [1955].

Historical drama about a T'ang dynasty emperor.

Tzu Yeh-Ko (late fourth century)

571 Mayhew, Leonore, and William McNaughton, trans. A GOLD ORCHID: THE LOVE POEMS OF TZU YEH. Rutland, Vt.: Charles E. Tuttle Co., 1972.

Attractive love poems allegedly written by a woman poet.

Wang Shih-Fu, supposed author (fl. 1295-1307)

572 Hart, Henry H., trans. THE WEST CHAMBER: A MEDIEVAL DRAMA. Stanford: Stanford Univ. Press, [1936].

Famous Chinese play taken from a story by Yüan Chen (776-831). Excellent translation with introduction and notes.

573 Hsiung, S.I., trans. THE ROMANCE OF THE WESTERN CHAMBER (HSI HSIANG CHI). New York: Liveright, 1936. Reprint. New York: Columbia Univ. Press, 1968.

The 1968 edition contains a new introduction by C.T. Hsia. Another good translation which includes the source story. Hsia's introduction is recommended.

Wang Wei (699-759)

574 Chang Yin-Nan, and Lewis C. Walmsley, trans. POEMS BY WANG WEI. Rutland, Vt.: Charles E. Tuttle Co., 1958.

A famous poet and painter. Generous selection in good translations. Illustrated.

575 Robinson, G.W., trans. THE POEMS OF WANG WEI. Baltimore: Penguin Books, [1973].

Perhaps the best of recent translations.

576 Yip Wai-Lim, trans. HIDING THE UNIVERSE: POEMS BY WANG WEI. New York: Grossman, [1972].

A good modern translation. Includes the Chinese text.

Wu Ch'eng-En (ca. 1500-1580)

TRANSLATIONS

577   Waley, Arthur, trans. MONKEY. London: Allen and Unwin, 1942.

      Delightful fantasy and almost untranslatable religious allegory, based on the pilgrimage to India of Hsuan Tsang (see above). The title HSI YU CHI is usually translated as RECORD OF A JOURNEY TO THE WEST.

578   Yang Hsien-Yi, and Gladys Yang, trans. "The Pilgrimage to the West. Chapter 59." CHINESE LITERATURE, No. 1 (1961), pp. 126-72.

579   Yu, Anthony C., trans. JOURNEY TO THE WEST. Chicago: Univ. of Chicago Press, vol. 1, 1977, vol. 2, 1979.

      This will be the definite, full-length translation, when completed. Only two volumes have appeared at this date.

STUDIES

580   Dudbridge, Glen. THE HSI-YU CHI: A STUDY OF THE ANTECEDENTS TO THE 16TH CENTURY CHINESE NOVEL. Cambridge, Engl.: Cambridge Univ. Press, 1970.

      Thorough, scholarly study of the background of the work.

581   Dye, Harriet. "Notes for a Comparison of the ODYSSEY and MONKEY." LITERATURE EAST & WEST, 8 (1964), 14-18.

582   Liu Ts'un-Yan. "The Prototypes of MONKEY (Hsi Yu Chi)." T'OUNG PAO, 51 (1964), 55-71.

Wu Ching-Tzu (1701-54)

TRANSLATIONS

583   Yang Hsien-Yu, and Gladys Yang, trans. THE SCHOLARS. Peking: Foreign Languages Press, 1957.

      The JU-LIN WAI-SHIH (UNOFFICIAL HISTORY OF OFFICIALDOM) is a vivid satire on bureaucracy.

STUDIES

584   Král, Oldrich. "Several Artistic Methods in the Classic Chinese Novel JU-LIN WAI SHIH." ARCHIV ORIENTÁLNÍ, 32 (1964), 16-43.

China

Yang Hsiung (53 B.C.-A.D. 18)

585   Knechtges, David R. THE HAN RHAPSODY. Cambridge, Engl.: Cambridge Univ. Press, 1976.

> Excellent study of a court poet and philosopher and the literary background of his age.

586   _____. TWO STUDIES OF THE HAN "FU." See entry no. 357.

> Not entirely superseded by Knechtges' later work, above.

O. MODERN LITERATURE

1. Bibliography and Reference

587   Boorman, Howard, and Richard C. Howard, eds. BIOGRAPHICAL DICTIONARY OF REPUBLICAN CHINA. 4 vols. New York: Columbia Univ. Press, 1967-71.

> Includes many writers, with bibliographies.

588   Gibbs, Donald A., and Li Yun-Chan, comps. A BIBLIOGRAPHY OF STUDIES AND TRANSLATIONS OF MODERN CHINESE LITERATURE, 1918-1942. Cambridge, Mass.: Harvard Univ. Press, 1975.

> Valuable. Especially useful in that it collects translations in periodicals for authors who have not yet appeared in book form.

589   Shu, Austin C.W., comp. MODERN CHINESE AUTHORS: A LIST OF PSEUDONYMS. 2d ed. [Taipei:] Chinese Materials and Research Aids Center, 1971.

590   Wang, James C.F. comp. CULTURAL REVOLUTION IN CHINA, AN ANNOTATED BIBLIOGRAPHY. New York: Garland Publications, 1976.

2. Anthologies

591   Berninghausen, John, and Ted Huters, eds. REVOLUTIONARY LITERATURE IN CHINA, AN ANTHOLOGY. White Plains, N.Y.: M. Sharpe, 1977.

> Essays and stories of the last sixty years, often by writers important in the Revolution.

592   Chi Pang-Yuan, et al, eds. ANTHOLOGY OF CONTEMPORARY
       CHINESE LITERATURE. 2 vols. Taiwan: National Institute for Com-
       pilation and Translation, 1975.

       Large, varied collection. Vol. 1: Poems and essays. Vol.
       2: Short stories.

593   Meserve, Walter J., and Ruth I. Meserve, eds. MODERN LITERA-
       TURE FROM CHINA. New York: New York Univ. Press, 1974.

       Excellent general anthology.

3. Literary History and Criticism

594   Birch, Cyril, ed. CHINESE COMMUNIST LITERATURE. New York:
       Praeger, [1963].

       Good collection of studies by experts in the field.

595   Buck, Pearl S. "Chinese Literature in Today's World." In CHINA,
       pp. 379-405. See entry no. 132.

596   Chao Chung. THE COMMUNIST PROGRAM FOR LITERATURE AND
       ART IN CHINA. Kowloon, Hong Kong: Union Research Institute,
       [1955].

597   Chou Yang. CHINA'S NEW LITERATURE AND ART; ESSAYS AND
       ADDRESSES. Peking: Foreign Languages Press, 1954.

598   Chow Tse-Tung [Chow Tsê-Tsung]. THE MAY FOURTH MOVEMENT:
       INTELLECTUAL REVOLUTION IN MODERN CHINA. Cambridge, Mass.:
       Harvard Univ. Press, 1960.

       Concentrates on the 4 May 1919 crisis and the literary revolu-
       tion of the Communist party.

599   Davis, A.R. "China's Entry into World Literature." JOURNAL OF
       THE ORIENTAL SOCIETY OF AUSTRALIA, 5 (1967), 43-50.

600   _____. "Revolution and Literature in Twentieth Century China."
       JOURNAL OF THE ORIENTAL SOCIETY OF AUSTRALIA, 3 (1963),
       55-64.

601   Grieder, Jerome B. HU SHIH AND THE CHINESE RENAISSANCE.
       Cambridge, Mass.: Harvard Univ. Press, 1970.

       About the revered founder of the Republic's literary renais-
       sance.

602   Hsia, C.T.   "Chinese Literature and the Modern Chinese Temper."
       LITERATURE EAST & WEST, 8 (1964), 55-58.

603   Hsia Tsi-An.   THE GATE OF DARKNESS: STUDIES ON THE LEFTIST
       LITERARY MOVEMENT IN CHINA.   Seattle: Univ. of Washington
       Press, 1968.

       Scholarly but negative account of the Maoist literary revolu-
       tion.

604   Hsiao Ch'ien.   ETCHINGS OF A TORMENTED AGE: A GLIMPSE OF
       CONTEMPORARY CHINESE LITERATURE.   London: Allen and Unwin,
       [1942].

       Interesting, especially because of its date.

605   Hsu Kai-Yu.   THE CHINESE LITERARY SCENE.   A WRITER'S VISIT TO
       THE PEOPLE'S REPUBLIC.   New York: Random House, 1975.

       Interesting account by an American professor and scholar who
       was born in China.

606   Lee, Leo Ou-Fan.   THE ROMANTIC GENERATION OF MODERN
       CHINESE WRITERS.   Cambridge, Mass.:   Harvard Univ. Press, 1973.

       Biographical-historical study concentrating on half-a-dozen
       major figures.

607   Li Tien-Yi.   "Continuity and Change in Modern Chinese Literature."
       ANNALS OF THE AMERICAN ACADEMY OF POLITICAL AND SOCIAL
       SCIENCES, 321 (1959), 90-99.

608   McDougall, Bonnie S.   THE INTRODUCTION OF WESTERN LITERARY
       THEORIES INTO MODERN CHINA, 1919-1925.   Tokyo: Centre for
       East Asian Cultural Studies, 1971.

       Detailed and systematic account of this important influence.

609   Ong, Joktik.   "The Literature and Language of Formosa."   FORMOSAN
       QUARTERLY, 2 (1963), 9-16.

610   Phelps, Dryden Lindsay.   "Letters and Arts in the War Years."   In
       CHINA, pp. 406-19.   See entry no. 132.

611   Prušek, Jaroslav, ed.   STUDIES IN MODERN CHINESE LITERATURE.
       Berlin: Akademie-Verlag, 1964.

       Studies largely on the relationship of literature to society.

612 _____. THREE SKETCHES OF CHINESE LITERATURE. Prague: Oriental Institute, 1969.

On Mao Tun, Yü Ta-Fu, and Kuo Mo-Jo.

613 Scott, A[dolphe] C. LITERATURE AND THE ARTS IN TWENTIETH-CENTURY CHINA. New York: Doubleday, 1963.

Excellent, brief account. Includes literature, drama, and film.

614 Ting Yi [Ting I]. A SHORT HISTORY OF MODERN CHINESE LITERATURE. Peking: Foreign Languages Press, 1959; rpt. Port Washington, N.Y.: Kennikat Press, 1970.

Covers 1919-49. A revolutionary history.

4. Poetry—Anthologies

615 Acton, Harold, and Ch'en Shih Hsiang, trans. MODERN CHINESE POETRY. London: Duckworth, [1936].

Good translations and account of modern poetry as it looked in the pre-war years.

616 Alley, Rewi, trans. THE PEOPLE SING: MORE TRANSLATIONS OF POEMS AND SONGS OF THE PEOPLE OF CHINA. Peking: 1958.

617 _____. POEMS OF REVOLT: SOME CHINESE VOICES OVER THE LAST CENTURY. Peking: New World Press, 1962.

Especially useful for earlier modern material.

618 Hsu Kai-Yu, trans. TWENTIETH-CENTURY CHINESE POETRY, AN ANTHOLOGY. New York: Doubleday, 1963; rpt. Ithaca, N.Y.: Cornell University Press, 1970.

The best anthology to date. More than four hundred poems, with biographical and historical preface and some notes.

619 Palandri, Angela J., trans. MODERN VERSE FROM TAIWAN. Berkeley: Univ. of California Press, 1972.

620 Payne, Robert, ed. CONTEMPORARY CHINESE POETRY. London: Routledge, 1947.

Good collection in usually good translations.

621 Yip Wai-Lim, ed. and trans. MODERN CHINESE POETRY: TWENTY

POETS FROM THE REPUBLIC OF CHINA, 1955-1965. Iowa City: Univ. of Iowa Press, [1970].

A well-translated collection.

5. Poetry—History and Criticism

622   Hsu Kai-Yu. "The Moon and the Beautiful Woman in Modern Chinese Poetry." EAST-WEST REVIEW, 2 (1966), 261-68.

623   Lin, Julia C. MODERN CHINESE POETRY: AN INTRODUCTION. Seattle: Univ. of Washington Press, 1972.

Detailed modern study.

624   Stolzova, M. "The Foundations of Modern Chinese Poetics; Theory and Criticism of the New Poetry, 1917-1935." ARCHIV ORIENTÁLNÍ, 36 (1968), 585-608.

6. Drama—Anthologies

625   Ebon, Martin, ed. FIVE CHINESE COMMUNIST PLAYS. New York: John Day Co., 1975.

Five well-known plays with commentary.

626   Gamble, Sidney D., ed. CHINESE VILLAGE PLAYS FROM THE TING HSIEN REGION (YANG KE HSUAN), A COLLECTION OF FORTY-EIGHT CHINESE RURAL PLAYS AS STAGED BY VILLAGERS. Amersterdam: Philo Press, 1970.

Chinese village drama is an old tradition now being revived by the government.

627   Meserve, Walter J., and Ruth I. Meserve, eds. MODERN DRAMA FROM COMMUNIST CHINA. New York: New York Univ. Press, 1970.

Good selection of good translations and data on the history and staging of the plays.

628   Mitchell, John D., ed. THE RED PEAR GARDEN: THREE GREAT DRAMAS OF REVOLUTIONARY CHINA. [Boston]: David R. Godine, [1973].

Extensive introduction by an expert on the theater and three plays.

7. Drama—History and Criticism

629   Alley, Rewi, ed. PEKING DRAMA, AN INTRODUCTION THROUGH
       PICTURES. Peking: New World Press, 1957.

       Valuable collection of pictures.

630   Chen, David Y. "Two Chinese Adaptations of Eugene O'Neill's THE
       EMPEROR JONES." MODERN DRAMA, 9 (1967), 431-39.

       Plays by Ts'ao Yu and Hung Shen.

631   Davis, A.R. "Out of UNCLE TOM'S CABIN, Tokyo, 1907: A Prelimi-
       nary Look at the Beginnings of Spoken Drama in China." JOURNAL
       OF THE ORIENTAL SOCIETY OF AUSTRALIA, 4 (1968-69), 33-49.

       Concerned with Chinese exiles in pre-revolution Japan and
       the influence of Western dramatic techniques.

632   Kalvodova-Sis-Vanis. CHINESE THEATRE. London: Spring Books,
       n.d.

       Valuable pictures and a good introduction.

633   Kuo Han-Cheng. "New Development in the Traditional Chinese
       Theater." CHINESE LITERATURE, 1 (1960), 127-39.

634   Mackerras, Colin. AMATEUR THEATRE IN CHINA, 1949-1966. Can-
       berra: Australian National Universities Press, 1973.

635   _____. THE CHINESE THEATRE IN MODERN TIMES, FROM 1840
       TO THE PRESENT DAY. [Amherst:] Univ. of Massachusetts Press, 1975.

       The first Mackerras title is a brief sketch of a little-treated
       subject. The second is a lengthy and essential work on the
       modern drama, its history, and nature.

8. Fiction—Anthologies

636   Ai Wu, et al. A NEW HOME AND OTHER STORIES BY CONTEMPO-
       RARY CHINESE WRITERS. Trans. Tso Cheng et al. Peking: Foreign
       Languages Press, 1955.

637   _____. WILD BULL VILLAGE. CHINESE SHORT STORIES BY AI WU
       AND OTHERS. Peking: Foreign Languages Press, 1965.

638   Chang Lin, ed. A SNOWY DAY AND OTHER STORIES BY CONTEM-
       PORARY CHINESE WRITERS. Peking: Foreign Languages Press, 1960.

639   Chou Li-Po, et al. SOWING THE CLOUDS: A COLLECTION OF
      CHINESE SHORT STORIES. Peking: Foreign Languages Press, 1961.

640   HOMEWARD JOURNEY AND OTHER STORIES. Peking: Foreign Lan-
      guages Press, 1957.

641   Hsia, C.T., trans. TWENTIETH-CENTURY CHINESE STORIES. New
      York: Columbia Univ. Press, 1971.

      Nine stories from 1921 to 1965 in good translations.

642   Hsiao Ch'ien, ed. SPINNERS OF SILK. London: Allen and Unwin,
      [1944].

643   Isaacs, Harold Robert, comp. STRAW SANDALS: CHINESE SHORT
      STORIES, 1918-1933. Cambridge: MIT Press, 1974.

      Large collection from a period of great intellectual ferment.
      Lengthy introduction and biographical sketches.

644   Jenner, W.J.F., ed. MODERN CHINESE SHORT STORIES. Trans.
      W.J.F. Jenner and Gladys Yang. London: Oxford Univ. Press, 1970.

      From the 1920s to the mid-1960s. The stories deal mostly
      with modern social problems--valuable historical collection.

645   Lau, Joseph F.M., and Timothy A. Ross, eds. CHINESE STORIES
      FROM TAIWAN, 1960-1970. New York: Columbia Univ. Press, 1976.

646   Ma Feng, et al. I KNEW ALL ALONG, AND OTHER STORIES BY
      CONTEMPORARY CHINESE WRITERS. Peking: Foreign Languages
      Press, 1960.

647   A NEW HOME AND OTHER STORIES BY CONTEMPORARY CHINESE
      WRITERS. Peking: Foreign Languages Press, 1956.

648   REGISTRATION, AND OTHER STORIES BY CONTEMPORARY CHINESE
      WRITERS. Peking: Foreign Languages Press, 1954.

649   Snow, Edgar, ed. LIVING CHINA: MODERN CHINESE SHORT
      STORIES. New York: John Day Co., [1936].

      Stories by major authors whom Snow knew, done in collabora-
      tive translations.

650   Wang Chi-Chen, ed. STORIES OF CHINA AT WAR. New York:
      Columbia Univ. Press, 1944.

Good selection (twenty-one stories by twelve authors) in a
fair translation.

651   [Wu, Lucien], trans. NEW CHINESE STORIES. Taipei: n.p., [1961].

652   Yuan Chia-Hua, and Robert Payne, eds. CONTEMPORARY CHINESE
       SHORT STORIES. London: Noel Carrington, 1946.

       Excellent collection of stories from 1920 to the 1940s, the
       war years.

9. Fiction—History and Criticism

653   Birch, Cyril. "Fiction of the Yenan Period." CHINA QUARTERLY, 4
       (1960), 1-11.

654   Borowitz, Albert. FICTION IN COMMUNIST CHINA. Cambridge:
       MIT Press, 1954.

655   Hsia Chih-Tsing. A HISTORY OF MODERN CHINESE FICTION, 1917-
       1957. New Haven: Yale Univ. Press, 1961.

       Comprehensive account, with an appendix on Taiwan.

656   Huang, Joe C. HEROES AND VILLAINS IN COMMUNIST CHINA:
       THE CONTEMPORARY CHINESE NOVEL AS A REFLECTION OF LIFE.
       New York: Pica Press, 1973.

       Writers of the last twenty or so years. A lengthy study.

657   Lu Hsün. A BRIEF HISTORY OF CHINESE FICTION. Trans. Yang
       Hsien-Yi and Gladys Yang. Peking: Foreign Languages Press, 1923.

       Lectures given 1920-24 by the celebrated writer of fiction.

658   Tsai Mei-Shih, ed. CCONTEMPORARY CHINESE NOVELS AND
       SHORT STORIES, 1949-1972, AN ANNOTATED BIBLIOGRAPHY.
       Cambridge, Mass.: Harvard Univ. Press, 1977.

       An essential bibliography.

10. Miscellaneous Writings

659   Liu Pai-Yu, et al. MIRAGES AND SEA-MARKETS, A COLLECTION
       OF MODERN CHINESE ESSAYS. Peking: Foreign Languages Press,
       1962.

11. Modern Authors and Works

AI WU [T'ANG TA-TENG] (1904-)

660   STEELED AND TEMPERED, A NOVEL. Peking: Foreign Languages Press, 1961.

CHANG AI-LING [EILEEN CHANG] (ca. 1920-)

661   NAKED EARTH. Hong Kong: Union Press, [ca. 1956].

662   THE RICE-SPROUT SONG. New York: Charles Scribner's Sons, 1955.

CHAO SHU-LI (1903-)

663   Yang, Gladys, trans. CHANGES IN LI VILLAGE. Peking: Foreign Languages Press, 1953.

    Winner of Stalin Second Prize for Literature, 1952.

CHEN CHI-TUNG (1916-)

664   THE LONG MARCH. Peking: Foreign Languages Press, 1956.

    A play. Illustrated edition, includes the songs.

CH'EN CHI-YING (1908-)

665   Chang, Eileen, trans. FOOL IN THE REEDS. [Hong Kong]: Rainbow Press, 1959.

CH'EN T'ENG-K'O [CHEN TENG-KE] (1918-)

666   Shapiro, Sidney, trans. LIVING HELL. Peking: Foreign Languages Press, 1955.

CHOU ERH-FU

667   Barnes, A.C., trans. MORNING IN SHANGHAI. Peking: Foreign Languages Press, 1962-- .

    A very lengthy novel. Illustrated. Volume 1 is all that has appeared thus far.

CHOU LI-PO (1908-)

668   Bryan, Derek, trans. GREAT CHANGES IN A MOUNTAIN VILLAGE.

Peking: Foreign Languages Press, 1961-- .

Only volume 1 has appeared thus far.

669 Hsü Meng-Hsiung, trans. THE HURRICANE. Peking: Foreign Languages Press, 1955.

CHO TSO-JEN (1885-1966)

670 Pollard, David E. A CHINESE LOOK AT LITERATURE: THE LITERARY VALUES OF CHOU TSO-JEN IN RELATION TO THE TRADITION. Berkeley: Univ. of California Press, [1973].

671 Wolff, Ernst. CHOU TSO-JEN. New York: Twayne, [1971].

Two good studies of a much persecuted writer.

HSIAO CHUN [LIU CHUN] (1908-)

672 VILLAGE IN AUGUST. New York: Smith and Durell, [1942].

HSIUNG SHIH-I (1902-)

673 THE BRIDGE OF HEAVEN. London: P. Davies, 1943; New York: G.P. Putnam, 1943.

A novel with a prefatory poem by John Masefield.

HSÜ CHIH-MO (1896-1931)

674 Birch, Cyril. "English and Chinese Metres in Hsü Chih-Mo." ASIA MAJOR, 8 (1961), 258-93.

675 Tsang, Winne Une-Shing. "Hsü Chih-Mo, Poet of the Twenties." TENGGARA, 2 (1968), 32-43.

HU SHIH (1891-1962)

676 THE CHINESE RENAISSANCE. Chicago: Univ. of Chicago Press, 1934; rpt. New York: Paragon Book Co., 1963.

An important document for literary studies.

Studies

677 Grieder, Jerome B. HU SHIH AND THE CHINESE RENAISSANCE. See entry no. 601.

678 Kwok, D.Y.W. "Hu Shih's Individualism, an Appreciation." JOUR-

NAL OF NANYANG UNIVERSITY, 1 (1967), 126-32.

KUO MO-JO (1892-)

Translations

679   Barnes, A.C. trans. SONGS OF THE RED FLAG. Peking: Foreign
       Languages Press, 1961.

680   Bester, John, and A.C. Barnes, trans. SELECTED POEMS FROM THE
       GODDESSES. Peking: Foreign Languages Press, 1958.

       Early poems of an important modern writer and thinker.

681   Yang Hsien-Yi, and Gladys Yang, trans. CHU YUAN. Peking:
       Foreign Languages Press, 1955.

       An imaginative story of a fourth century B.C. poet.

Studies

682   Dolezelová-Velingerova, Milená. "Kuo Mo-Jo's Autobiographial
       Works." In STUDIES IN MODERN CHINESE LITERATURE, pp. 45-75.

       See entry no. 611.

683   Gálik, Marián. "Studies in Modern Chinese Literary Criticism, IV:
       The Proletarian Criticism of Kuo Mo-Jo." ASIAN AND AFRICAN
       STUDIES [Bratislava], 6 (1970), 145-60.

684   Roy, David E. KUO MO-JO, THE EARLY YEARS. Cambridge, Mass.:
       Harvard Univ. Press, 1971.

685   Schultz, William. "Kuo Mo-Jo and the Romantic Aesthetic." JOUR-
       NAL OF ORIENTAL LITERATURE, 6 (1955), 49-81.

LAO SHE (LAO SHAW, LAO SHEH, LAU SHAW) [SHU CH'ING-CH'UN]
       (1899-1966)

Translations

686   Kao, George, trans. "Fruits in the Spring." CHINA MAGAZINE,
       17, No. 3 (March 1947), 37-53; No. 4 (April 1947), 37-48; No. 5
       (May 1947), 37-50; No. 6 (June 1947), 37-48.

       An important play by this satirical writer.

687   King, Eva, trans. DIVORCE. St. Petersburg, Fla.: King Publica-
       tions, [1948].

688   _____. RICKSHAW BOY. New York: Reynal and Hitchcock, 1945.

Vivid picture of social disorder in China before 1938.

689   Kuo, Helena, trans. THE DRUM SINGERS. New York: Harcourt, Brace and Co., 1952.

690   _____. THE QUEST FOR LOVE OF LAU LEE. New York: Reynal and Hitchcock, [1948].

691   Liao Hung-Ying, trans. DRAGON BEARD DITCH. Peking: Foreign Languages Press, 1956.

Realistic satire on corruption under the Nationalists.

692   Lyall, William A., trans. CAT COUNTRY: A SATIRICAL NOVEL OF CHINA IN THE 1930'S. Columbus: Ohio State Univ. Press, 1970.

A vicious satire on modern China with the scene set in a Chinese spaceship.

693   Pruitt, Ida, trans. THE YELLOW STORM. New York: Harcourt, Brace and Co., [1951].

Abridged translation of parts of this novel.

Studies

694   Birch, Cyril. "Lao She: The Humourist in his Humour." CHINA QUARTERLY, 8 (1961), 45-62.

A good introduction to the author's main contribution.

695   Slupski, Zbigniew. THE EVOLUTION OF A MODERN CHINESE WRITER: AN ANALYSIS OF LAO SHE'S FICTION WITH BIOGRAPHI-CAL AND BIBLIOGRAPHICAL APPENDICES. Prague: Oriental Institute, 1966.

696   Vohra, Ranbir. LAO SHE AND THE CHINESE REVOLUTION. Cambridge, Mass.: Harvard Univ. Press, 1974.

Both Slupski's and Vohra's are good books on Lao She. The latter is more biographical and includes discussion of his diffi-culties with the Communist government.

LIU E. [LIU T'IEH-YÜN] (1857-1909)

Translations

697   Lin Yutang, trans. A NUN OF TAISHAN AND OTHER TRANSLATIONS.

Shanghai: Commercial Press, 1936.

This and the three translations below are of THE TRAVELS OF LAO TS'AN, an episode and entertaining autobiographical novel. Lin translates chapters 20-26 in this, plus some humorous stories.

698 _____. WIDOW, NUN AND COURTESAN: THREE NOVELETTES FROM THE CHINESE. Westport, Conn.: Greenwood Press, 1971.

A revised version, first published in 1951, of NUN OF TAISHAM.

699 Shadick, Harold, trans. THE TRAVELS OF LAO TS'AN. Ithaca: Cornell Univ. Press, [1952].

Most versions contain only chapters 1-20, as this does.

700 Yang, H.Y. [Yang Hsien-Yi], and G.H. Taylor, trans. London: Allen and Unwin, [1948].

An abridged version.

Studies

701 Hsia, C.T. "The TRAVELS OF LAO TS'AN, an Exploration of its Art and Meaning." TSING HUA JOURNAL OF CHINESE STUDIES, 7 (1969), 40-66.

LIU PAI-YU (1915-)

Translations

702 FLAMES AHEAD. Peking: Foreign Languages Press, 1954.

703 SIX A.M. AND OTHER STORIES. Peking: Foreign Languages Press, 1953.

Studies

704 Chen Tan-Chen. "Liu Pai-Yu's Writings." CHINESE LITERATURE, 3 (1963), 88-94.

LU HSUN (LU XUN, LUSIN) [CHOU SHU-JEN] (1881-1936)

Translations of AH Q

705 Leung, George Kin, trans. THE TRUE STORY OF AH Q. Shanghai: Commercial Press, 1927.

706   THE TRUE STORY OF AH Q. Peking: Foreign Languages Press, 1953.

707   Wang Chu-Chen, trans. AH Q AND OTHERS: SELECTED STORIES OF LUSIN. New York: Columbia Univ. Press, 1941.

Eleven of his best stories about the wastrel Ah Q. Good introduction.

Translated Collections

708   Yang, Gladys, and Hsien-Yi Yang, trans. COMPLETE WORKS OF LU XUN. 4 vols. Peking: Foreign Languages Press, 1956-60.

709   Yang, Gladys, ed. SILENT CHINA: SELECTED WRITINGS OF LU XUN. London: Oxford Univ. Press, 1973.

710   Yang Hsien-Yi, and Gladys Yang, trans. OLD TALES RETOLD. Peking: Foreign Languages Press, 1961.

711   _____. SELECTED STORIES OF LU HSÜN. 2d ed. Peking: Foreign Languages Press, 1963; rpt. New York: Oriole Editions, 1972.

Studies

712   Chinnery, J.D. "The Influence of Western Literature on Lu Xun's 'Diary of a Madman.'" BULLETIN OF THE SCHOOL OF ORIENTAL AND AFRICAN STUDIES, 23 (1960), 309-22.

713   Hanan, Patrick D. "The Technique of Lu Hsün's Fiction." HARVARD JOURNAL OF ASIATIC STUDIES, 34 (1974), 53-96.

714   Huang Sung-K'ang. LU HSÜN AND THE NEW CULTURE MOVEMENT OF MODERN CHINA. Amsterdam: Djambatan, 1957; rpt. Westport, Conn.: Hyperion Books, 1975.

Good study of the cultural milieu.

715   Krebasová, Berta. "Lu Hsün and his Collection 'Old Tales Retold." ACTA ORIENTALIA, 28 (1960), 640-56.

716   _____. "Lu Hsün's Contribution to Modern Chinese Literature and Thought." NEW ORIENT, 7 (February 1968), 9-13.

717   Mills, Harriet. "Lu Hsün and the Communist Party." CHINA QUAR-
      TERLY, No. 4 (October–December 1960), pp. 17–27.

718   Prušek, Jaroslav. "Lu Hsün the Revolutionary and the Artist."
      ORIENTALISTISCHE LITERATURZEITUNG, 55 (1960), 230–35.

719   _____. "Lu Hsün's 'Huai Chiu,' a Precursor of Modern Chinese
      Literature." HARVARD JOURNAL OF ASIATIC STUDIES, 29 (1969),
      169–76.

720   Schultz, William Rudolph. LU HSÜN: THE CREATIVE YEARS.
      Seattle: Univ. of Washington Press, 1955.

          A thorough, scholarly study.

721   Wang Chi-Chen. "Lusin: A Chronological Record, 1881–1936."
      CHINA INSTITUTE BULLETIN, 3 (1939), 99–125.

          A major work of scholarship for its time.

722   Weakland, John H. "Lusin's AH Q, a Rejected Image of Chinese
      Character." PACIFIC SPECTATOR, 10 (1956), 137–46.

MAO TSE-TUNG (1893-1976)

Poetry—Translations

723   Barnstone, Willis, trans. THE POEMS OF MAO TSE-TUNG. New
      York: Harper and Row, [1972].

          Good introduction and notes, with the Chinese text.

724   Boyd, Andrew, and Gladys Yang, trans. NINETEEN POEMS.
      Peking: Foreign Languages Press, 1958.

          Small collection of patriotic poems.

725   Engle, Hua-Ling, and Paul Engle, trans. POEMS. New York:
      Simon and Schuster, 1972.

726   Wong Man, trans. POEMS. Hong Kong: Eastern Horizon Press, 1966.

727   _____. TEN MORE POEMS OF MAO TSE-TUNG. Hong Kong:
      Eastern Horizon Press, 1966.

Two small, carefully translated volumes, with Chinese text
included.

Poetry—Studies

728   Ho Ping-Ti. "Two Major Poems by Mao Tse-Tung, a Commentary with
Translation." QUEEN'S QUARTERLY, 65 (1958), 251-58.

729   Lee, Cyrus. "Mao Tse-Tung's Poems and their Impact on Chinese Education." REVUE DE L'UNIVERSITÉ D'OTTAWA, 38 (1968), 393-404.

730   Tay, C.N. "From SNOW to PLUM BLOSSOMS: A Commentary on
Some Poems by Mao Tse-Tung." JOURNAL OF ASIAN STUDIES, 25
(1966), 287-303.

731   _____. "Two Poems of Mao Tse-Tung in the Light of the Chinese
Literary Tradition." JOURNAL OF ASIAN STUDIES, 29 (1970),
633-55.

Other Writings—Translations

732   Freemantle, Anne, ed. MAO TSE-TUNG: AN ANTHOLOGY OF HIS
WRITINGS. New York: New American Library, [1962].

    Good selection, well translated.

733   ON ART AND LITERATURE. 2d ed. Peking: Foreign Languages
Press, 1960.

Studies

734   Boorman, Harold L. "The Literary World of Mao Tse-Tung." In
CHINESE COMMUNIST LITERATURE, pp. 15-38. See entry no. 594.

    An important article on the whole literary scene of Mao.

MAO TUN [SHEN YEN-PING] (1896-)

Translations

735   MIDNIGHT. Peking: Foreign Languages Press, 1957.

736   Shapiro, Sidney, trans. SPRING SILKWORMS AND OTHER STORIES.
Peking: Foreign Languages Press, 1956.

    Thirteen stories from the 1930s.

Studies

737   Gálik, Marián. "From CHUANG-TZU to Lenin: Mao Tun's Intellectual Development." ASIAN AND AFRICAN STUDIES [Bratislava], 3 (1967), 98-110.

738   _____. MAO TUN AND MODERN CHINESE LITERARY CRITICISM. Wiesbaden: Steiner, 1969.

> Good study of the ideas of this writer by an expert on literary criticism.

739   _____. "The Names and Pseudonyms Used by Mao Tun." ARCHIV ORIENTÁLNÍ, 31 (1963), 80-108.

PA CHIN [LI FEI-KAN] (1904-)

Translations

740   "How I Wrote the Novel FAMILY." CHINA RECONSTRUCTS, 7 (1958), 15-17.

741   Hung, Josephine Huang, trans. THE GRAND GARDEN AND OTHER PLAYS. Taipei: n.p., 1958.

742   Jen, Richard L., trans. STAR. Shanghai: n.p., 1947.

743   Shapiro, Sidney, trans. THE FAMILY. 2d ed. Peking: Foreign Languages Press, 1964; rpt. New York: Doubleday and Co., 1972.

> Family novel about the decline of life in the twenties. The reprint has a preface by Pa Chin and a supplementary part of the novel translated by Lu Kuang-Huan.

Studies

744   Chen Tan-Chen. "Pa Chin the Novelist." CHINESE LITERATURE, No. 6 (1963), pp. 84-92.

745   Lang, Olga. PA CHIN AND HIS WRITINGS: CHINESE YOUTH BETWEEN THE TWO REVOLUTIONS. Cambridge, Mass.: Harvard Univ. Press, 1967.

> Detailed scholarly study of the life and works.

PING HSIN [HSIEH WAN-YUNG] (1902-)

746   Boušková, Marcela. "On the Origins of Modern Chinese Prosody: An

Analysis of the Prosodic Components in the Work of Ping Hsin."
ARCHIV ORIENTÁLNÍ, 32 (1964), 619-43.

747   Pao King-Li.   "Ping Hsin, a Modern Chinese Poetess."   LITERATURE
       EAST & WEST, 8 (1964), 58-72.

SHEN TS'UNG-WEN (1902-)

Translations

748   Ching Ti, and Robert Payne, trans.   THE CHINESE EARTH: STORIES.
       London: Allen and Unwin, [1947].

Studies

749   Nieh Hua-Ling.   SHEN TS'UNG-WEN.   New York: Twayne, [1972].

SU MAN-SHU (OR MANDJU) [SU HSUAN-YING] (1884-1918)

Translations

750   Leung, George Kin, trans.   THE LONE SWAN: THE AUTOBIOG-
       RAPHY OF A GREAT SCHOLAR AND MONK, THE REVERED MANDJU.
       Shanghai: Commercial Press, 1934.

Studies

751   Liu Wu-Chi.   SU MAN-SHU.   New York: Twayne, [1972].

       Good introduction to the writer, a Sino-Japanese poet, short-
       story writer, and radical thinker.

752   McAleavy, Henry.   SU MAN-SHU (1884-1918), A SINO-JAPANESE
       GENIUS.   London: China Society, 1960.

T'IEN HAN (1898-)

Translations

753   Yang Hsien-Yi, and Gladys Yang, trans.   THE WHITE SNAKE.   Peking:
       Foreign Languages Press, 1957.

       Popular adaptation of a Peking opera.

Studies

754   Tung, Constantine.   "Lonely Search into the Unknown: T'ien Han's
       Early Plays, 1920-1930." COMPARATIVE DRAMA, 2 (1968): 44-54.

755 _____. "T'ien Han and the Romantic Ibsen." MODERN DRAMA, 9 (1967), 389-95.

TS'AO YÜ [WAN CHIA-PAO] (ca. 1905-)

Translations

756 Barnes, A.C., trans. SUNRISE, A PLAY IN FOUR ACTS. Peking: Foreign Languages Press, 1960.

Part II of a trilogy, of which THUNDERSTORM is first.

757 Chang Pei-Chi, trans. BRIGHT SKIES. Peking: Foreign Languages Press, 1960.

Antiimperialist and anti-American novel. Written 1954.

758 Ho Yong, trans. THE SUNRISE. Shanghai: Commercial Press, 1940.

Contains an introduction on Chinese drama.

759 Wang Tso-Liang, and A.C. Barnes, trans. THUNDERSTORM. Peking: Foreign Languages Press, 1958.

Part I of a trilogy (see SUNRISE). Part III, THE WILDER-NESS, does not seem to have been translated.

760 Winters, Lily, trans. "Peking Man." RENDITIONS, No. 4 (Autumn 1974), pp. 66-80.

Excerpts from Act I of this important play.

Studies

761 Hu, John Yaw Herng. TS'AO YU. New York: Twayne, [1972].

Good study of the life and works.

762 _____. "Ts'ao Yü: An Evaluation of his Dramatic Works." TAM-KANG REVIEW, 1 (1970): 89-103.

763 Lau, Joseph S.M. TS'AO YÜ: THE RELUCTANT DISCIPLE OF CHEKHOV AND O'NEIL, A STUDY IN LITERARY INFLUENCE. Hong Kong: Hong Kong Univ. Press, 1970.

Good comparative study of a writer much indebted to Western literature.

764 Mekada, Makoto. "On Ts'ao Yü's Plays." STUDIES IN LITERATURE, KYUSHU UNIVERSITY, No. 5 (1959), pp. 65-97.

WANG CH'ING-WEI [WANG CHAO-MING] (1883-1944)

765   Shu Seyuan, trans. POEMS OF WANG CH'ING WEI. Foreword by
       T. Sturge Moore. London: Allen and Unwin, [1938].

       Short selection of poems by a traditional poet.

WEN I-TO (1899-1946)

Translations

766   Olney, Charles V., trans. "The Chinese Poet Wen I-To." JOURNAL
       OF ORIENTAL LITERATURE, 7 (1966), 8-17.

767   _____. "More Poems by Wen I-To." JOURNAL OF ORIENTAL
       LITERATURE, 8 (1967), 38-42.

768   Sanders, Tao-Tao, trans. RED CANDLE: SELECTED POEMS BY WEN
       I-TO. London: Jonathan Cape, 1972.

       Wen was important in the introduction of Western poetry to
       China.

Studies

769   Hsu Kai-Yu. "The Life and Poetry of Wan I-To." HARVARD JOUR-
       NAL OF ASIATIC STUDIES, 21 (1958), 134-79.

       Excellent scholarly study, with some translations.

YANG SHUO (1913-)

770   SNOWFLAKES. Peking: Foreign Languages Press, 1961.

771   Yuan Ko-Chia, trans. A THOUSAND MILES OF LOVELY LAND.
       Peking: Foreign Languages Press, 1957.

       Novel about the Korean War.

YEH CHUN-CHAN (1916-)

Translations

772   THE IGNORANT AND THE FORGOTTEN, NINE STORIES. London:
       Sylvan Press, 1946.

773   MOUNTAIN VILLAGE, A NOVEL. New York: G.P. Putnam, [1947].

774   THEY FLY SOUTH. London: Sylvan Press, 1948.

775   THREE SEASONS AND OTHER STORIES. London: Staples Press, [1946?].

The first of these was translated by the author. The others may have been also.

YEH SHENG-T'AO [YEH SHAO-CHUN] (1893- .)

Translations

776   Barnes, A.C., trans. SCHOOLMASTER. Peking: Foreign Languages Press, 1958.

A long novel.

Studies

777   Průšek, Jaroslav. "Yeh Sheng-Ta'o and Anton Chekhov." ARCHIV ORIENTÁLNÍ, 38 (1970), 437-52.

YU TA-FU (1896-1945)

778   Dolezalova, Anna. YU TA-FU: SPECIFIC TRAITS OF HIS LITERARY CREATION. Bratislava: Slovak Academy of Sciences; New York: Praeger, 1971.

779   Melyan, Gary. "The Enigma of Yu Ta-Fu's Death." MONUMENTA SERICA, 29 (1970-71), 557-88.

780   Průšek, Jaroslav. "Yu Ta-Fu." In THREE SKETCHES OF CHINESE LITERATURE, pp. 44-98. See entry no. 612.

12. Periodicals

781   CHINESE LITERATURE. Peking: Foreign Languages Press, 1951-- .

An essential journal for translations and criticism of modern Chinese literature. Also contains some translations and criticism of earlier literature.

782   MONUMENTA SERICA. Tokyo: Catholic Univ. of Peking, 1935-- .

Scholarly journal devoted mostly to history and culture, including literature.

783   TAMKANG REVIEW. Taipei: Tamkang College of Arts and Science, 1970-- .

Covers all aspects of Chinese culture.

784   T'OUNG PAO: ARCHIVES CONCERNANT L'HISTOIRE, LES LANGUES,
       LA GEOGRAPHIE, L'ETHNOGRAPHIE ET LES ARTS DE L'ASIE. Leiden:
       E.J. Brill [and various other publishers], 1890-- .

       Largely concerned with Chinese culture.

Chapter 3
JAPAN

A. BIBLIOGRAPHY

785 BIBLIOGRAPHY OF THE JAPANESE EMPIRE, 1477-1926. 4 vols.
Leiden, Netherlands: E.J. Brill [and other publishers], 1885-1928.
Continued as BIBLIOGRAPHIE VON JAPAN, 1927-1937. 4 vols.
Leipzig: Hiersmann Verlag, 1931-1940. Vol. 1 of BIBLIOGRAPHY
covers 1477-1893, ed. Friedrich von Wenckstern (Brill, 1885); Vol. 2
covers 1894-1906, (Tokyo, Maruzen, 1907); Vols. 3-4 covers 1906-26,
ed. Oskar Nachod (London: Goldston, 1928). Vol. 3 of BIBLIOG-
RAPHIE covers 1933-35, ed. Hans Praesent and Wolf Haenisch.

This work is a comprehensive bibliography of books and articles
in Western languages on Japan (and for Korea, 1906-26; and
Manchuria, 1933-35). Divided by subjects. A major historical work, the completeness of which allows it to include much
ephemeral material.

786 Borton, Hugh, comp. JAPAN. Ithaca: Cornell Univ. Pres, 1951.

Excellent selected bibliography, especially good for the modern period.

787 Cordier, Henri. BIBLIOTHECA JAPONICA. DICTIONNAIRE BIBLIOG-
RAPIQUE DES OURAGES RELATIF A L'EMPIRE JAPONAIS. Paris:
Leroux, 1912; rpt. Hildesheim: Georg Olms Verlag, 1969.

An important work for its time but now largely superseded.
Covers 1870-1912.

788 Hisamatsu, Sen'ichi, ed. BIOGRAPHICAL DICTIONARY OF JAPANESE
LITERATURE. New York: Kodansha International, 1976.

Over three hundred entries on writers ancient and modern, with
bibliography.

789 Japaninstitut und Deutsches Forschunginstitut. BIBLIOGRAPHISCHER-ALT-

JAPAN-KATALOG, 1542-1853. Kyoto: Deutsches Forschunginstitut, 1940.

A supplement to Cordier, entry no. 787.

790   Japan P.E.N. Club. JAPANESE LITERATURE IN EUROPEAN LAN-
       GUAGES. Tokyo: 1961. Supp., 1964.

       Excellent brief literary bibliography.

791   Marks, Alfred H., and Barry D. Bort, comps. GUIDE TO JAPANESE
       PROSE. Boston: G.K. Hall, 1975.

       Useful bibliography which concentrates on works available in
       English translation. Useful introduction and lengthy annota-
       tions.

792   Silberman, Bernard S., comp. JAPAN AND KOREA: A CRITICAL
       BIBLIOGRAPHY. Tucson: Univ. of Arizona Press, 1962.

       Needs to be updated, but perhaps the best selective guide
       available because of its bibliographical essays and notes.

B. REFERENCE

793   Chamberlain, Basil Hall. 6th ed. rev. and corrected. THINGS
       JAPANESE. London: Kegan Paul, 1939.

       Still useful guide to many aspects of Japanese life by a
       pioneer in Japanese studies.

794   Hall, John W. JAPANESE HISTORY: NEW DIMENSIONS OF AP-
       PROACH AND UNDERSTANDING. Washington, D.C.: American
       Historical Association, 1961.

       Substantial bibliographical essay on Japanese history and
       histories of Japan.

795   Ienaga, Saburo. HISTORY OF JAPAN. Tokyo: Japan Travel Bureau,
       1959.

       Good brief history by a well-known historian.

796   JAPAN: ITS LAND, PEOPLE AND CULTURE. Tokyo: Ministry of
       Education, 1958.

       A good account of the beginnings of modern Japan.

797   Keene, Donald. LANDSCAPES AND PORTRAITS: APPRECIATIONS OF
       JAPANESE CULTURE. Tokyo: Kodansha, [1971].

Series of essays by a leading American scholar of Japanese literature and culture. Some are noted separately below.

798   _____. LIVING JAPAN. Garden City, N.Y.: Doubleday, 1959.

A popular but especially useful introduction to Japanese life. Illustrated.

799   Morris, Ivan. THE NOBILITY OF FAILURE: TRAGIC HEROES IN THE HISTORY OF JAPAN. New York: New American Library, 1976.

Excellent history of the subject, important for the literature.

800   _____. THE WORLD OF THE SHINING PRINCE: COURT LIFE IN ANCIENT JAPAN. Oxford: Oxford Univ. Press, 1964.

Very readable, scholarly history of the society of the period that produced the TALE OF GENJI and other major literary works.

801   Reischauer, Robert K. EARLY JAPANESE HISTORY (40 B.C.-1167 A.D.) 2 vols. Princeton: Princeton Univ. Press, 1937.

Valuable compendium of information. For the specialist.

802   Roggendorf, J., ed. STUDIES IN JAPANESE CULTURE. Tokyo: Sophia Univ. Press, 1963.

Varied essays on Japanese culture. Scholarly.

803   Sansom, George. A HISTORY OF JAPAN TO 1334. Stanford: Stanford Univ. Press, 1958.

804   _____. A HISTORY OF JAPAN, 1615-1867. Stanford: Stanford Univ. Press, 1963.

The first two of Sansom's volumes constitute a very detailed history which includes cultural material. They are useful for the historical background of the wars so often depicted in literature. The third volume is more social and political.

805   _____. A HISTORY OF JAPAN, 1334-1615. Stanford: Stanford Univ. Press, 1961.

806   _____. JAPAN, A SHORT CULTURAL HISTORY. Rev. ed. New York: Appleton-Century Co., 1962.

Perhaps the best introduction to Japan for the ordinary reader. Not short (558 p.).

807 _____. JAPAN IN WORLD HISTORY. New York: Institute of Pacific Relations, 1951.

Brief but penetrating analysis.

808 _____. THE WESTERN WORLD AND JAPAN: A STUDY IN THE INTERACTION OF EUROPEAN AND ASIATIC CULTURES. New York: Alfred A. Knopf, 1950.

Some attention to literary culture in this general study.

809 Shively, Donald H., ed. TRADITION AND MODERNIZATION IN JAPANESE CULTURE. Princeton: Princeton Univ. Press, 1971.

A large collection of essays by specialists.

810 Storry, Richard. A HISTORY OF MODERN JAPAN. Baltimore: Penguin Books, [1961].

Begins with the Meiji restoration of 1868. A good short history.

811 Tiedemann, Arthur E., ed. AN INTRODUCTION TO JAPANESE CIVILIZATION. New York: Columbia Univ. Press, [1974].

Historical survey by a group of specialists, followed by essays on various aspects of the culture, including literature.

812 Tsunoda, Ryusaku, trans. JAPAN IN THE CHINESE DYNASTIC HIS-TORIES: LATER HAN THROUGH MING DYNASTIES. Ed. L.C. Goodrich. South Pasadena, Calif.: P.D. and Ione Perkins, 1951.

Translation of passages about Japan in Chinese histories, with notes.

813 Varley, H. Paul. JAPANESE CULTURE: A SHORT HISTORY. New York: Praeger, 1973.

Up to date, reliable cultural history.

814 _____. A SYLLABUS OF JAPANESE CIVILIZATION. New York: Columbia Univ. Press, 1972.

Brief outline of the important events in Japanese civilization from the beginnings, with bibliography and maps.

815 Webb, Herschel. AN INTRODUCTION TO JAPAN. New York: Columbia Univ. Press, 1955.

An excellent short survey. This and Varley (entry no. 813) are perhaps the best books for the general reader.

C. ANTHOLOGIES

816   Daniels, Frank James, ed. SELECTIONS FROM JAPANESE LITERATURE
       (12TH TO 19TH CENTURIES). Texts, with Notes, Transcriptions, and
       Translations by Members of the Japanese Seminar, School of Oriental
       and African Studies. London: Lund Humphries, [1959].

       Short selections designed to help the student of the language,
       but some material of interest to the general reader.

817   Dickins, Frederick V., ed. and trans. PRIMITIVE AND MEDIEVAL
       JAPANESE TEXTS. 2 vols. Oxford: Oxford Univ. Press, 1906.

       Vol. 1 contains translations of older texts, mostly mythological
       and religious. Largely superseded by better translations.

818   Keene, Donald ed. AN ANTHOLOGY OF JAPANESE LITERATURE
       FROM THE EARLIEST ERA TO THE MID-NINETEENTH CENTURY. New
       York: Grove Press, 1955.

       Excellent selection in good translations of a wide variety of
       literary types. Good introduction.

819   Reischauer, Edwin O., and Joseph K. Yamagiwa, trans. TRANSLA-
       TIONS FROM EARLY JAPANESE LITERATURE. Cambridge, Mass.:
       Harvard Univ. Press, 1951.

       Important selection of lengthy translations, with full notes, of
       some important works. Contents noted in appropriate sections
       below.

820   Tsunoda, Ryusaku, W.T. De Bary, and Donald Keene, eds. SOURCES
       OF JAPANESE TRADITION. 2 vols. New York: Columbia Univ.
       Press, 1958.

       Large selection of documents, mostly historical, but some
       literary and cultural material, especially in vol. I.

821   Watson, Burton, trans. JAPANESE LITERATURE IN CHINESE. See
       entry no. 152.

822   Wheeler, Post, trans. THE SACRED SCRIPTURES OF THE JAPANESE.
       New York: Henry Schuman, [1952].

       Attempts to reconstruct the Japanese system of mythology from
       ancient texts, beginning with the KOJIKI AND NIHONGI.
       The translations listed below under individual authors and works
       are preferable.

D. LITERARY HISTORY AND CRITICISM

823   Aston, W.G. A HISTORY OF JAPANESE LITERATURE. Rutland, Vt.: Charles E. Tuttle Co., 1972.

An important work for its time (first published in 1899) but now outdated and critically superseded.

824   Bruhl, Odette. "Japanese Mythology." In LAROUSSE ENCYCLOPEDIA OF MYTHOLOGY. Ed. Felix Guirand. New York: Prometheus Press, 1959, pp. 412-26.

An excellent brief article.

825   Bryan, John Thomas Ingram. THE LITERATURE OF JAPAN. New York: Henry Holt and Co., 1930.

A short history, now superseded.

826   Ceadel, E[ric] B. "Japanese Literature." In LITERATURES OF THE EAST, pp. 161-88. See entry no. 46.

827   Gatenby, E.V. THE CLOUD MEN OF YAMATO, BEING AN OUT-LINE OF MYSTICISM IN JAPANESE LITERATURE. London: John Murray, [1929].

A brief sketch.

828   Hisamatsu, Sen'ichi. THE VOCABULARY OF JAPANESE LITERARY AESTHETICS. Tokyo: Centre for East Asian Cultural Studies, 1963.

A diction of cultural and literary terms which occur in both literary works and criticism for early times to modern.

829   Keene, Donald. "Feminine Sensibility in the Heian Era." In LAND-SCAPES AND PORTRAITS, pp. 26-39. See entry no. 797.

Concentrates on the era of the early great poetical miscel-lanies and the TALE OF GENJI.

830   _____. "Individuality and Pattern in Japanese Literature." In LAND-SCAPES AND PORTRAITS, pp. 41-51. See entry no. 797.

Discusses an important problem in Japanese society as it affects literature.

831   _____. "Japanese Aesthetics." In LANDSCAPES AND PORTRAITS, pp. 11-25. See entry no. 797.

See entry no. 797.

832   . JAPANESE LITERATURE, AN INTRODUCTION.   London:
John Murray, [1955]; New York: Grove Press, 1955.

An excellent brief history, both historical and critical.   Does
not cover the modern period.

833   . WORLD WITHIN WALLS: JAPANESE LITERATURE OF THE
PRE-MODERN ERA.   New York: Holt, Rinehart and Winston, 1976.

The first volume of what promises to be the standard history of
the literature for some time to come.   Both historical and
critical.

834   Kokusai Bunka Shinkōkai.   INTRODUCTION TO CLASSICAL JAPANESE
LITERATURE.   Tokyo: 1948.

Much useful detail, including synopses of works, but a handbook rather than a history.

835   Komiya, Toyotaka, ed.   JAPANESE MUSIC AND DRAMA IN THE
MEIJI ERA.   Trans. Edward G. Seidensticker and Donald Keene.
Tokyo: Obunsha, 1956.

Covers 1868-1912.   Detailed and somewhat difficult, thorough
account of music, dance, and drama in the first period of
Western influence on literature and drama.

836   Meskill, John.   JAPANESE VIEWPOINTS: EXPRESSIONS IN FICTION,
POETRY, DRAMA, THOUGHT.   New York: Japan Society, [1965].

Focuses on certain important topics in Japanese literature.
Includes materials for discussion.

837   Okazaki, Yoshie.   JAPANESE LITERATURE IN THE MEIJI ERA.   Trans.
Valdo H. Viglielmo.   [Tokyo]:   Obunsha, 1955.

A companion volume to Komiya (entry no. 835).   A thorough
study of the period 1868-1912, but not for beginners--much
detail.

838   Putzar, Edward.   JAPANESE LITERATURE, AN HISTORICAL OUTLINE.
Tucson: Univ. of Arizona Press, 1973.

A detailed chronological outline, useful for reference in
conjunction with critical histories.

839   Rogers, Effie B.   AN OUTLINE OF THE HISTORY OF EARLY JAPA-
NESE LITERATURE.   New York: Greenwich Book Publishers, [1965].

A brief, readable account.

840   Saunders, E. Dale. "Japanese Mythology." In MYTHOLOGIES OF
        THE ANCIENT WORLD, pp. 409-42. See entry no. 56.

        An excellent brief survey.

841   Ueda, Makoto. LITERARY AND ART THEORIES IN JAPAN. Cleve-
        land: Western Reserve Univ. Press, [1967].

        Useful survey, much concerned with poetics from earliest
        times.

E. POETRY—ANTHOLOGIES

842   Blyth, R[eginald] H., trans. EDO SATIRICAL VERSE ANTHOLOGIES.
        Tokyo: Hokuseido Press, 1961.

        With English translations and commentary, and Japanese text
        in both characters and Romanization.

843   _____. HAIKU. 4 vols. Tokyo: Hokuseido Press, 1942-1952; rpt.
        1957.

        A major collection of the popular short form with comments
        on meanings and some references to Western analogues. Not
        very critical. Japanese texts included.

844   _____. JAPANESE LIFE AND CHARACTER IN SENRYU. Tokyo:
        Hokuseido Press, 1960.

        Translations of the short satiric or comic form. Convenient
        topical arrangement, with comments and a valuable historical
        introduction from the sixteenth century to the early twentieth
        century.

845   _____. SENRYŪ, JAPANESE SATIRICAL VERSES. Tokyo: Hokuseido
        Press, 1949.

846   Bownas, Geoffrey, and Anthony Thwaite, trans. THE PENGUIN BOOK
        OF JAPANESE VERSE. Baltimore: Penguin Books, [1964].

        Very good selection and translation, and useful introduction.
        No notes.

847   Chamberlain, Basil Hall, trans. CLASSICAL POETRY OF THE JAPA-
        NESE. London: Trubner, 1880.

        An important work for its time, but now superseded by more
        modern translations.

848   Clack, Robert Wood, ed. THE SOUL OF YAMATO, AN HISTORICAL
        ANTHOLOGY OF JAPANESE POETRY. New York: Gordon Press,
        1976.

        A good collection.

849   Hearn, Lafcadio, trans. JAPANESE LYRICS. Boston: Houghton
        Mifflin Co., 1915.

        With the Japanese text and notes. Probably more interesting
        historically than for the translations because it is by the
        great American expatriate.

850   Henderson, Harold, trans. THE BAMBOO BROOM: AN INTRODUC-
        TION TO JAPANESE HAIKU. Boston: Houghton Mifflin Co., 1934.

        By a translator who has made a major contribution to the
        understanding of the haiku form. The predecessor of the
        INTRODUCTION (see entry 852) below.

851   _____. HAIKU IN ENGLISH. Rutland, Vt.: Charles E. Tuttle Co.,
        1967.

        Lengthy essay on this form, which has been much imitated in
        the West.

852   _____. AN INTRODUCTION TO HAIKU. Garden City, N.Y.:
        Doubleday, 1958.

        Perhaps the best introduction to this form. Historical and
        critical, with word-for-word translations, Romanization, and
        literary translations.

853   Ichikawa, Sanki, ed. HAIKA AND HAIKU. Tokyo: Nippon Gaku-
        jutsu Shinkōkai, 1958.

        Good collection with useful introduction and biographies of
        the poets.

854   Miyamori, Asatarō, ed. AN ANTHOLOGY OF HAIKU, ANCIENT
        AND MODERN. Tokyo: Maruzen, 1932; rpt. Westport, Conn.:
        Greenwood Press, 1971.

        Very large collection with lengthy introduction and good trans-
        lations. Includes early material.

855   _____. HAIKU POEMS, ANCIENT AND MODERN. Tokyo: Maruzen,
        1940.

        A revision of the 1932 edition, above.

856   _____. MASTERPIECES OF JAPANESE POETRY, ANCIENT AND MODERN. 2 vols. Tokyo: Maruzen, 1936; rpt. Westport, Conn.: Greenwood Press, 1970.

> A good collection, chronologically arranged. Still useful though many of the poems are available in more modern trans-lations.

857   Page, Curtis H., trans. JAPANESE POETRY, AN HISTORICAL ESSAY WITH TWO HUNDRED AND THIRTY TRANSLATIONS. Boston: Hough-ton Mifflin Co., 1923.

> Translations into rhymed verse. Now superseded.

858   Philippi, Donald L., trans. THIS WINE OF PEACE, THIS WINE OF LAUGHTER: A COMPLETE ANTHOLOGY OF JAPAN'S EARLIEST SONGS. New York: Grossman Publishers, 1968.

> Excellent collection of songs from pre-classical, early sources. With notes.

859   Sackheim, Eric, trans. THE SILENT FIREFLY: JAPANESE SONGS OF LOVE AND OTHER THINGS. Tokyo: Kodansha, 1963.

> Traditional folk songs, with introduction.

860   Waley, Arthur, trans. JAPANESE POETRY, THE UTA. London: Lund Humphries, 1965.

> Excellent introduction and good translations first published in 1919. Includes the Japanese texts.

861   [Yasuda, Kenneth], trans. A PEPPER POD: CLASSICAL JAPANESE POEMS, TOGETHER WITH ORIGINAL HAIKU BY SHOSON. New York: Alfred A. Knopf, 1947.

> Translations by a historian of the haiku form with some of his own attempts in the form.

F. POETRY—HISTORY AND CRITICISM

862   Blyth, R[eginald] H. A HISTORY OF HAIKU. 2 vols. Tokyo: Hokuseido Press, 1963-64.

> Useful if somewhat rambling account with translations. Illus-trated.

863   Brower, Robert H., and Earl Miner. "Formative Elements in the Japa-nese Poetic Tradition." JOURNAL OF ASIAN STUDIES, 16 (1957), 502-27.

Excellent brief sketch of the nature of the poetry from the
fifty to the thirteenth centuries.

864 _____. JAPANESE COURT POETRY. Stanford: Stanford Univ. Press,
1961.

The major study of the rise of poetry in the great age--forms,
schools, technique. Full notes. Ends with the fourteenth
century.

865 Harich-Schneider, Eta. RŌEI: THE MEDIEVAL COURT SONGS OF
JAPAN. Tokyo: Sophia Univ. Press, 1965.

Scholarly study of court poems as they were set to music in
the Heian period, with the music in Western notation.

866 Hibbett, Howard. "The Japanese Comic Linked-Verse Tradition."
HARVARD JOURNAL OF ASIATIC STUDIES, 23 (1966), 76-92.

Valuable article on an important poetic technique which is
also a popular pastime.

867 Hisamatsu, Sen'ichi, and Nobuyoshi Shida. CONCEPT OF KAMI IN
ANCIENT JAPANESE SONG AND POETRY. Tokyo: Daiichi Shobo,
1967.

Lengthy scholarly study of the role of the gods or kami.

868 Konishi, Jin'inchi. "Association and Progression: Principles of Integra-
tration in Anthologies and Sequences of Japanese Court Poetry." Trans.
and adapted by Robert H. Brower and Earl Miner. HARVARD JOURNAL
OF ASIATIC STUDIES, 21 (1968), 67-127.

The anthology is the major vehicle of transmission of early
Japanese poetry. This is a valuable study of the structure of
the anthologies.

869 Miner, Earl. AN INTRODUCTION TO JAPANESE COURT POETRY.
Stanford: Stanford Univ. Press, 1968.

Both critical and historical with much material on the social
scene. Many translations by Miner and Robert H. Brower. A
better book for beginners than Brower, entry no. 864.

870 Nippon Gakujutsu Shinkōkai. HAIKAI AND HAIKU. Tokyo: 1958.

Useful, chronologically arranged reference material on the
form.

871 Rimer, J. Thomas, and Robert E. Morrell. GUIDE TO JAPANESE

POETRY. Boston: G.K. Hall, 1975.

An essential guide. The introduction provides an excellent
outline sketch of the history of the poetry from the earliest
times to the present, and there are lengthy comments on
translations.

872   Watson, Burton. "Some Remarks on the Kanshi." JOURNAL-
NEWSLETTER OF THE ASSOCIATION OF TEACHERS OF JAPANESE,
5 (July 1968), 15-21.

On Chinese poetry as written by Japanese.

873   Yasuda, Kenneth. THE JAPANESE HAIKU: ITS ESSENTIAL NATURE,
HISTORY AND POSSIBILITIES IN ENGLISH, WITH SELECTED EXAMPLES.
Rutland, Vt.: Charles E. Tuttle, 1957.

Along with Henderson (entry no. 852), a good introduction to
the form. Yasuda discusses the problems of translation and
makes comparisons with Western poets.

874   Yoshikawa, Kōjirō. "Chinese Poetry in Japan: Influence and Reac-
tion." CAHIERS D'HISTOIRE MONDIALE, 2 (1955), 883-94.

Important study of this major influence.

G. DRAMA—ANTHOLOGIES

875   Brandon, James R., trans. KABUKI: FIVE CLASSIC PLAYS. Cambridge, Mass.: Harvard Univ. Press, 1975.

Good translations of popular plays by a drama scholar who
has directed many kabuki plays on the Western stage.

876   Ernst, Earle, trans. THREE JAPANESE PLAYS FROM THE TRADITIONAL
THEATRE. London: Oxford Univ. Press, 1959.

Also translations adaptable to the Western stage. A no play,
a puppet play, and a kabuki play. Good introductions.

877   Hirano, Umeyo, trans. BUDDHIST PLAYS FROM JAPANESE LITERA-
TURE. Tokyo: CIIB, [1962].

Useful for plays not usually translated.

878   Keene, Donald, ed. 20 PLAYS OF THE NŌ THEATRE. New York:
Columbia Univ. Press, 1970.

Very careful translations and with excellent introduction and
full notes.

879   McKinnon, Richard N., trans. SELECTED PLAYS OF KYŌGEN.
       Tokyo: Uniprint, 1968.

       Ten plays well translated with excellent photographs of the
       traditional comic interlude. Excellent critical introduction
       to the form.

880   Nippon Gakujutsu Shinkōkai. JAPANESE NOH DRAMA. 3 vols.
       Rutland, Vt.: Charles E. Tuttle Co., 1955-66.

       A substantial collection (thirty plays in all) in good transla-
       tions and with introductory material and some illustrations.

881   Pound, Ezra, and Ernest Fenollosa, trans. THE CLASSIC NOH
       THEATRE OF JAPAN. New York: New Directions, 1958.

       Important work in its influence on Western poets and drama-
       tists, but the translations are now obsolete. First published
       in 1917.

882   Richie, Donald, and Miyoto Watanabe, trans. SIX KABUKI PLAYS.
       Tokyo: Hokuseido Press, 1963.

       Plays translated and adapted for performance by a Japanese
       troup in the United States, with a record of American
       reactions.

883   Sadler, A[rthur] L., trans. JAPANESE PLAYS: NŌ, KYŌGEN,
       KABUKI. Sydney: Angus and Robertson, 1934.

       Large collection, well translated, of the three major forms of
       Japanese drama.

884   Sakanishi, Shio, trans. JAPANESE FOLK-PLAYS: THE INK-SMEARED
       LADY AND OTHER KYŌGEN. Rutland, Vt.: Charles E. Tuttle Co.,
       1960.

       About twenty short comic plays with good introduction.

885   Ueda, Makota, trans. THE OLD PINE TREE AND OTHER NOH PLAYS.
       Lincoln: Univ. of Nebraska Press, 1962.

       Presents a cycle of five plays, each of a different type.
       Valuable critical comments.

886   Waley, Arthur, trans. THE NŌ PLAYS OF JAPAN. London: Allen
       and Unwin, 1921; rpt. New York: Grove Press, 1950.

       A classic of translation by one of the age's great scholar-
       translators. Valuable introduction. Few notes.

887   Wells, Henry W. THE CLASSICAL DRAMA OF THE ORIENT. See
       entry no. 276.

       Part II deals with Japan.

H. DRAMA—HISTORY AND CRITICISM

888   Ando, Tsuruo. BUNRAKU: THE PUPPET THEATRE. Trans. Don Kenny.
       New York: Weatherhill, 1970.

       An appreciative book by a "fan" of this traditional theater
       which is still popular in the great cities of Japan.

889   Araki, James T. THE BALLAD DRAMA OF MEDIEVAL JAPAN.
       Berkeley: Univ. of California Press, 1964.

       Scholarly study of the kōwaka, a musical type of drama of
       early Japan.

890   Arnott, Peter D. THE THEATRES OF JAPAN. New York: St.
       Martin's Press, 1969.

       By a specialist in and translator of classical Greek drama.
       Valuable comparative study.

891   Ashihara, Eiryo. THE JAPANESE DANCE. Tokyo: Japan Travel
       Agency, 1964.

       Good introductory book on the dance, which is a component
       of the nō and kabuki.

892   Bowers, Faubion. JAPANESE THEATRE. New York: Hermitage Books,
       1952.

       Lively survey by a specialist in world theater. Translations
       of three plays from the kabuki repertoire.

893   Dunn, Charles J. THE EARLY JAPANESE PUPPET DRAMA. London:
       Luzac and Co., 1966.

       Specialized study on the early development of the art.

894   Ernst, Earle. THE KABUKI THEATRE. Oxford: Oxford Univ. Press,
       1956.

       Perhaps the best general guide to this form. By a scholar
       who for many years directed kabuki plays on the Western
       stage.

895   Gunji, Masakatsu. BUYŌ: THE CLASSICAL DANCE. Trans. Don
       Kenny. Tokyo: Weatherhill, 1970.

Includes analysis of the use of dance in the kabuki drama.

896 _____. KABUKI. Trans. John Bester. Tokyo: Kodansha, 1969.

Splendidly illustrated volume with good text and notes.

897 Haar, Francis. JAPANESE THEATRE IN HIGHLIGHT: A PICTORIAL COMMENTARY. Text by Earle Ernst. Rutland, Vt.: Charles E. Tuttle Co., 1952.

Excellent studies by a master photographer with precise comments by a scholar of the drama. Covers nō, bunraku, and kabuki.

898 Halford, Aubrey S., and M. Halford. THE KABUKI HANDBOOK. Rutland, Vt.: Charles E. Tuttle Co., [1956].

Indispensible collection of summaries of almost all of the plays and much other information about the form.

899 Hamamura, Yonezo, et al. KABUKI. Tokyo: Kenkyushu, 1956.

A good study especially as it concerns itself with the continuing popularity of kabuki and its recent developments.

900 Hironaga, Shuzaburo. BUNRAKU: AN INTRODUCTION TO THE JAPANESE PUPPET THEATRE. Osaka: Bunrakuza Theatre, 1959.

Good brief introduction for beginners.

901 _____. BUNRAKU; JAPAN'S UNIQUE PUPPET THEATRE. Rev. D. Warren Knott. Tokyo: Tokyo News Service, 1964.

Synopses of about one hundred of the plays. Good photographs. Largely a revision of the entry above.

902 Inoura, Yohinobu. A HISTORY OF JAPANESE THEATRE, I: UP TO NOH AND KYŌGEN. Tokyo: Kokusai Bunka Shinkokai, 1971.

Very able study of the nō and the kyōgen interludes which went with it. See also entry no. 904.

903 Kawatake, Shigetoshi. KABUKI JAPANESE DRAMA. Tokyo: Foreign Affairs Association of Japan, 1958.

Useful but largely superseded by other works.

904 Kawatake, Toshio. A HISTORY OF JAPANESE THEATRE, II: BUNRAKU AND KABUKI. Tokyo: Kokusai Bunka Shinkokai, 1971.

Companion volume to entry no. 902. Scholarly study of the

development of these two forms from the seventeenth century
to the end of the nineteenth century.

905   Keene, Donald. BUNRAKU: THE ART OF THE JAPANESE PUPPET
THEATRE. Tokyo: Kodansha International, 1965.

A superior study accompanied by excellent large-sized photographs.

906   _____. NŌ: THE CLASSICAL THEATRE OF JAPAN. Tokyo:
Kodansha International, 1966.

Like the foregoing entry, important for the expert and also
as an illustrated introduction for the novice.

907   _____. "Realism and Unreality in Japanese Drama." In LANDSCAPES
AND PORTRAITS, pp. 52-70. See entry no. 797.

Perceptive critical paper which includes both the nō and
kabuki.

908   Kenny, Don. A GUIDE TO KYŌGEN. Tokyo: Hinoki Shoten, 1968.

Summarizes about 250 plays of the comic interlude tradition.

909   Kincaid, Zoe. KABUKI: THE POPULAR STAGE OF JAPAN. New
York: Benjamin Blom, 1965.

Good material on actors and stage technique. A pioneering
work on the subject, first published in 1925.

910   Kurahashi, Takeshi. "Western Drama in Japan--The Japanese SHINGEKI
Movement." JAPAN QUARTERLY, 5 (1958), 178-85.

Useful article on the Western type of drama written and
staged by Japanese.

911   Kusano, Eisaburō. STORIES BEHIND NOH AND KABUKI PLAYS.
Tokyo: Tokyo News Service, 1962.

Concentrates on the supernatural rather than the historical
stories which are the sources for many plays.

912   Lombard, Frank A. AN OUTLINE HISTORY OF THE JAPANESE
DRAMA. London: Allen and Unwin, 1928; Boston: Houghton Mifflin
Co., 1929.

Good handbook to the Japanese drama despite its age, but
the translations have been superseded.

913   Malm, William P. JAPANESE MUSIC AND MUSICAL INSTRUMENTS.
       Rutland, Vt.: Charles E. Tuttle Co., 1959.

       Important scholarly study which includes the music of the
       drama.

914   _____. NAGAUTA: THE HEART OF KABUKI MUSIC. Rutland, Vt.:
       Charles E. Tuttle Co., 1963.

       A major contribution, though highly technical. Includes
       musical transcriptions.

915   Maruoka, Daiji, and Tatsuo Yoshikoshi. NOH. Trans. Don Kenny.
       Osaka: Hoikusha Publishing Co., 1969.

       Valuable illustrations.

916   Miyake, Shūtarō. KABUKI DRAMA. 8th ed. Tokyo: Japan Travel
       Bureau, 1961.

       A good introductory volume, with synopses of plays.

917   Nakamura, Tasue. NOH: THE CLASSICAL THEATER. Trans. Don
       Kenny. New York: Weatherhill, 1971.

       A good history with many photographs.

918   Nogami, Toyochirō. NOH PLAYS: HOW TO SEE THEM. Tokyo:
       Nogaku Shorin, 1954.

       Brief guide which classifies plays by subject matter. Also
       contains comments by G.B. Shaw and Paul Claudel on nō
       plays. Illustrated.

919   O'Neill, P.G. EARLY NŌ DRAMA, ITS BACKGROUND, CHARACTER
       AND DEVELOPMENT 1300-1450. London: Lund Humphries, 1959.

       Major scholarly study of the rise of the form from its folk
       drama origins to the great age of Zeami.

920   _____. A GUIDE TO NŌ. Tokyo: Hinoki Shoten, 1953.

       Valuable handbook containing summaries of over two hundred
       plays currently performed, classified by type and school.

921   Pauly, Herta. "Inside KABUKI: An Experience in Comparative
       Aesthetics." JOURNAL OF AESTHETICS AND ART CRITICISM, 25
       (1967), 293-304.

       Useful in its attempts to separate Western and Japanese reac-
       tions to a form which has superficial similarities to Western
       drama.

922   Pronko, Leonard C. GUIDE TO JAPANESE DRAMA. Boston: G.K. Hall, 1973.

Especially useful for its very full annotations on some seventy-five works. Good brief introduction.

923   Rimer, J. Thomas. TOWARDS A MODERN JAPANESE THEATRE: KISHIDA KUNIO. Princeton: Princeton Univ. Press, 1974.

Kunio (1890-1954) was a playwright, director, and critic who pioneered the development of Western-type drama in Japan. The study focuses on him, but has much other useful material on modern Japanese drama and the stage.

924   Saitō, Seijirō, et al. MASTERPIECES OF JAPANESE PUPPETRY: SCULPTURED HEADS OF THE UNRAKU THEATRE. Trans. and adapted by Roy Andrew Miller. Rutland, Vt.: Charles E. Tuttle Co., 1958.

Handsome, large photographs of the puppets with precise notes.

925   Sakanishi, Shio, et al. A LIST OF TRANSLATIONS OF JAPANESE DRAMA INTO ENGLISH, FRENCH AND GERMAN. Washington, D.C.: American Council of Learned Societies, 1935.

More useful as an index of Western interest than as a guide to translations because of its date.

926   Scott, A[dolphe] C. THE KABUKI THEATRE OF JAPAN. London: Allen and Unwin, 1955.

Very solid study of the form by a specialist in Chinese and Japanese theatre. A good book for beginners.

927   Shaver, Ruth M. KABUKI COSTUME. Rutland, Vt.: Charles E. Tuttle Co., 1966.

An historical study with detailed information. Essential to interpreting the live theater and the photographic records that are available.

928   Shively, Donald L. "Bakufu versus Kabuki." HARVARD JOURNAL OF ASIATIC STUDIES, 18 (1955), 326-56.

Historical study of attempts to control the theater during the Tokugawa period.

929   Sieffert, René. BIBLIOGRAPHIE DU THÉÂTRE JAPONAIS. Tokyo: Maison Francaise Japonnaise, 1953.

Includes works in Western languages and in Japanese.

930 Teele, Roy E. "Formal and Linguistic Problems in Translating a Noh Play." STUDIES ON ASIA, 4 (1963), 43-54.

Reveals some of the language problems in translating these difficult texts.

931 _____. "Translations of Noh Plays." COMPARATIVE LITERATURE, 9 (1957), 345-68.

Very good bibliography and guide.

932 Togi, Masataro. GAGAKU: COURT MUSIC AND DRAMA. Trans. Don Kenny. Tokyo: Weatherhill, [1971].

An explanation of court dance, drama, and music by a musician. Well illustrated.

933 Toita, Yasuji. KABUKI, THE POPULAR THEATRE. Trans. Don Kenny. New York: Walker, Weatherhill, [1970].

Another source of good photographs.

934 Toki, Zemmaro. JAPANESE NŌ PLAYS. Tokyo: Japan Travel Bureau, [1954].

Considers both the nature of the type and gives details of performance and summaries of plays. Illustrated.

935 Upton, Murakami. A SPECTATOR'S HANDBOOK OF NOH. Tokyo: Wanya Shoten, 1963.

A very brief introduction, with summaries of plays and photographs.

936 Yoshida, Chiaki. KABUKI. Tokyo: Japan Times, 1971.

Mostly useful for its photographs.

I. FICTION—ANTHOLOGIES

937 Hakutani, Toshinobu, and Arthur O. Lewis, comps. THE WORLD OF JAPANESE FICTION. New York: D.P. Dutton, 1973.

Generous selection from the TALE OF GENJI to the present.

938 Seki, Keigo, ed. FOLKTALES OF JAPAN. Trans. Robert J. Adams. Chicago: Univ. of Chicago Press, [1963].

Well-translated collection of important tales.

J. FICTION—HISTORY AND CRITICISM

939   Feldman, Horace. "The Meiji Political Novel: A Brief Survey."
       FAR EASTERN QUARTERLY, 9 (1950), 245-56.

       Down to 1890. A good account of a somewhat neglected
       type.

940   Hibbett, Howard. THE FLOATING WORLD IN JAPANESE FICTION.
       New York: Oxford Univ. Press, 1959.

       Full study of the writers and their world, 1680-1740, which
       is valuable to readers interested in other types. Includes
       translations of selections.

941   Ikeda, Hiroko. A TYPE AND MOTIF INDEX OF JAPANESE FOLK
       LITERATURE. Helsinki: Suomalainen Tiedeakatemia, 1971.

       Valuable finding list for subjects, plots, and themes in popu-
       lar literature. Uses the Thompson motif-index numbers. See
       entry no. 63.

942   Miyoshi, Masao. ACCOMPLICES OF SILENCE: THE MODERN JAPA-
       NESE NOVEL. Berkeley: Univ. of California Press, 1974.

       Perceptive critical analysis of modern trends.

K. MISCELLANEOUS WRITINGS—ANTHOLOGIES

943   Miner, Earl, trans. JAPANESE POETIC DIARIES. Berkeley: Univ.
       of California Press, 1969.

       Excellent translations of a very popular Japanese literary form.
       Includes work by Basho, Ki no Tsurauki, Izumi Shikubu, and
       Masaoka Shiki.

944   Omori, Annie Shepley, and Kochi Doi, trans. DIARIES OF THE
       COURT LADIES OF OLD JAPAN. Tokyo: Kenkyusha, [1961].

       Selections from the SARASHINA DIARY, Murasaki Shikubu,
       and Izumi Shikubu. With a introduction by Amy Lowell.
       First published in 1935.

945   Philippi, Donald L., trans. NORITO: A NEW TRANSLATION OF
       THE ANCIENT JAPANESE RITUAL PRAYERS. Tokyo: Institute for
       Japanese Culture and Classics, Kogakuin Univ., 1959.

       Prayers from the early period as found in the KOJIKI, NI-
       HONGI, and elsewhere. A valuable contribution.

L. COMPARATIVE STUDIES

946   Brower, Gary L., comp. HAIKU IN MODERN LANGUAGES, AN
       ANNOTATED BIBLIOGRAPHY. Metuchen, N.J.: Scarecrow Press,
       1972.

       The haiku form has had a vogue in America and Europe.
       Good bibliography of English, Spanish, Portuguese, Italian,
       French, and German experiments.

947   Ishibashi, Hiro. YEATS AND THE NŌ. Ed. Anthony Kerrigan.
       Dublin: Dolmen Press, 1966.

       A sensitive but somewhat subjective account.

948   Janeira, Armando Martins. JAPANESE AND WESTERN LITERATURE,
       A COMPARATIVE STUDY. Rutland, Vt.: Charles E. Tuttle Co.,
       [1970].

       Compares the different genres of Japanese literature with their
       Western equivalents. Also contains valuable comment on the
       Japanese writers themselves.

949   Japan P.E.N. Club. FOOTPRINTS OF FOREIGN LITERATURE IN
       JAPAN. [Tokyo]: [1957].

       Quantitative. Some twenty folding charts showing the number
       of translations from various foreign literatures, including
       twentieth-century European and American writers.

950   Kaneseki, Hisao. "HAIKU and Modern American Poetry." EAST-WEST
       REVIEW, 3 (1967-68), 223-41.

       The popularity of the Japanese short form goes back to the
       beginnings of the century. This article shows how American
       poets have understood some aspects of the art and misunder-
       stood other aspects.

951   Keene, Donald. THE JAPANESE DISCOVERY OF EUROPE, 1720-1830.
       Rev. ed. Stanford: Stanford Univ. Press, 1969.

       An important study of the earliest period of modern influence.

952   _____. MODERN JAPANESE NOVELS AND THE WEST. Charlottes-
       ville: Univ. of Virginia Press, [1961].

       Good brief survey of the conflict between Western influences
       and the Japanese search for a modern literary idiom.

953   Milward, Peter. "Shakespeare in Japanese Translation." In STUDIES
       IN JAPANESE CULTURE, pp. 187-207. See entry no. 802.

954   Miner, Earl. THE JAPANESE TRADITION IN BRITISH AND AMERI-
       CAN LITERATURE. Princeton: Princeton Univ. Press, 1958.

       Excellent study concentrating on the major effects of Japanese
       influence.

955   Miyata, Shimpachiro. "Translated Literature in Japan." JAPAN
       QUARTERLY, 4 (1957), 169-77.

       Analysis of Japanese taste in foreign literature as evidenced
       in translations.

956   Nakamura, Mitsuo. "The French Influence in Modern Japanese Litera-
       ture." JAPAN QUARTERLY, 7 (1960), 57-65.

957   Qamber, Akhtar. YEATS AND THE NOH, WITH "TWO PLAYS FOR
       DANCERS" BY YEATS AND TWO NOH PLAYS. New York: Weather-
       hill, 1975.

       A good sketch of Yeats's somewhat minimal involvement with
       Japanese ideas.

958   Seidensticker, Edward G. "Through Foreign Eyes: Redskins in Japan."
       KENYON REVIEW, 22 (1960), 374-91.

       Aspects of some popular Western ideas as adapted by the
       Japanese.

959   Senuma, Shigeki. "The Influence of Russian Literature in Japan."
       JAPAN QUARTERLY, 7 (1960), 341-49.

960   Stucki, Yasuko. "Yeat's Drama and the Nō: A Comparative Study in
       Dramatic Theories." MODERN DRAMA, 9 (1946), 101-22.

961   Sugiyama, Yoko. "The Wasteland and Contemporary Japanese Poetry."
       COMPARATIVE LITERATURE, 13 (1961), 264-78.

       A study of Japanese poets who have been influenced by Eliot.
       With translations.

962   Takahashi, Kenji. "German Literature in Japan." JAPAN QUARTERLY,
       7 (1960), 193-99.

963   Taylor, Richard. THE DRAMA OF W.B. YEATS: IRISH MYTH AND
       THE JAPANESE NŌ. New Haven: Yale Univ. Press, 1976.

       Perhaps the best of the studies on Yeats and the nō.

964   Tezuka, Tomio. "Goethe and the Japanese." JAPAN QUARTERLY,
       11 (1964), 481-85.

965 Ueda, Makoto. ZEAMI, BASHŌ, YEATS, POUND: A STUDY IN
JAPANESE AND ENGLISH POETICS. The Hague: Mouton, 1965.

A superior critical study based on Ueda's 1962 Univ. of
Washington dissertation.

M. EARLIER AUTHORS AND WORKS

Abutsu (1233-83)

966 Reischauer, Edwin O., and Joseph K. Yamigiwa, trans. "Izayoi
Nikki." In TRANSLATIONS FROM EARLY JAPANESE LITERATURE,
pp. 1-135. See entry no. 819.

A diary interspersed with verse, a favorite Japanese genre.
By a woman poet describing a journey from Kyoto to Kamakura. Superior translation with good notes. The title can
be translated as DIARY OF A WANING MOON.

Bashō Matsuo [Munefuso Masuo] (1664-94)

967 Nobuyuki, Yuasa, trans. THE NARROW ROAD TO THE DEEP NORTH
AND TRAVEL SKETCHES. Baltimore: Penguin Books, 1966.

Good selection of Bashō's sketches in an adequate translation.

GENJŪAN NO KI (UNREAL DWELLING)

968 Keene, Donald, trans. In AN ANTHOLOGY OF JAPANESE LITERA-
TURE, pp. 374-76. See entry no. 818.

NOZARASHI KIKŌ (JOURNEY OF 1684)

969 Hayashi, Eiichi, trans. "NOZARASHI KIKŌ (The Journal of a Weather-
beaten Wayfarer)." THE REEDS, 9 (1963), 24-25.

970 Keene, Donald, trans. "Bashō's Journey of 1684." In LANDSCAPES
AND PORTRAITS, pp. 94-108. See entry no. 797.

Keene's is the better translation, but both his and Hayashi's
have merit and a comparison is interesting.

OKU NO HOSOMICHI (NARROW ROAD)

971 Britton, Dorothy, trans. A HAIKU JOURNEY: BASHŌ'S THE NAR-
ROW ROAD TO THE FAR NORTH AND SELECTED HAIKU. New

York: Kodansha, 1975.

Rather free translation. Good introduction.

972   Corman, Cid, and Kamaike Susumu, trans. BACK ROADS TO FAR
       TOWNS. New York: Grossman Publishers, 1968.

       Poetical, very modern translation by an American poet and a
       Japanese associate.

973   Keene, Donald, trans. "The Narrow Road of Oku." In AN ANTHOL-
       OGY OF JAPANESE LITERATURE, pp. 363-71. See entry no. 818.

974   Lane, Richard, trans. "Bashō the Wanderer." JOURNAL OF ORI-
       ENTAL LITERATURE, 4 (1951), 59-66.

975   Miner, Earl, trans. "The Narrow Road Through the Provinces." In
       JAPANESE POETIC DIARIES, pp. 157-197. See entry no. 943.

       All three of these translations are excellent and all done by
       experts.

976   Nobuyuki, Yuasa, trans. THE NARROW ROAD TO THE DEEP NORTH.
       See entry no. 967.

SAGA DIARY

977   Terasaki, Etsuko, trans. "The Saga Diary." LITERATURE EAST &
       WEST, 15 (1971), 701-18.

       Bashō's personality is more evident in this work than in some
       of the others.

SARASHINA KIKO (JOURNEY TO SARASHINA)

978   Keene, Donald, trans. "Bashō's Journey to Sarashina." In LAND-
       SCAPES AND PORTRAITS, pp. 109-30. See entry no. 797.

       Excellent translation, introduction, and notes.

SARUMINO (MONKEY'S RAINCOAT)

979   Cana, Maeda, trans. MONKEY'S RAINCOAT. New York: Grossman
       Publishers, 1973.

       One of the great anthologies of haiku. Good notes.

STUDIES

980   Chamberlain, Basil Hall. "Bashō and the Japanese Poetic Epigram."
       TRANSACTIONS OF THE ASIATIC SOCIETY OF JAPAN, 30 (1972),
       242-362.

       Extensive study, somewhat outmoded but useful.

981   Keene, Donald. "Individuality and Pattern in Japanese Literature." In
       LANDSCAPES AND PORTRAITS, pp. 41-51. See entry no. 797.

       Discusses Bashō and other writers of his age.

982   Ueda, Makoto. "Bashō and the Poetics of Haiku." JOURNAL OF
       AESTHETICS AND ART CRITICISM, 21 (1963), 423-31.

       Good essay on the technique. See also entry no. 965.

983   _____. MATSUO BASHŌ. New York: Twayne, 1970.

       Well-rounded study of the life, works, and contribution.

Busokusekika (Buddha's Stone Poems) (ca. 752)

984   Mills, D.F., trans. "The Buddha's Footprint Stone Poems." JOURNAL
       OF THE AMERICAN ORIENTAL SOCIETY, 80 (1960), 229-42.

985   Philippi, Donald L., trans. In THIS WINE OF PEACE. See entry no.
       858.

       Two good translations of a poem engraved on a tablet in the
       old capital of Nara.

Chikamatsu Monzaemon (1653-1725)

TRANSLATIONS

986   Keene, Donald, trans. FOUR MAJOR PLAYS OF CHIKAMATSU. New
       York: Columbia Univ., [1951].

       Paperback reprint of four of the plays included in entry no. 987.

987   _____. MAJOR PLAYS OF CHIKAMATSU. New York: Columbia
       Univ. Press, 1961.

       Excellent, very readable translations of the master of plays for
       the puppet stage and the kabuki. Introduction and very full
       notes.

988   Miyamori, Asatarō, trans. MASTERPIECES OF CHIKAMATSU, THE
       JAPANESE SHAKESPEARE. London: Kegan Paul, 1926.

       Important for its time but now superseded by Keene.

KOKUSEN'YA KASSEN (BATTLE OF COXINGA)

989   Keene, Donald, trans. THE BATTLE OF COXINGA: CHIKAMATSU'S
       PUPPET PLAY, ITS BACKGROUND AND IMPORTANCE. London:
       Taylor's Foreign Press, 1951.

       A scholarly background study of the play and a translation
       more literal than the one in MAJOR PLAYS, entry no. 987.
       Also included in entry no. 986.

TEN NO AMIJIMA (LOVE SUICIDE AT AMIJIMA)

990   Shively, Donald H., trans. THE LOVE SUICIDE AT AMIJIMA. Cam-
       bridge, Mass.: Harvard Univ. Press, 1953.

       Very scholarly translation and study with full notes. The
       play is also translated by Keene in entries nos. 986-87.

Ennin (ninth century)

991   Reischauer, Edwin O., trans. ENNIN'S DIARY: THE RECORD OF A
       PILGRIMAGE TO CHINA IN SEARCH OF THE LAW. New York:
       Ronald Press, 1955.

992   _____. ENNIN'S TRAVELS IN T'ANG CHINA. New York: Ronald
       Press, 1955.

       The diary of a Buddhist monk who travelled to China and a
       good study of the man and the importance of the journey.

Fujiwara Michitsuna no Haha (ca. 954-74)

993   Seidensticker, Edward, trans. THE GOSSAMER YEARS: THE DIARY
       OF A NOBLEWOMAN OF HEIAN JAPAN. Rutland, Vt.: Charles
       E. Tuttle Co., [1964].

       Important diary (earliest by a woman) in an excellent transla-
       tion. With introduction and notes.

Fujiwara Shunzei (eleventh century)

994   Hisamatsu, Senichi. "Fujiwara Shunzei and Literary Theories of the
       Middle Ages." ACTA ASIATICA, 1 (1960), 29-42.

Fukuzawa Yukichi (1834-1901)

995   Dilworth, David A., and Umayo Hirano, trans. AN ENCOURAGE-
       MENT TO LEARNING. Tokyo: Sophia Univ., 1969.

996   Kiyoota, Eiichi, trans. THE AUTOBIOGRAPHY OF FUKUZAWA
       YUKICHI. Tokyo: Hokuseido Press, 1960.

       A treatise by and the autobiography of an important thinker
       of the transition period in Japan's modern history.

Genshin (942-1017)

997   Reischauer, August Karl, trans. "Genshin's Ōjō Yō Shū. Collected
       Essays on Birth and Paradise." TRANSACTIONS OF THE ASIATIC
       SOCIETY OF JAPAN, 7 (1930), 16-97.

       Meditative essays by a religious man.

Gikeki Monogatari (fifteenth century)

998   McCullough, Helen Clark, trans. YOSHITSUNE: A FIFTEENTH
       CENTURY JAPANESE CHRONICLE. Stanford: Stanford Univ. Press,
       1966.

       Valuable as a translation and also as a study of Yoshitsune,
       the prince of the Heike and a popular figure of the feudal
       wars in later literature and drama.

Go-Toba, Emperor of Japan (1180-1239)

999   Brower, Robert H., trans. "Ex-Emperor Go-Toba's Secret Teachings: GO
       TOBA MO IN GOKUDEN." HARVARD JOURNAL OF ASIATIC
       STUDIES, 32 (1972), 5-70.

       Scholarly, well-annotated translation of a poetic treatise.

Hachimonjiya Jishō (d. 1745)

1000   Dunn, Charles J., and Bunzo Torigoe, trans. THE ACTOR'S ANALECTS.
       Tokyo: Univ. of Tokyo Press, 1969.

       The YAKUSHA RONGO, a work on dramatic theory and
       practice.

Heiji Monogatari (early thirteenth century)

1001   Reischauer, Edwin O., and Joseph K. Yamagiwa, trans. In TRANSLA-

TIONS FROM EARLY JAPANESE LITERATURE, pp. 375-457. See entry no. 819.

Narrative of the Heike-Minamoto wars covering the events of 1159-60. A very popular chronicle.

Heike Monogatari (early thirteenth, late fourteenth centuries)

1002   Kitagawa, Hiroshi, and Bruce T. Tsuchida, trans. THE TALE OF THE HEIKE. [Tokyo]: Univ. of Tokyo Press, [1975].

1003   Sadler, A.L., trans. THE HEIKE MONOGATARI. 2 vols. Tokyo: Kimiwada Shoten, 1942. Also in THE TEN-FOOT SQUARE HUT (see entry no. 1025).

Two good translations of a chronicle of the Heike-Minamoto wars. Much adapted by later writers.

1004   Yoshikawa, Eiji, trans. and adaptor. THE HEIKE STORY. See entry no. 1362.

Hōgen Monogatari (early thirteenth century?)

1005   Watson, William R., trans. HŌGEN MONOGATARI: TALES OF THE DISORDER IN HŌGEN. Tokyo: Sophia Univ. Press, 1971.

A narrative of the prelude to the Heike-Minamoto rivalries which bring the golden age of the Heian court to an end. Well translated.

Hōnen Shōnen (1173-1212)

1006   Coates, Harper Havelock, and Ryugaki Ishizuka, trans. HŌNEN, THE BUDDHIST SAINT, HIS LIFE AND TEACHINGS. 5 vols. Kyoto: Society for the Publication of Sacred Books, 1949.

Complete translation of an official thirteenth-century account of the founder of Pure Land Buddhism.

Hyaku Nin Isshu (1209)

1007   Brower, Robert H., and Earl Miner, trans. FUJIWARA TEIKA'S SUPERIOR POEMS OF OUR TIME: A THIRTEENTH CENTURY POETIC TREATISE AND SEQUENCE. Stanford: Stanford Univ. Press, 1967.

An anthology compiled by Fujiwara no Sadaie, also called Teika, which sets the standards of taste in poetry for the age. Excellent translation with introduction and full notes.

1008   Honda, Heichachiro, trans. A HUNDRED POEMS FROM A HUNDRED POETS, BEING A TRANSLATION OF THE OGURA-HYAKU-NIN-ISSHU. Tokyo: Hokuseido Press, 1956.

1009   Macauley, Clay, and F. Victor Dickins, trans. HYAKU-NIN-ISSHU, OR SINGLE SONGS OF A HUNDRED POETS. Tokyo: Sankakusha, 1934.

1010   Porter, William N., trans. A HUNDRED VERSES FROM OLD JAPAN. Oxford: Clarendon Press, 1909.

1011   Saito, Hidesaburo, trans. THE HUNDRED CLASSIC JAPANESE POETS. Tokyo: Kobunsha, 1909.

1012   Sharman, Grant, trans. ONE HUNDRED POEMS: A JAPANESE ANTHOLOGY. Los Angeles: Monograph Committee, 1965.

1013   Yasuda, Ken, trans. POEM CARD. Tokyo: Kamakura Bunko, 1948.

>   Of the above translations, Honda's and Sharman's are the most modern and most useful.

Ikku Jippensha (1765-1831)

1014   Satchell, Thomas, trans. SHANK'S MARE, BEING A TRANSLATION OF THE TOKAIDO VOLUMES OF "HIZAKURIGE," JAPAN'S GREAT COMIC NOVEL OF TRAVEL AND RIBALDRY. Rutland, Vt.: Charles E. Tuttle Co., 1960.

>   Amusing account of two adventurers who walk the Tokaido Road between Tokyo and Kyoto.

Ikkyū Sōjun (1394-1481)

1015   Arntzen, Sonja, trans. IKKYŪ SŌJUN: A ZEN MONK AND HIS POETRY. Bellingham: West Washington State College, 1973.

>   Poems in Chinese by a Japanese monk. Introduction, translation with notes, and Romanized Chinese text.

Ise Daijingū Sankeiki (tenth century)

1016   Sadler, A.L., trans. THE ISE DAIJINGŪ SANKEIKI. Tokyo: Meiji Japan Society, 1940.

>   A travel diary.

Ise Monogatari (tenth century)

TRANSLATIONS

1017 McCullough, Helen Craig, trans. TALES OF ISE: LYRICAL EPISODES FROM TENTH CENTURY JAPAN. Stanford: Stanford Univ. Press, 1968.

> Excellent translation and study with full notes. An early verse narrative mixed with prose of court life and love.

STUDIES

1018 Vos, Fritz, trans. A STUDY OF THE ISE MONOGATARI. 2 vols. The Hague: Mouton, 1957.

> Both an authoritative study and a translation.

Issa Kobayashi (1763-1827)

1019 Mackenzie, Lewis, trans. THE AUTUMN WIND: A SELECTION FROM THE POEMS OF ISSA. London: John Murray, 1957.

> Good translation with an essay on his life.

1020 Yuasa, Nobuyuki, trans. THE YEAR OF MY LIFE: A TRANSLATION OF ISSA'S "ORAGA HARU." Berkeley: Univ. of California Press, 1960.

> A diary of the inner life of the writer during the year 1819.

Izumi Shikubu (ca. 970-1030)

1021 Cranston, Edwin A., trans. THE IZUMI SHIKUBU DIARY: A RO-MANCE OF THE HEIAN COURT. Cambridge, Mass.: Harvard Univ. Press, 1969.

> An intimate diary of life and love at court by a prominent poetess.

Kamo no Chōmei (1154-1216)

TRANSLATIONS

1022 Dickins, F. Victor, trans. HŌ-JŌ-KI: NOTES FROM A TEN FOOT SQUARE HUT. London: Gowans and Gray, 1921.

1023 Itakura, Junji, trans. THE HŌ-JŌ-KI: PRIVATE PAPERS OF KAMO NO CHŌMEI OF THE TEN FOOT SQUARE HUT. Tokyo: Maruzen, 1935.

1024 Keene, Donald, trans. In AN ANTHOLOGY OF JAPANESE LITERA-
TURE, pp. 197-212. See entry no. 818.

1025 Sadler, A.L., trans. THE TEN-FOOT SQUARE HUT AND TALES OF
THE HEIKE. Sydney: Angus and Robertson, 1928; rpt. Rutland, Vt.:
Charles E. Tuttle Co., 1972.

Account of life in the woods by a meditative recluse who
invites comparison with Thoreau. Keene's and Sadler's translations are to be preferred to others.

Karasumaru Mitsuhiro (1579-1638)

1026 Putzar, Edward trans. "CHIKUSAI MONOGATARI: A Partial Translation." MONUMENTA NIPPONICA, 16 (1960-61), 161-95.

Kawatake Mokuami (1816-93)

1027 Motofuji, Frank T., trans. THE LOVE OF IZAYOI AND SEISHIN.
Rutland, Vt.: Charles E. Tuttle Co., 1966.

Realistic play by the nineteenth-century master of domestic
drama on the kabuki stage. Four out of seven acts are translated.

Ki no Tsurayuki (884-946)

1028 Ceadel, E.B., trans. "The Ōi River Poems and Preface." ASIA
MAJOR, 1 (1953), 65-106.

1029 _____. "Tadamine's Preface to the Ōi River Poems." BULLETIN OF
THE SCHOOL OF ORIENTAL AND AFRICAN STUDIES, 18 (1956),
331-43.

Poems by an important diarist, editor, and poet.

1030 Miner, Earl, trans. "TOSA DIARY." In JAPANESE POETIC DIARIES,
pp. 59-91. See entry no. 943.

An excellent translation of a poetic diary.

1031 Porter, William N., trans. THE TOSA DIARY. London: Frowde,
1912.

A somewhat old-fashioned translation.

Kizan Fujimoto (1626-1704)

1032 Keene, Donald, trans. "Fujimoto Kizan and the GREAT MIRROR OF LOVE."

In LANDSCAPES AND PORTRAITS, pp. 242-49. See entry no. 797.

A study of the social behavior of a night-life quarter.

Kojiki (Records of Ancient Matters) (712)

1033 Chamberlain, Basil Hall, trans. TRANSLATION OF "KO-JI-KI" OR "RECORDS OF ANCIENT MATTERS." Kobe: J.L. Thompson and Co., 1932.

1034 Philippi, Donald L., trans. KOJIKI. Tokyo: Univ. of Tokyo Press; Princeton: Princeton Univ. Press, 1968.

The major source of myth and legend of the Japanese people. Chamberlain's translation, first published in 1882, was the standard for many years, but Philippi's (with full apparatus and a valuable introduction) has now superseded it.

Kokinshū (905)

1035 Ceadel, E.B., trans. "The Two Prefaces to the Kokinshū." ASIA MAJOR, 7 (1957), 40-51.

A major early anthology with a first preface in Japanese and another later one in Chinese with borrowings from Chinese sources--the prefaces are critically important.

1036 Dickins, F. Victor, trans. In PRIMITIVE AND MEDIEVAL JAPANESE TEXTS, pp. 378-91. See entry no. 817.

Translation of the Japanese preface.

1037 Wakameda, Takeji, trans. EARLY JAPANESE POETS. London: Eastern Press, 1922.

Complete translation of the poems.

1038 Waley, Arthur, Kenneth Rexroth, and Donald Keene, trans. In AN ANTHOLOGY OF JAPANESE LITERATURE, pp. 76-81. See entry no. 818.

Konjaku Monogatari (ca. 1120)

1039 Jones, Susan Wilbur, trans. AGES AGO: THIRTY-SEVEN TALES FROM THE KONJAKU MONOGATARI COLLECTION. Cambridge, Mass.: Harvard Univ. Press, 1959.

Selections from a major collection of folktales.

Manyōshū (ca. 759)

TRANSLATIONS

1040   Arrowsmith, William, trans.   "Translation from Hitomaro."   HUDSON
        REVIEW, 8 (1955), 346-50.

        A translation by a distinguished translator of the Greek
        classics.

1041   Dickins, F. Victor, trans.   In PRIMITIVE AND MEDIEVAL JAPANESE
        TEXTS, pp. 1-303.   See entry no. 817.

1042   Honda, H.H., trans.   "The MANYŌSHŪ, Book I."   THE REEDS, 9
        (1963), 3-24.

1043   Miner, Earl, and Robert H. Brower, trans.   "Kakinomoto no Hitomaro:
        Two Poems, with a Note about the Poet."   JAPAN QUARTERLY, 6
        (1959), 448-52.

1044   Nippon Gakujutsu Shinkōkai, trans.   THE MANYOSHU: THE NIPPON
        GAKUJUTSU KINKOKAI TRANSLATION OF ONE THOUSAND POEMS.
        Foreword by Donald Keene.   New York: Columbia Univ. Press, 1965.

        About one hundred poems from the over four thousand in this
        major anthology.   Good translations and Romanized Japanese
        text.   Perhaps the best introduction to the work.

1045   Okado, Tetsuzō, trans.   THREE HUNDRED POEMS FROM THE MANYŌ-
        SHŪ, POETICAL COLLECTION OF EARLY JAPAN.   Tokyo: Seikanso,
        1935.

1046   Pierson, J.L., ed. and trans.   THE MANYŌSŪ, TRANSLATED AND
        ANNOTATED.   12 vols.   Leiden: E.J. Brill, 1929-60.

        The major scholarly edition, with translations and extensive
        philological notes.   Pierson attempts to reconstruct the origi-
        nal form of the language.

1047   Yasuda, Kenneth, trans.   LAND OF THE REED PLAINS: ANCIENT
        JAPANESE LYRICS FROM THE MANYŌSHŪ.   Rutland, Vt.: Charles E.
        Tuttle Co., 1960.

        Includes the interpretative paintings of Inoue Sanko, about
        one hundred poems, and a good preface.   The reader may
        prefer these more modern renditions to those of entry no.
        1044, but the latter offers more variety.

Japan

1048 _____. MYRIAD LEAVES (THE MANYŌSHŪ). Tokyo: Hosokawa
Shoten, 1949-- .

   Projected complete translation with texts in characters and
   Romanization. May be the definitive translation when completed.

STUDIES

1049 Pierson, J.L. THE MAKURA-KOTOBA OF THE MANYŌSŪ. Leiden:
D.J. Brill, 1964.

   A study of the elements of the figures of speech.

Minase Sangin Hyakuin (1488)

1050 Yasuda, Kenneth, trans. MINASE SANGIN HYAKUIN: A POEM OF
ONE HUNDRED LINKS COMPOSED BY THREE POETS AT MINASE.
Tokyo: Kogakusha, 1956.

   A famous collection of "linked verse"--each poem being built
   on an element of the previous one, a favorite Japanese pastime here raised to a high level.

Motoori Norinaga (1730-1801)

1051 Matsumoto, Shigeru. MOTOORI NORINAGA. Cambridge, Mass.:
Harvard Univ. Press, 1970.

   Study of a famous poet and literary critic.

Murasaki Shikubu (978?-1916?)

GENJI MONOGATARI (TALE OF GENJI)

Translations

1052 Seidensticker, Edward G., trans. THE TALE OF GENJI. 2 vols.
New York: Alfred A. Knopf, 1976.

   Lady Murasaki's novel is one of the earliest and greatest of
   psychological novels. Seidensticker's translation is a remark-
   able achievement which will take the place of Waley's version
   for most readers.

1053 Waley, Arthur, trans. THE TALE OF GENJI. New York: Modern
Library, [1960].

   First published 1925-33, Waley's elegant, somewhat abridged
   translation has been standard for most of this century.

Studies

1054   Keene, Donald. "The TALE OF GENJI." In APPROACHES TO THE
        ORIENTAL CLASSICS, pp. 186-95. See entry no. 50.

        An excellent brief introduction to the work.

1055   Maki, J.M. "Lady Murasaki and the GENGI MONOGATARI."
        MONUMENTA NIPPONICA, 3 (1940), 122-43.

        Useful literary and historical background.

1056   Morris, Ivan. "Translating the Tale of Genji." ORIENT/WEST 9
        (January-February 1964), 21-24.

1057   Mudrick, Marvin. "Genji and the Age of Marvels." HUDSON
        REVIEW, 8 (1955), 327-45.

        Acritical appreciation by a specialist in Western fiction.

1058   Oyama, Atsuko. "How was the Genji Monogatari Written?" ACTA
        ASIATICA, 2 (1961), 59-67.

        On the literary background.

1059   Seckel, Dietrich. EMAKIMONO: THE ART OF THE JAPANESE
        PAINTED HAND SCROLL. Foreword and photos by Akihisa Hase.
        London: Jonathan Cape, 1959.

        Plates 1-13 of this work depict the TALE OF GENJI
        in pictures.

Murasaki Shikubu Nikki

1060   Omori, Annie Shepley, and Kōchi Doi, trans. In DIARIES OF THE
        COURT LADIES OF OLD JAPAN, pp. 69-145. See entry no. 944.

        The diary of Lady Murasaki.

Namiki Gohei III (1747-1808)

1061   Brandon, James R., and Tamiko Niwa, trans. "Kanjinchō." EVER-
        GREEN REVIEW, 4 (September-October 1960), 28-57.

1062   Scott, A[dolphe] C., trans. KANJINCHŌ, A JAPANESE KABUKI
        PLAY. Tokyo: Hokuseido Press, [1953].

        A masterpiece of the jidaimono or historical kabuki play.

The Brandon-Niwa translation, above, is lively and intended for the Western stage. Scott's is faithful and has a good scholarly apparatus.

Nihongi or Nihon Shoki (Chronicles of Japan) (720)

1063   Aston, W.G., trans. NIHONGI: CHRONICLES OF JAPAN FROM THE EARLIEST TIMES TO A.D. 697. London: Allen and Unwin, 1956.

The second oldest sacred chronicle, the first being the KOJIKI. This is mostly early history and of less literary interest. First published in this translation in 1896.

Nijō no Tsubone (b. 1258)

1064   Brazell, Karen, trans. THE CONFESSIONS OF LADY NIJŌ. New York: Doubleday and Co., 1973.

1065   Whitehouse, Wilfrid, and Eizo Yanagisawa, trans. LADY NIJŌ'S OWN STORY: THE CANDID DIARY OF A 13TH CENTURY JAPANESE IMPERIAL COURT CONCUBINE. Rutland, Vt.: Charles E. Tuttle, Co., 1974.

An uninhibited account of court life. Both translations above are good.

Ochikubo Monogatari (Tales of Lady Ochikubo) (tenth century)

1066   Whitehouse, Wilfrid, and Ezio Yamagisawa, trans. OCHIKUBO MONO-GATARI, OR TALES OF THE LADY OCHIKUBO. London: Kegan Paul, Trench, Trubner, [1934]; rpt. Garden City, N.Y.: Doubleday, 1971.

A romantic novel, one of the earliest in Japanese literature.

Ōkagami (The Great Mirror) (ca. 1025)

1067   Yamagiwa, Joseph K., trans. THE ŌKAGAMI, A JAPANESE HISTORI-CAL TALE. London: Allen and Unwin, 1967.

An anecdotal history of the intrigues of court life. Good translation with scholarly apparatus and map. Part of this translation is in TRANSLATIONS FROM EARLY JAPANESE LITERATURE, entry no. 819.

Ōkuma Kotomichi (1789-1868)

1068   Uyehara, Yukio, and Marjorie Sinclair, trans. A GRASS PATH:

SELECTED POEMS FROM SOKEISHU. Honolulu: Univ. of Hawaii Press, 1955.

Good translations of an important minor poet.

Ryōkan (1785-1831)

1069   Kodama, Misao, and Yanagishima Hikosakie, trans. RYŌKAN THE GREAT FOOL. Kyoto Seika Junior College Press, 1969.

Ryōkan, a Buddhist monk, wrote poetry in both Chinese and Japanese. Includes Chinese and Japanese texts.

1070   Watson, Burton, trans. RYŌKAN, ZEN MONK-POET OF JAPAN. New York: Columbia Univ. Press, 1977.

Excellent translation and introduction to the poet.

Saikaku Ihara (1642-93)

TRANSLATIONS

Koshoku Gonin Onna

1071   De Bary, William T., trans. FIVE WOMEN WHO LOVED LOVE. Rutland, Vt.: Charles E. Tuttle Co., 1956.

Five love stories set in the "floating world" of the Japanese city. Good introductory essay by Richard Lane.

1072   Hibbett, Howard, trans. "The Woman Who Spent Her Life in Love." In THE FLOATING WORLD IN JAPANESE FICTION, pp. 154-217. See entry no. 940.

Ten chapters of the twenty-four in an excellent translation.

Koshoku Ichidai Onna

1073   Morris, Ivan, trans. THE LIFE OF AN AMOROUS WOMAN. Norfolk, Conn.: New Directions, [1963].

Excellent translation. Also includes extracts from entry no. 1072 and NIPPON EITAIGURA, entries 1076-77.

1074   Rahder, Johannes, trans. "Saikaku's Life of a Voluptuous Woman." ACTA ORIENTALIA, 13 (1934), 292-318.

A good translation of Book II, with annotations.

Koshoku Ichidai Otoko

1075   Hamada, Kengi, trans. THE LIFE OF AN AMOROUS MAN. Rutland, Vt.: Charles E. Tuttle Co., [1964].

    Adventures in the night-life quarter of Kyoto. Free translation.

Nippon Eitaigura

1076   Mizuno, Sōji, trans. IBARA SAIKAKU'S NIPPON EITAIGURA: THE WAY TO WEALTH. 2d ed. Tokyo: Hokuseido Press, [1961].

1077   Sargent, G.W., trans. THE JAPANESE FAMILY STOREHOUSE, OR THE MILLIONAIRE'S GOSPEL MODERNIZED. Cambridge, Engl.: Cambridge Univ. Press, 1959.

    Stories of success and failure in the world of business. Sargent's translation is fuller than Mizuno's and has useful notes.

Seken Munesan'yo

1078   Takatsuka, Masanori, and David D. Stubbs, trans. THIS SCHEMING WORLD. Rutland, Vt.: Charles E. Tuttle Co., [1965].

    Also about the merchant world of Japan's great cities.

STUDIES

1079   Hibbett, Howard. "Saikaku." In THE FLOATING WORLD IN JAPANESE FICTION, pp. 36-49. See entry no. 940.

    Good brief picture of the novelist in his social setting.

1080   _____. "Saikaku and Burlesque Fiction." HARVARD JOURNAL OF ASIATIC STUDIES, 20 (1957), 53-73.

1081   _____. "Saikaku as a Realist." HARVARD JOURNAL OF ASIATIC STUDIES, 15 (1952), 408-18.

    Two important critical studies.

1082   Keene, Donald. "Individuality and Pattern in Japanese Literature." In LANDSCAPES AND PORTRAITS, pp. 41-51. See entry no. 797.

1083   Lane, Richard. "Postwar Japanese Studies of the Novelist Saikaku." HARVARD JOURNAL OF ASIATIC STUDIES, 18 (1955), 181-99.

1084 ____. "Saikaku and Boccaccio." MONUMENTA NIPPONICA, 15 (1959), 87-118.

1085 ____. "Saikaku and the Japanese Novel of Realism." JAPAN QUARTERLY, 4 (1957), 178-88.

1086 ____. SAIKAKU, NOVELIST OF THE JAPANESE RENAISSANCE. New York: Columbia Univ. Press, 1957.

1087 ____. "Saikaku's Contemporaries and Followers, the Ukiyozoshi 1680-1780." MONUMENTAL NIPPONICA, 14 (1958), 125-37.

1088 ____. "Saikaku's Prose Works, a Bibliographical Study." MONU-MENTA NIPPONICA, 14 (1958), 1-26.

Lane is probably the greatest Western authority on Saikaku, and all of these studies are valuable.

Lady Sarashina (eleventh century)

1089 Morris, Ivan, trans. AS I CROSSED THE BRIDGE OF DREAMS: RECOLLECTIONS OF A WOMAN IN ELEVENTH-CENTURY JAPAN. New York: Dial Press, 1971.

A superior translation of a diary of everyday life by an aristocratic woman. Full notes.

Sarugenji-Zōshi (Monkey Genji)

1090 Putzar, Edward D., trans. "The Tale of Monkey Genji--SARUGENJI-ZŌSHI." MONUMENTA NIPPONICA, 18 (1963), 286-312.

A work of popular fiction. Good introduction.

Segawa Jokō III (1806-81)

1091 Scott, A[dolphe] C., trans. "GENYADANA," A JAPANESE KABUKI PLAY. Tokyo: Hokuseido Press, 1953.

Excellent translation of a popular kabuki play.

Sei Shōnagon (b. ca. 967)

1092 Cranmer-Byng, L., trans. THE SKETCH-BOOK OF THE LADY SEI SHŌNAGON. Forest Hills, N.Y.: Transatlantic Arts, 1947.

1093   Kobayashi, Nobuko, trans. THE SKETCH-BOOK OF THE LADY SEI
SHŌNAGON. New York: E.P. Dutton, 1930.

1094   Morris, Ivan, trans. THE PILLOW BOOK OF SEI SHŌNAGON.
2 vols. New York: Columbia Univ. Press, 1967.

    Very full notes (also of vol. 2).

1095   Waley, Arthur, trans. THE PILLOW BOOK OF SEI SHŌNAGON.
London: George Allen, 1928; rpt. New York: Grove Press, [1960].

    A great diary by a court lady in the service of the empress--
an amazing picture of the age. Waley's translation has been
the best for many years, but Morris' elegant and complete
translation, above, supersedes it.

Shin Kokinshū (1205)

1096   Honda, H.H., trans. THE SHIN KOKINSHŪ: THE 13TH CENTURY
ANTHOLOGY EDITED BY IMPERIAL EDICT. [Tokyo]: Hokuseido
Press, 1970.

    A complete translation.

1097   Keene, Donald, trans. In AN ANTHOLOGY OF JAPANESE LITERA-
TURE, pp. 192-96. See entry no. 818.

    A brief selection from the SHIN ("new") KOKINSHŪ, the
eighth anthology of poetry created by imperial edict.

Taiheki Monogatari (fourteenth century)

1098   McCullough, Helen Craig, trans. THE TAIHEKI, A CHRONICLE OF
MEDIEVAL JAPAN. New York: Columbia Univ. Press, 1959.

    Narrative of the feudal wars of the first half of the fourteenth
century. Excellent translation with valuable introduction.

Takeda Izumo II (1756-1822)

CHŪSHINGURA

Translations

1099   Allyn, John. THE FORTY-SEVEN RONIN STORY. Rutland, Vt.:
Charles E. Tuttle Co., 1970.

    A historical reconstruction of the story, made popular on the
kabuki stage, of loyalty and suicide by a lord's devoted band
of followers.

1100 Dickins, F. Victor, trans. CHŪSHINGURA, OR THE LOYAL LEAGUE. London: George Allen, 1880.

1101 Inoue, Jūkichi, trans. CHŪSHINGURA, OR THE TREASURY OF LOYAL RETAINERS. Tokyo: Nakanshi-ya, 1910.

This and entry no. 1100 represent two older and somewhat out-of-date translations.

1102 Keene, Donald, trans. CHŪSHINGURA, OR THE TREASURY OF THE LOYAL RETAINERS. New York: Columbia Univ. Press, [1971].

Superior translation with critical and historical introduction.

1103 Masefield, John. THE FAITHFUL, A TRAGEDY IN THREE ACTS. London: William Heinemann, 1915.

An adaptation of the play by the late poet-laureate of England.

Studies

1104 Sakae, Shioya. CHŪSHINGURA, AN EXPOSITION. 2d ed. Tokyo: Hokuseido Press, 1956.

The background of the work and a detailed summary.

Sugawara Denju Tenarai Kagami (House of Sugawara)

1105 Steed, Louis, and Earle Ernst, trans. "The House of Sugawara." In THREE JAPANESE PLAYS FROM THE TRADITIONAL THEATRE, pp. 53-128. See entry no. 876.

Another popular kabuki drama of intrigue and adventure.

Takenori Monogatari (early tenth century?)

1106 Keene, Donald, trans. "TAKENORI MONOGATARI: The Tale of the Bamboo Cutter." MONUMENTA NIPPONICA, 11 (1956), 1-28.

Excellent translation of a group of stories.

Takizawa Bakin [Takizawa Kyokutei] (1767-1848)

TRANSLATIONS

1107 Gowans, Adam L., trans. TWO WIVES EXCHANGE SPIRITS AND TALES. London: Gowans and Gray, 1930.

Japan

STUDIES

1108   Zolbrod, Leon M. TAKIZAWA BAKIN. New York: Twayne, [1967].

   A popular writer of short stories.

Teitoku Matsunaga (1571-1653)

1109   Keene, Donald. "Masunaga Teitoku and the Beginnings of haikai
   Poetry." In LANDSCAPES AND PORTRAITS, pp. 71-94. See entry
   no. 797.

      An early experimenter with the short form. Includes some
      translations.

Tsutsumi Chunagon Monogatari (Tales of the Lesser Commander) (eleventh century)

1110   Hirano, Umeyo, trans. TSUTSUMI CHŪNAGON MONOGATARI, A
   COLLECTION OF 11TH CENTURY SHORT STORIES OF JAPAN.
   Tokyo: Hokuseido Press, [1963].

1111   Reischauer, Edwin O., and Joseph K. Yamigiwa, trans. "Tsutsumi
   Chūnagon Monogatari." In TRANSLATIONS FROM EARLY JAPANESE
   LITERATURE, pp. 137-268. See entry no. 819.

1112   Waley, Arthur, trans. THE LADY WHO LOVED INSECTS. London:
   Blackmore, 1929.

      All of these three are good translations of this interesting
      collection of tales. The Reischauer-Yamagiwa translation is
      scholarly, with full notes. Waley translates only the most
      popular story, MUSHI MEZURU HIMEGIMI.

Ueda Akinari (1734-1809)

TRANSLATIONS

1113   Jackson, Barry, trans. TALES OF THE SPRING RAIN. Tokyo: Univ.
   of Tokyo Press, 1976.

1114   Whitehouse, Wilfrid, trans. "UGETSU MONOGATARI: Tales of a
   Clouded Moon." MONUMENTA NIPPONICA, 1 (1938), 257-74; 4
   (1941), 166-91.

1115   Zolbrod, Leon M., trans. UGETSU MONOGATARI: TALES OF MOON-
   LIGHT AND RAIN, A COMPLETE ENGLISH VERSION. Vancouver:

Univ. of British Columbia Press, 1974; London: Allen and Unwin, 1974.

Three good translations of a collection of mysterious stories. Zolbrod's is very thorough and closest to the original.

1116 Araki, James T. "A Critical Approach to the Ugetsu Monogatari." MONUMENTA NIPPONICA, 22 (1967), 49-64.

An excellent introduction to the work.

Uji Shūi Monogatari (twelfth century)

1117 Ballard, S., trans. "Some Tales from the UJI SHŪI MONOGATARI." TRANSACTIONS OF THE ASIATIC SOCIETY OF JAPAN, 28 (1900), 31-45.

1118 Brower, Robert H., trans. "Tales from the Uji Collection." In AN ANTHOLOGY OF JAPANESE LITERATURE, pp. 213-23. See entry no. 818.

1119 Mills, D.E., trans. A COLLECTION OF TALES FROM UJI. A STUDY AND TRANSLATION OF UJI SHŪI MONOGATARI. Cambridge, Engl.: Cambridge Univ. Press, 1970.

Good translation, with introduction and full notes, of a collection of folktales.

Yamato Monogatari (ca. 951-52)

1120 Tahara, Mildred, trans. "YAMATO MONOGATARI." MONUMENTA NIPPONICA, 27 (1927), 1-37.

Romantic stories. Good translation and critical material.

STUDIES

1121 Tahara, Mildred. "Heichū, as Seen in the YAMATO MONOGATARI." MONUMENTA NIPPONICA, 26 (1971), 17-48.

Yoshida Kenkō [Yoshida Kaneyoshi] (fl. 1283-1350)

1122 Keene, Donald, trans. ESSAYS IN IDLENESS: THE TSUREZUREGUSA OF KENKO YOSHIDA. New York: Columbia Univ. Press, 1967.

Amusing and penetrating anecdotes by a Buddhist monk. Good translation with introduction.

1123 Kurata, Ryūkichi, trans. THE HARVEST OF LEISURE, TRANSLATED

FROM THE TSURE-ZURE GUSA. London: John Murray, [1931]; rpt. New York: Grove Press, 1962.

1124   Porter, William N., trans. THE MISCELLANY OF A JAPANESE PRIEST, BEING A TRANSLATION OF TSURE-ZURE-GUSA. London: H. Milford, 1914; rpt. Rutland, Vt.: Charles E. Tuttle Co., 1974.

1125   Sansom, G[eorge] B., trans. "The TSUREZURE GUSA of Yoshida no Kaneyoshi." TRANSACTIONS OF THE ASIATIC SOCIETY OF JAPAN, 39 (1911), 1-146.

Still an important, complete translation.

Zeami (or Seami) Motokiyo (1363-1444)

TRANSLATIONS

[Translations of Zeami's plays are in most anthologies of nō plays. See entries nos. 878, 880-81, 883, 885-86.]

1126   Shidehara, Michitaro, and Wilfrid Whitehouse, trans. "Seami's JORUKI BUSHU: Seami's SIXTEEN TREATISES." MONUMENTA NIPPONICA, 4 (1941), 204-39; 5 (1942), 180-214.

Important treatise on the nature of the nō play and the staging and acting by the great master of the form.

STUDIES

1127   McKinnon, Richard N. "The Nō and Zeami." FAR EASTERN QUARTERLY, 11 (1952), 355-61.

A valuable introduction to the dramatist and his work.

1128   _____. "Zeami on the Art of Training." HARVARD JOURNAL OF ASIATIC STUDIES, 16 (1953), 200-225.

Discussion of Zeami's theoretical treatises.

1129   Nogami, Toyochirō. ZEAMI AND HIS THEORIES ON NOH. Trans. Matsumoto Ryozo. Tokyo: Hinoki Shoten, 1955.

Analysis of Zeami's theory and literary terminology. Useful on the nō play in general. Illustrated.

1130   O'Neill, P.G. "The Nō Plays KOI NO OMONI and YUYA." MONUMENTA NIPPONICA, 10 (1954), 203-26.

1131   Ortolani, Benito. "Zeami's Aesthetics of the Nō and Audience Participation." EDUCATIONAL THEATER JOURNAL, 24 (1972), 109-17.

Study of Zeami's theory as it involves interaction between the audience and the actors.

1132 Tsubaki, Andrew T. "Zeami and the Transition of the Concept of Yugen." JOURNAL OF AESTHETICS AND ART CRITICISM, 30 (1971), 55-67.

1133 Ueda, Makoto. "Zeami on Art: A Chapter for the History of Japanese Aesthetics." JOURNAL OF AESTHETICS AND ART CRITICISM, 20 (1961), 73-79.

A good general view of Zeami's ideas on dramatic art.

N. MODERN LITERATURE

1. Bibliography

1134 Bonneau, Georges. BIBLIOGRAPHIE DE LA LITTÉRATURE JAPONAISE CONTEMPORAINE. Tokyo: Kokusai Shuppan Insatusha, [1938].

1135 Borton, Hugh, ed. A SELECTED LIST OF BOOKS AND ARTICLES ON JAPAN IN ENGLISH, FRENCH AND GERMAN. Cambridge, Mass.: Harvard Univ. Press, 1954.

Both of these lists are still useful, but they need to be supplemented by entry no. 1.

1136 Fujino, Yukio. MODERN JAPANESE LITERATURE IN WESTERN TRANSLATIONS, A BIBLIOGRAPHY. Tokyo: International House of Japan, 1972.

Very useful. From the Meiji restoration (1868) to modern times.

2. Reference

1137 Beasley, W.G., ed. MODERN JAPAN: ASPECTS OF HISTORY, LITERATURE AND SOCIETY. Berkeley: Univ. of California Press, 1975.

Useful collection by experts on various aspects of modern Japanese life.

1138 Borton, Hugh, ed. JAPAN BETWEEN EAST AND WEST. New York: Harper, 1957.

Another good collection emphasizing the Westernization of Japan.

1139　Reischauer, Edwin O. JAPAN, PAST AND PRESENT. New York: Alfred A. Knopf, 1946.

Short historical survey with emphasis on the modern age.

1140　_____. THE UNITED STATES AND JAPAN. Cambridge, Mass.: Harvard Univ. Press, 1957.

On American-Japanese relations but also on the institutions and traditions by which the Japanese react against the West.

1141　Tiedeman, Arthur F. MODERN JAPAN, A BRIEF HISTORY. Rev. ed. Princeton: Van Nostrand, [1962].

Good concise outline of modern history.

1142　Yanaga, Chitoshi. JAPAN SINCE PERRY. New York: McGraw-Hill, 1949.

Detailed reference work on the modern period.

3. Anthologies

1143　Bell, Eric S., and Eiji Ukai, comps. EMINENT AUTHORS OF CONTEMPORY JAPAN: ONE ACT PLAYS AND SHORT STORIES. 2 vols. Tokyo: Kaitakusha, 1930-31.

1144　Keene, Donald, ed. MODERN JAPANESE LITERATURE. New York: Grove Press, 1960.

An excellent selection in good translations. Large number of authors represented.

1145　Matsumoto, Ryōzō, ed. JAPANESE LITERATURE NEW AND OLD. Tokyo: Hokuseido Press, [1961].

Good selection of modern authors.

4. Literary History and Criticism

1146　Bailey, Don C. A GLOSSARY OF JAPANESE NEOLOGISMS. Tucson: Univ. of Arizona Press, 1962.

A dictionary of words borrowed from Western languages in modern times by the Japanese. Valuable for cultural history.

1147 Keene, Donald. "The Japanese and the Landscape of War." In LANDSCAPES AND PORTRAITS, pp. 259–321. See entry no. 797.

Good study of major and minor writers and attitudes during the "Greater East Asian War," 1894–95.

1148 _____. "Literary and Intellectual Currents in Postwar Japan and their International Implications." In JAPAN BETWEEN EAST AND WEST, pp. 153–98. See entry no. 1138.

1149 _____. "Modern Japanese Literature." UNIVERSITY OF TORONTO QUARTERLY, 30 (1961): 336–44.

1150 Kikuchi, Kan. HISTORY AND TRENDS OF MODERN JAPANESE LITERATURE. Tokyo: Kokusai Bunka Shinkokai, [1936?].

A brief essay by an important early modern critic.

1151 Kimura, Ki, ed. JAPANESE LITERATURE: MANNERS AND CUSTOMS IN THE MEIJI-TAISHO ERA. Trans. Philip Yampolsky. Tokyo: Obunsha, [1957].

Good socioliterary material, including the impact of the West on Japanese literature.

1152 Kokusai Bunka Shinkōkai. INTRODUCTION TO CONTEMPORARY JAPANESE LITERATURE, 1902–35. Tokyo: 1939.

1153 _____. INTRODUCTION TO CONTEMPORARY JAPANESE LITERA-TURE, 1936–1955. Tokyo: 1959.

Many works are summarized in these two volumes and they give an indication of the range of the literature within the dates notes.

1154 Kunitomo, Tadao. JAPANESE LITERATURE SINCE 1868. Tokyo: Hokuseido Press, 1938.

Still useful. Considerable emphasis on the new Western-type novel.

1155 Miner, Earl. "Traditions and Individual Talents in Recent Japanese Fiction." HUDSON REVIEW, 10 (1957), 302–8.

1156 Sakanishi, Shio. "Women Writers of Today." JAPAN QUARTERLY, 2 (1955), 489–95.

Notes the growing importance of women writers in postwar Japan.

1157   Shea, George Tyson. LEFTWING LITERATURE IN JAPAN: A BRIEF
       HISTORY OF THE PROLETARIAN LITERARY MOVEMENT. Tokyo:
       Hosei Univ. Press, [1964].

           Good study of a somewhat neglected area.

1158   Tsuneari, Fukuda, et al. INTRODUCTION TO CONTEMPORARY
       JAPANESE LITERATURE 1956-1970. SYNOPSES OF MAJOR WORKS.
       Tokyo: Univ. of Tokyo Press, 1972.

           About seventy authors are included.

1159   Ueda, Makoto. MODERN JAPANESE WRITERS AND THE NATURE OF
       LITERATURE. Stanford: Stanford Univ. Press, 1976.

           Good critical study of eight major writers: Soseki, Nagai
           Kafu, Tanizaki, Shiga, Akutagawa, Dazai, Kawabata, and
           Mishima.

1160   Yamagiwa, Joseph K., comp. JAPANESE LITERATURE OF THE SHOWA
       PERIOD: A GUIDE TO JAPANESE REFERENCE AND RESEARCH MATE-
       RIALS. Ann Arbor: Univ. of Michigan Press, 1959.

           Despite the fact that this is a guide to Japanese materials,
           good introductions to the major trends and writers are included
           in English. From 1926.

1161   _____. "The Old and the New in Twentieth-Century Japanese Litera-
       ture." In PAPERS OF THE INDIANA CONFERENCE, pp. 87-104.
       See entry no. 53.

           Particularly useful on schools and literary movements.

5. Poetry—Anthologies

1162   Fitzsimmons, Thomas, trans. JAPANESE POETRY NOW. London:
       Rapp and Whiting, 1972.

           Imaginative reactions of poems by recent generation.

1163   Guest, Harry, Lynn Guest, and Kajima Shozo, trans. POST-WAR
       JAPANESE POETRY. Baltimore: Penguin, [1972].

           Good selection in very modern translation with introduction
           on the techniques.

1164   Kijima, Hajime, ed. THE POETRY OF POSTWAR JAPAN. Iowa City:
       Univ. of Iowa Press, 1975.

           Some thirty wrters, most of whom have radical views on mod-
           ern issues.

1165   Kono, Ichiro, and Rikutarō Fukuda, trans. AN ANTHOLOGY OF
       MODERN JAPANESE POETRY. Tokyo: Kenkyusha, 1957.

       Good cross-section of modern poets--over one hundred repre-
       sented in good translations.

1166   Ninomiya, Takamichi, trans. THE POETRY OF LIVING JAPAN, AN
       ANTHOLOGY. London: John Murray, 1957.

       Good selection for its date. Some thirty authors in good
       translations with background material.

1167   Sato, Hiroaki, ed. "Anthology of Modern Japanese Poets." CHICAGO
       REVIEW, 25 (1973), 1-146.

1168   _____. TEN JAPANESE POETS. Hanover, N.H.: Granite Publica-
       tions, 1973.

       Two collections in excellent modern translations.

1169   Sato, Kiyoshi, et al. GREEN HILL POEMS. Tokyo: Hokuseido
       Press, 1953.

1170   Shiffert, Edith M., and Yuki Sawa, trans. ANTHOLOGY OF MOD-
       ERN JAPANESE POETRY. Rutland, Vt.: Charles E. Tuttle Co., 1972.

       Good selection of adequate translations.

1171   Ueda, Makota, trans. MODERN JAPANESE HAIKU, AN ANTHOLOGY.
       Toronto: Univ. of Toronto Press, 1975.

       Late nineteenth- and twentieth-century writers of haiku in
       superior translation with a literal translation attached. Ro-
       manized Japanese text. Good introduction.

1172   Wilson, Graham, and Atsumi Ikuko, trans. THREE CONTEMPORARY
       JAPANESE POETS. London: Magazine Editions, 1972.

       Excellent translations of three important modern poets: Anzai
       Hitoshi, Shirashi Kazuko, and Tanikawa Suntaro.

6. Poetry—History and Criticism

1173   Keene, Donald. "Modern Japanese Poetry." In LANDSCAPES AND
       PORTRAITS, pp. 131-56. See entry no. 797.

       Good historical sketch from the Meiji restoration. Notes
       heavy European influence.

1174   Wright, Harold P. "The Poetry of Japan." ASIA, 16 (1969), 61-90.

        Brief survey of poetry from the earliest times to the present, especially useful on the modern age.

7. Drama—Anthologies

1175   Hikata, Noboru, trans. THE PASSION BY S. MUSHAKOJI AND THREE OTHER JAPANESE PLAYS. Honolulu: Univ. of Hawaii Press, 1933.

        Early modern plays, all domestic tragedies.

1176   Iwasaki, Y.T., and Glenn Hughes, trans. NEW PLAYS FROM OLD JAPAN. New York: Appleton and Co., 1930.

1177   _____. THREE MODERN JAPANESE PLAYS. New York: Stewart-Kidd, 1923.

        Both volumes include early modern plays much influenced by Western models.

1178   Scott, A[dolphe] C. FIVE PLAYS FOR A NEW THEATRE. New York: New Directions, 1956.

        Three recent plays which demonstrate a modern, distinctly Japanese approach.

8. Drama—History and Criticism

1179   Japan. National Commission for UNESCO. THEATRE IN JAPAN. Tokyo: Ministry of Finance, 1963.

        Studies by Japanese experts on various aspects of the modern theater.

1180   Ortolani, Benito. "Shingeki: The Maturing New Drama of Japan." In STUDIES IN JAPANESE CULTURE, pp. 163-85. See entry no. 802.

9. Fiction—Anthologies

1181   Gluck, Jay, ed. UKIYO: STORIES OF THE "FLOATING WORLD" OF POSTWAR JAPAN. New York: Grosset's Universal Library, 1963.

        Good collection illustrating the stresses of life under the occupation and immediately after the peace.

1182   Keene, Donald. THE OLD WOMAN, THE WIFE, AND THE ARCHER: THREE MODERN JAPANESE SHORT NOVELS. New York: Viking Press, 1961.

   Three important short novels in a superior translation.

1183   McKinnon, Richard N., ed. THE HEART IS ALONE: A SELECTION OF 20TH CENTURY JAPANESE SHORT STORIES. Tokyo: Hokuseido Press, 1957.

   Well-known writers. Good translations and biographical notes.

1184   Morris, Ivan, ed. MODERN JAPANESE STORIES, AN ANTHOLOGY. Rutland, Vt.: Charles E. Tuttle Co., [1962.

   Large collection of works by twenty-five authors. Perhaps the best collection available.

1185   Saeki, Shoichi, ed. THE SHADOW OF SUNRISE: SELECTED STORIES OF JAPAN AND THE WAR. Tokyo: Kodansha International, 1966.

   Stories concerning the domestic scene during the war years. Adequate translations.

1186   Seidensticker, Edward G., John Bester, and Ivan Morris, trans. MODERN JAPANESE SHORT STORIES. Tokyo: Japan Publications Trading Co., 1961.

   Excellent translations of modern stories of a psychological nature.

10. Fiction—History and Criticism

1187   Beauchamp, Nancy Junko, comp. THE MODERN JAPANESE NOVEL IN ENGLISH TRANSLATION, A SELECT BIBLIOGRAPHY. [Honolulu: Graduate School of Library Studies, Univ. of Hawaii, 1973].

   Useful brief list.

1188   Hibbett, Howard. "Tradition and Trauma in the Contemporary Japanese Novel." DAEDALUS, 95 (1966), 925-40.

1189   Kimball, Arthur G. CRISIS IN IDENTITY: STUDIES IN THE CONTEMPORARY JAPANESE NOVEL. Rutland, Vt.: Charles E. Tuttle Co., [1973].

   Concentrates on ten outstanding works and their depiction of this modern theme.

1190   Lane, Richard. "The Beginnings of the Modern Japanese Novel: Kanazoshi, 1600–1682." HARVARD JOURNAL OF ASIATIC STUDIES, 20 (1957), 644–701.

Discusses the popular fiction which is the immediate ancestor of the modern popular novel.

1191 Miyoshi, Masao. ACCOMPLICES OF SILENCE: THE MODERN JAPANESE NOVEL. Berkeley: Univ. of California Press, 1974.

Perceptive critical analysis of trends in the modern novel.

1192 Morris, Ivan. "Fiction in Japan Today, an Exchange of Views." JAPAN QUARTERLY, 4 (1957), 159–68.

1193 Morrison, John. MODERN JAPANESE FICTION. Salt Lake City: Univ. of Utah Press, 1955.

Survey of fiction from 1868.

1194 Nakajima, Kenzo, and Edward G. Seidensticker. "Two Views of the Novel." ATLANTIC MONTHLY, 195 (January 1955), 165–69.

Brief but stimulating perspectives on fiction.

1195 Nakamura, Mitsuo. MODERN JAPANESE FICTION 1926–1968. Rev. ed. 2 vols. in 1. Tokyo: Kokusai Banka Shinkokai, 1968.

Uncritical summaries of works. Useful facts on a great many writers.

1196 Seidensticker, Edward G. "Strangely Shaped Novels: A Scattering of Examples." In STUDIES IN JAPANESE CULTURE, pp. 209–24. See entry no. 802.

On modern experiments with the form of the novel.

1197 Yamagiwa, Joseph K. "Fiction in Post-War Japan." FAR EASTERN QUARTERLY, 13 (1953), 3–22.

On the schools and movements.

11. Modern Authors and Works

ABE, KŌBŌ [ABE KIMIFUSA] (1924-)

Dai Yon Kampyō-Ki

1198 Saunders, E. Dale, trans. INTER ICE AGE 4. New York: Alfred A. Knopf, 1970.

Abe's works are symbolic and psychological studies of the plight of modern man. All of the works are novels except for TOMODACHI (FRIENDS).

Moetsukita Chizu

1199   _____. THE RUINED MAP. New York: Alfred A. Knopf, 1969.

Suna No Onna

1200   _____. THE WOMAN IN THE DUNES. New York: Alfred A. Knopf, 1964.

Tanin No Kao

1201   _____. THE FACE OF ANOTHER. New York: Alfred A. Knopf, 1966.

Tomodachi

1202   Keene, Donald, trans. FRIENDS. New York: Grove Press, 1969.

Modern play influenced by the theater of the absurd.

AKUTAGAWA, RYŪNOSUKE (1892-1927)

Collections

1203   Kojima, Takashi, trans. JAPANESE SHORT STORIES. New York: Liveright, 1961.

The stories including HELL SCREEN, one of Akutagawa's most famous.

1204   _____. RASHOMON AND OTHER STORIES. New York: Bantam Books, 1959.

The story IN A GROVE provides the plot for the noted movie RASHOMON, rather than the title story.

1205   Kojima, Takashi, and John McVittie, trans. EXOTIC JAPANESE STORIES. New York: Liveright, 1964.

Large collection with good introduction. Translations adequate.

1206   Norman, W.H.H., trans. HELL SCREEN AND OTHER STORIES. Tokyo: Hokuseido Press, 1948; rpt. Westport, Conn.: Greenwood Press, 1970.

Japan

1207 Shaw, Glenn W., trans. TALES GROTESQUE AND CURIOUS. Tokyo: Hokuseido Press, 1930.

1208 Takamasa, Sasaki, trans. THE THREE TREASURES. Tokyo: Hokuseido Press, 1951.

Kappa

1209 Bownas, Geoffrey, trans. KAPPA. Rutland, Vt.: Charles E. Tuttle Co., 1976.

1210 Shiojiro, Seiichi, trans. KAPPA. Tokyo: Hokuseido Press, 1919.

Satire on Japanese society in the pre-war years using fantastic mythological creatures, the Kabbas. The Bownas translation above, is probably the better, but both are good.

To Shi Shun

1211 Britton, Dorothy, trans. TU TZE-CHUN. Tokyo: Kodansha International, 1965.

A fantasy of a man who suddenly becomes rich.

ARISHIMA, TAKEO (ALSO TAKERŌ) [ARISHIMA YUKIMASA] (1878-1923)

1212 Fujita, Seiji, trans. THE AGONY OF COMING INTO THE WORLD. Tokyo: Hokuseido Press, 1955.

Translation of UMARE IZURU NAYAMI, story of the relation between art and nature.

DAZAI, OSAMU (1909-48)

Translations

NINGEN SHIKKAKU

1213 Keene, Donald, trans. NO LONGER HUMAN. Norwalk, Conn.: New Directions, 1958.

SHAYŌ

1214 _____. THE SETTING SUN. Norwalk, Conn.: New Directions, 1954.

Two novels on the decline of values for the individual man.

Studies

1215 Keene, Donald. "Dazai Osamu." In LANDSCAPES AND PORTRAITS, pp. 186-203. See entry no. 797.

1216 O'Brien, James A. DAZAI OSAMU. New York: Twayne, 1975.

A good critical essay and a full study of the life and work are represented by these two above titles.

EDOGAWA ALEMPO (1894-1965)

1217 Harris, James E., trans. JAPANESE TALES OF MYSTERY AND IMAGINATION. Rutland, Vt.: Charles E. Tuttle Co., 1956.

Popular stories of murder and crime.

ENDŌ, SHŪSAKU (1923-)

Chinmoku

1218 Johnson, William, trans. SILENCE. Rutland, Vt.: Charles E. Tuttle Co., 1969.

An excellent novel about the Jesuits in Japan in the seventeenth century.

Ogo No Kuni

1219 Mathy, Francis, trans. THE GOLDEN COUNTRY: A PLAY ABOUT MARTYRS IN JAPAN. Rutland, Vt.: Charles E. Tuttle Co., 1970.

A modern play on the persecutions of Christians in early Japan. Much praised.

FUTABATEI, SHIMEI [TATSUNOSUKE HASEGAWA] (1864-1909)

Heibon

1220 Shaw, Glenn W., trans. MEDIOCRITY. Tokyo: Hokuseido Press, 1927.

First-person narrative of a tortured personality.

Sono Omokage

1221 Mitsui, Buchachiro, and Gregg Sinclair, trans. AN ADOPTED HUSBAND. New York: Alfred A. Knopf, 1919.

Japan

A novel of the problems of modern life. An important early modern novel influenced by European models.

Ukigumo

1222 Ryan, Marleigh Grayer, trans. JAPAN'S FIRST MODERN NOVEL: UKIGUMO OF FUTABATEI SHIMEI. New York: Columbia Univ. Press, 1967.

Full scholarly study of the author and translation of his most important work, published 1887–89. A psychological novel which was a pioneering effort at the time.

HAGIWARA, SAKUTARŌ (1886-1942)

1223 Wilson, Graeme, trans. FACE AT THE BOTTOM OF THE WORLD AND OTHER POEMS. Rutland, Vt.: Charles E. Tuttle Co., 1969.

Collection of his poetry from about 1917. A symbolist poet.

HAYASHI, FUMIKO (1904-51)

1224 Koitabashi, Yoshiyuki, and Martin C. Collcott, trans. THE FLOATING CLOUD. Tokyo: Hara Shobo, 1965.

Novel of post-war Japan (UKIGUMO) by a well-known woman writer.

IBUSE, MASUJI (1898-)

Jon Manjiro Hyōryuki

1225 Kaneko, Hisakazu, trans. JOHN MANJIRO, THE CAST-AWAY: HIS LIFE AND ADVENTURES. Tokyo: Hokuseido Press, 1940.

Kuroi Ame

1226 Bester, John, trans. BLACK RAIN. Tokyo: Kodansha International, 1969; London: Secker and Warburg, 1971.

Yohai Taicho

1227 _____. LIEUTENANT LOOKEAST AND OTHER STORIES. Tokyo: Kodansha International, 1969.

Three highly imaginative novels. BLACK RAIN is concerned with Hiroshima.

INOUE, YASUSHI (1907-)

Collections

1228   Picon, Leon, trans. THE COUNTERFEITER AND OTHER STORIES.
Rutland, Vt.: Charles E. Tuttle Co., 1965.

Ryōjū

1229   Yokoo, Sadamichi, and Sanford Goldstein, trans. THE HUNTING
GUN. Rutland, Vt.: Charles E. Tuttle Co., 1961.

A major psychological novel.

Saiiki Monogatari

1230   Furuta, Gyo, and Gordon Sager, trans. JOURNEY BEYOND SAMAR-
CAND. Tokyo: Kodansha International, 1971.

ISHIKAWA, TAKUBOKU (1885-1912)

1231   Hondo, Heihachiro, trans. THE POETRY OF ISHIKAWA TAKUBOKO.
Tokyo: Hokuseido Press, 1959.

Good translations, but more pedestrian than those in the
following entry.

1232   Sesar, Carl, trans. POEMS TO EAT. Tokyo: Kodansha International,
1966.

Poems by an important early modern poet. Well translated.

ISHIKAWA, TATSUZŌ (1905-)

1233   Kazuma, Nakayama, trans. RESISTANCE AT FORTY-EIGHT. Tokyo:
Hokuseido Press, 1960.

Translation of SHIJŪHASSAI NO TEIKO, a novel of the inner
life of a middle-aged man. Not a good translation.

KAGAWA, TOYOHIKO (1888-1960)

Collections

1234   Erickson, Lois J., trans. SONGS FROM THE LAND OF THE DAWN.
New York: Friendship Press, 1949; rpt. New York: Books for Libraries
Press, 1968.

1235 _____. SONGS FROM THE SLUMS. Nashville, Tenn.: Cokesbury Press, 1935.

> Collections of poetry by a well-known Christian thinker and activist.

SHISEN WO KOETE

1236 Fukumoto, I., and Thomas Satchell, trans. BEFORE THE DAWN. New York: Doran and Co., 1925.

> Appeared earlier in Japan as ACROSS THE DEATH LINE. Novel of a man who tries to live by Christian principles.

KAWABATA, YASUNARI (1899-1972)

Essays

BI NO SONZAI TO HAKKEN

1237 Viglielmo, V.H. trans. THE EXISTENCE AND DISCOVERY OF BEAUTY. Tokyo: Mainichi Shimuhunsha, 1969.

> A lengthy essay which shed much light on the fiction of the first Japanese writer to win the Nobel Prize.

UTSUKUSHII NIHON NO WATAKUSHI

1238 Seidensticker, Edward G., trans. JAPAN THE BEAUTIFUL AND MY-SELF. Tokyo and Palo Alto, Calif. Kodansha International, [1969].

> The 1968 Nobel Prize acceptance speech. A peculiarly Japanese essay on aesthetics.

Fiction

IZO NO ODORIKO

1239 Seidensticker, Edward G., trans. THE IZO DANCER. Tokyo: Hara Shobo, 1963; rpt. Rutland, Vt.: Charles E. Tuttle Co., 1974.

MEIJIN

1240 _____. THE MASTER OF GO. New York: Alfred A. Knopf, 1972.

MIZUUMI

1241 Tsukimura, Reiko, trans. THE LAKE. Tokyo: Kodansha International, [1974].

NEMURERU BIJO

1242   Seidensticker, Edward G., trans.   HOUSE OF THE SLEEPING BEAUTIES
AND OTHER STORIES.   Tokyo: Kodansha International, 1969.

A strange and erotic short novel and some stories.

SENBAZURU

1243   _____.   THOUSAND CRANES.   New York: Alfred A. Knopf, 1958.

All of these novels and this one in particular, perhaps, demonstrate the qualities that make Kawabata a very Japanese writer
as well as an international one.

YAMA NO OTO

1244   _____.   THE SOUND OF THE MOUNTAIN.   New York: Alfred A.
Knopf, 1970.

The theme is the sensual impulses of an aging man.

YUKIGUNI

1245   _____.   SNOW COUNTRY.   New York: Alfred A. Knopf, 1956.

Novel of a love affair in a resort area.   Perhaps his most
popular and most accessible novel for the Westerner.

Studies

1246   Oi, Koji, ed. and trans.   "Snow Country: Some Critical Views."
THE REEDS, 9 (1963), 47-70.

KIKUCHI, KAN (1888-1948)

1247   Nishi, Kiichi, trans.   VICTORY OR DEFEAT.   Tokyo: Kairyudo, 1934.

A novel (SHOKAI) by this important playwright of the pre-war era.

1248   Shaw, Glenn W., trans.   TOJURO'S LOVE AND FOUR OTHER PLAYS.
Tokyo: Hokuseido Press, 1925.

Plays largely concerned with domestic situations.

KINOSHITA, JUNJI (1914-)

Translations

1249   Kurashi, Takeshi, trans.   TWILIGHT OF A CRANE.   Tokyo: Miraisha, 1952.

1250   Scott, A[dolphe] C., trans. TWILIGHT CRANE. New York: New Directions, 1956.

       Two translations of YŪZURU. Scott's is preferable. A play.

Studies

1251   Brazell, Karen Woodward. "Kinoshita Junji's Use of Tradition in Modern Japanese Drama." PAPERS OF THE MICHIGAN ACADEMY OF ARTS AND SCIENCES. ARTS AND LETTERS, 49 (1963) 261-69.

KINOSHITA, NAOE (1869-1937)

1252   Lloyd, Arthur, trans. THE CONFESSIONS OF A HUSBAND. 2 vols. Tokyo: Yurakusha, 1905-06.

       Distinctly nineteenth- century, rambling novel (OTTO NO JIHAKU).

1253   Strong, Kenneth, trans. PILLAR OF FIRE. London: Allen and Unwin, 1972.

       Published in 1904. Moralistic novel of opposition to the Russo-Japanese war (HI NO HISHIRA).

KOBAYASHI, TAKIJI (1903-33)

1254   THE CANNERY BOAT AND OTHER JAPANESE SHORT STORIES. New York: International Publishing Co., 1933; rpt. Westport, Conn.: Greenwood Press, 1968.

       The title work is a Marxist novel about fishery workers. The other stories also depict the plight of the working man.

KŌDA, ROHAN (1867-1947)

1255   Nagura, Jiro, trans. LEAVING THE HERMITAGE. London: Allen and Unwin, 1925.

1256   Shioya, Sakae, trans. THE PAGODA. Tokyo: Okura Shoten, 1909.

       Translations of SHUTSURO and GOJU NO TŌ. A very learned writer of fiction whose work is permeated by Buddhist themes.

Studies

1257   Mulhern, Cheiko I. KŌDA ROHAN. Boston: Twayne, 1977.

       Brief study of the life and works.

MEIJI TENNO, EMPEROR OF JAPAN (1852-1912)

1258   Lloyd, Arthur, trans. IMPERIAL SONGS. Tokyo: Kinkodo, 1905.

Many of the emperors of Japan both wrote poetry and judged
poetry contests as well as commissioning anthologies.

MISHIMA, YUKIO [HIRAOKA, KIMITAKE] (1955-)

Translations—Fiction

AI NO KAWAKI

1259   Marks, Alfred H., trans. THIRST FOR LOVE. New York: Alfred A.
Knopf, 1969.

A well-translated novel of sexual intrigue and jealousy.

GOGO NO EIKO

1260   Nathan, John, trans. THE SAILOR WHO FELL FROM GRACE WITH
THE SEA. New York: Alfred A. Knopf, 1965.

A morbid tale of a boy, his mother, and her sailor lover.

HŌJŌ NO UMI

1261   Gallagher, Michael, trans. THE SEA OF FERTILITY. 4 vols. New
York: Alfred A. Knopf, 1971-74.

I.   SPRING SNOW [HARU NO YUKI], 1971; II.   RUNAWAY
HORSES [HOMBA], 1973; III.   THE TEMPLE OF THE DAWN
[AKATSUKI NO TERA], 1973; IV.   THE DECAY OF THE
ANGEL [TENNIN GOSUI], 1974.   A long and complex
tetralogical parable of modern social disorder.

KAMEN NO KOKUHAKU

1262   Weatherby, Meredith, trans. CONFESSIONS OF A MASK. New
York: New Directions, 1958.

Portrait of a homosexual in a world of sadism and violence.

KINJIKI

1263   Marks, Alfred H., trans. FORBIDDEN COLORS. New York: Alfred
A. Knopf, 1968.

Depicts the many facets of amorous behavior of a young man.
One of Mishima's major works, well translated.

KINKAKUJI

1264   Morris, Ivan, trans. THE TEMPLE OF THE GOLDEN PAVILLION.
        New York: Alfred A. Knopf, 1958.

>   Perhaps his most important work. Story based on a real-life
>   incident of a young monk who burns down the Golden Pavil-
>   lion in Kyoto. Excellent translation.

SHIOSAI

1265   Weatherby, Meredith, trans. THE SOUND OF WAVES. New York:
        Alfred A. Knopf, 1956.

>   Perhaps his most attractive novel. Idyllic picture of young
>   love in a village on the seacoast.

UTAGE NO ATO

1266   Keene, Donald, trans. AFTER THE BANQUET. New York: Alfred A.
        Knopf, 1963.

>   Marital problems of a middle-aged successful business woman.

Translations—Plays

KINDAI NŌGAKUSHŪ

1267   Keene, Donald, trans. FIVE MODERN NŌ PLAYS. New York:
        Alfred A. Knopf, 1956.

>   Imaginative modernizations of classic nō plays: SOTOBA
>   KOMACHI, THE DAMASK DRUM, KĀN-TAN, PRINCESS
>   AOI, and HANJO. Critical analysis by Keene.

NETTAIJU

1268   Strong, Kenneth, trans. "Tropical Tree." JAPAN QUARTERLY, 11
        (1964), 174-210.

>   Modern tragedy of violent domestic passions.

SADO KŌSHAKU FUKIN

1269   Keene, Donald, trans. MADAME DE SADE. New York: Grove Press,
        1967.

>   The philosophy of De Sade through a woman's eyes.

YORU NO HIMAWARI

1270 Shinozaki, Shigeho, and Virgil A. Warren, trans. TWILIGHT
SUNFLOWER. Tokyo: Hokuseido Press, 1958.

A play, set in modern times, about family relations.

Translations—Essays

1271 Bester, John, trans. SUN AND STEEL. New York: Grove Press,
1972.

In his later life, Mishima's association with a paramilitary
organization dedicated to restoring Japanese patriotic principles
led to his suicide. His later philosophy is embodied in this
long essay, and is reflected in some of the essays below.

1272 Gallagher, Michael, trans. "Testament of a Samurai." SPORTS
ILLUSTRATED, 34 (11 January 1971), 24-27.

1273 Introd. HOUSE OF THE SLEEPING BEAUTIES. By Yasunari Kawabata.
Tokyo: Kodansha, 1969.

1274 Introd. "On Nakedness and Shame." NAKED FESTIVAL: A PHOTO
ESSAY. By T. Yato. New York: Walker, Weatherhill, 1969.

1275 Introd. YOUNG SAMURAI: BODY BUILDERS OF JAPAN. By T.
Yato. New York: Grove Press, 1967.

1276 Keene, Donald, trans. "Party of One." HOLIDAY, 30 (October
1961), 9-13.

Studies

1277 Boardman, Gwen R. "Greek Hero and Japanese Samurai: Mishima's
New Aesthetic." CRITIQUE, 12 (1970), 103-15.

1278 Dana, Robert. "Stutter of Eternity: A Study of the Themes of Isolation
and Meaninglessness in Three Novels of Yukio Mishima." CRITIQUE,
12 (1970), 87-102.

1279 Duus, Louise. "Novel as Koan: Mishima Yukio's THE TEMPLE OF
THE GOLDEN PAVILLION." CRITIQUE, 10 (1968), 120-29.

1280 Eschelbach, Claire John, comp. "Yukio Mishima in America: A Bibliography 1956-1974." BULLETIN OF BIBLIOGRAPHY, 32 (1975), 1-2, 44.

Useful list. Includes many ephemeral articles.

1281   Goldstein, Bernice, and Sanford Goldstein. "Observations on THE SAILOR WHO FELL FROM GRACE WITH THE SEA." CRITIQUE, 12 (1970), 116-26.

1282   Keene, Donald. "Mishima and the Modern Scene. TIMES [LONDON] LITERARY SUPPLEMENT, No. 3625 (20 August 1971), pp. 989-90.

1283   _____. "Mishima Yukio." In LANDSCAPES AND PORTRAITS, pp. 204-25. See entry no. 797.

An important essay by a scholar personally acquainted with Mishima.

1284   Korges, James. "Gide and Mishima: Homosexuality as Metaphor." CRITIQUE, 12 (1970), 127-37.

1285   Miller, Henry. REFLECTIONS ON THE DEATH OF MISHIMA. Santa Barbara, Calif.: Capra Press, 1972.

1286   Nathan, John. MISHIMA, A BIOGRAPHY. Boston: Little, Brown, 1974.

A picture of Mishima's artistic life and development which is the best available at the moment. Considers also his interest in politics which set up the circumstances for his tragic death.

1287   Scott-Stokes, Henry. THE LIFE AND DEATH OF YUKIO MISHIMA. New York: Farrar, Straus and Giroux, 1974.

A personal memoir of Mishima by a friend. Especially useful for the last years.

1288   Seidensticker, Edward G. "Mishima Yukio." HUDSON REVIEW, 24 (1971), 272-82.

1289   Shorer, Mark. "Weight Lifting, Nihilism, and the Japanese Novel." REPORTER, 15 (29 November 1956), 41-44.

Brief critical comment by a distinguished critic of American literature.

1290   Vidal, Gore. "The Death of Mishima." In his HOMAGE TO DANIEL SHAYE. New York: Random House, 1972, pp. 376-88.

1291   Wolf, Barbara. "Mishima's Testimony, Wanton and Reverent." THE NATION, 214 (12 June 1972), 758-62.

MIYAZAWA, KENJI (1806-1933)

Translations

1292 Hiroaki, Sato, trans. SPRING AND AZURA. Chicago: Chicago Review Press, 1973.

Good selection of poems with a substantial introduction by Burton Watson.

Studies

1293 Nakajima, Kenzo. "Miyazawa Kenji, the Man and his Work." JAPAN QUARTERLY, 5 (1958): 59-62.

MORI, ŌGAI (1862-1922)

1294 Fukuda, Tsutomu, trans. SANSHŌ-DAYU AND OTHER STORIES. Tokyo: Hokuseido Press, 1952.

A fair translation of a short story set in medieval Japan, with some other stories.

1295 Ninomiya, Kazuji, and Sanford Goldstein, trans. VITA SEXUALIS. Rutland, Vt.: Charles E. Tuttle Co., [1972].

The story of a young man's awakening sexuality (ITA SEKU-SUARISU). Banned by the authorities when it first appeared in 1909.

1296 Ochiai, Kingo, and Sanford Goldstein, trans. THE WILD GEESE. Rutland, Vt.: Charles E. Tuttle Co., 1959.

A romantic story (GAN) set in pre-war Tokyo.

MUSHANOKŌJI, SANEATSU (1885-)

Translations

AI TO SHI

1297 Marquardt, William F., trans. LOVE AND DEATH. New York: Twayne, 1958.

1298 Yamamura, Saburo, trans. LOVE AND DEATH. Tokyo: Hokuseido Press, 1967.

A melancholy novel about the death of a loved one. Both translations are satisfactory.

Japan

YŪJŌ

1299   Matsumoto, Ryuzo.   FRIENDSHIP.   Tokyo: Hokuseido Press, 1958.

A novel about love and friendship.

NAGAI, KAFŪ [NAGAI, SOKICHI] (1879-1959)

Translations

1300   Meissner, Kurt, and Ralph Friederich, trans.   GEISHA IN RIVALRY.
Rutland, Vt.:   Charles E. Tuttle Co., 1963.

First published in 1918, this novel depicts the Shimbashi
night-life quarter of Tokyo.

Studies

1301   Seidensticker, Edward G.   KAFŪ THE SCRIBBLER: THE LIFE AND
WRITINGS OF NAGAI KAFŪ, 1879-1959.   Stanford: Stanford Univ.
Press, 1965.

Major biographical account and critical analysis of the works.
Translations of excerpts from the longer works and some stories.

NAKAGAWA, YOICHI (1897-)

Translations

SHITSURAKU NO NIWA

1302   Negishi, Yoshitaro, trans.   THE GARDEN OF LOST JOY.   Tokyo:
Kokuseido Press, [1953].

TEN NO YŪGAO

1303   Ingalls, Jeremy, trans.   NAKAGAWA'S TENNO YŪGAO, WITH A
COMMENTARY ON THE RELEVANCE OF YOICHI NAKAGAWA'S
NOVEL IN JAPANESE LITERATURE.   Boston: Twayne, [1975].

Good critical material in this translation.

1304   Ota, Akira, trans.   A MOONFLOWER IN HEAVEN.   Tokyo: Hokuseido Press, [1949].

A romantic novel about a couple who cannot marry.

NIWA, FUMIŌ (1905-)

1305 Strong, Kenneth, trans. THE BUDDHA TREE. London: Peter Owen; Rutland, Vt.: Charles E. Tuttle Co., 1966.

Long novel about a weak and sensual priest of the Pure Land sect.

NOGAMI, YAEKO (1885-)

1306 Matsumoto, Ryōsō, trans. THE NEPTUNE AND THE FOXES. Tokyo: Kenkyusha, [1957].

Two short novels, KAIZAN-MARU and KITSUNE, by an early modern naturalistic writer.

NOMA, HIROSHI (1915-)

1307 Frechtman, Bernard, trans. ZONE OF EMPTINESS. Cleveland: World Publishing Co., [1956].

A story of the Japanese army in the final days of World War II. A re-translation from the French and not very satisfactory.

ŌE, KENZABURŌ (1935-)

1308 Bester, John, trans. THE SILENT CITY. New York: Kodansha International, 1974.

1309 Nathan, John, trans. A PERSONAL MATTER. Tokyo: Charles E. Tuttle Co., [1969].

Two novels (MAN'EN GANNEN NO FUTTOBORU and KOJINTEKI NA TAIKEN) by a writer concerned with existential ideas who is a serious adaptor of Western techniques.

ŌOKA SHŌHEI (1909-)

1310 Morris, Ivan, trans. FIRES ON THE PLAIN. New York: Alfred A. Knopf, 1957; rpt. Baltimore: Penguin Books, [1966].

Symbolic novel about the horrors of life behind the lines in the war.

OSARAGI, JIRO [NOJIRI KIYOHIKO] (1897-)

1311 Horwitz, Brewster, trans. HOME COMING. New York: Alfred A. Knopf, [1955].

A novel (KIKYŌ) of the experiences of a returning soldier after the Japanese defeat.

1312   Morris, Ivan, trans. THE JOURNEY. New York: Alfred A. Knopf, 1960.

TABIJI is a novel of the disorders in various parts of Asia at the end of the war.

OZAKI, KŌYŌ (1867-1903)

1313   Lloyd, A., and M. Lloyd, trans. THE GOLDEN DEMON. Tokyo: Seibundo, 1905.

A period piece. Early modern love story in a dated translation.

SŌSEKI, NATSUME (1867-1916)

Translations

BOTCHAN

1314   Sasaki, Umeji, trans. BOTCHAN. Rutland, Vt.: Charles E. Tuttle Co., [1968].

1315   Turney, Alan, trans. BOTCHAN. Tokyo: Kodanska International, [1972]; London: Peter Owen, [1972].

1316   Watson, Burton, trans. "Botchan." In MODERN JAPANESE LITERATURE, pp. 124-33. See entry no. 1144.

1317   Yasataro, Mori, trans. BOTCHAN. Tokyo: Kinseido, 1951.

A humorous story of a young man's adventures with a distinctly pre-war flavor. Watson's translation is the best of these four.

GARASUDO NO NAKA

1318   Matushara, Iwao, and E.T. Englehart, trans. WITHIN MY GLASS DOORS. Tokyo: Shin-Seido, [1928].

Impressionistic sketches of modern life.

KŌJIN

1319   Yu, Beongcheon, trans. THE WAYFARER. Detroit: Wayne State Univ. Press, 1967.

A good translation of a long novel.

KOKORO

1320   McClellan, Edwin, trans. KOKORO. Chicago: Henry Regnery Co.,
        1957.

1321   Sato, Ineko, trans. KOKORO. [Tokyo]: Hokuseido Press for the
        Japan Writers' Society, [1941].

> The title means "the heart of things." A subtle novel explain-
> ing why withdrawal from the world is desirable. This novel
> and I AM A CAT (WAGAHAI WA NEKO DE ARU) are perhaps
> Soseki's major works. McClellan's translations, above, is
> preferable.

KUSA MAKURA

1322   Turney, Alan, trans. THE THREE-CORNERED WORLD. London: Peter
        Owen, 1965. Chicago: Henry Regnery Co., [1967].

> KUSA MAKURA a "grass pillow" signifies sleeping in the
> countryside on a journey. Highly personal story of withdrawal
> from the world.

1323   Umeji, Sasabi, trans. KUSAMAKURA AND BUNCHO. Tokyo:
        Iwanami Shoten, 1927.

> A satisfactory translation. Turney's is preferable.

MICHIKUSA

1324   McClellan, Edwin, trans. GRASS ON THE WAYSIDE. Chicago: Univ.
        of Chicago Press, [1969].

> About the duties of the world and the lack of understanding
> between human beings. Excellent translation.

MON

1325   Mathy, Francis, trans. MON. London: Peter Owen, 1972.

> MON (THE GATE) depicts the problems of modern man in
> 1910.

WAGAHAI WA NEKO DE ARU

1326   Itō, Aiko, and Graeme Wilson, trans. I AM A CAT. Rutland, Vt.:
        Charles E. Tuttle Co., [1972].

1327 Shibata, Katsue, and Kai Motonari, trans. I AM A CAT, A NOVEL. Tokyo: Kenkyusha, [1962]; rpt. London: Peter Owen, 1971.

A cat makes satiric observations about the human scene. One of Sōseki's best novels. Both translations are satisfactory.

YUMEJŪYA

1328 Hata, Sankichi, and Shirai Dofu, trans. TEN NIGHTS' DREAMS AND OUR CAT'S GRAVE. Tokyo: Tokyo News Service, 1949.

1329 Itō, Aiko, and Graeme Wilson, trans. TEN NIGHTS OF DREAM, HEARING THINGS, THE HEREDITY OF TASTE. Rutland, Vt.: Charles E. Tuttle Co., [1974].

Humorous stories. The Itō-Wilson translation is preferable for the title story.

Studies

1330 Japan National Commission for UNESCO. ESSAYS ON NATSUME SŌSEKI'S WORKS. [Tokyo]: Japan Society for Promotion of Science, [1970].

Useful collection of critical material with bibliography.

1331 McClellan, Edwin. "The Implications of Sōseki's KOKORO." MONUMENTA NIPPONICA, 14 (1958-59), 110-24.

Excellent critical article on this major work.

1332 _____. "An Introduction to Sōseki." HARVARD JOURNAL OF ASIATIC STUDIES, 22 (1959), 150-208.

A major guide to the works, historical and critical.

1333 _____. TWO JAPANESE NOVELISTS: SŌSEKI AND TŌSON. Chicago: Univ. of Chicago Press, [1969].

Good critical study of Sōseki and Tōson Shimazaki (see also the entry for the latter, below).

1334 Viglielmo, Valdo H. "An Introduction to the Later Novels of Sōseki." MONUMENTA NIPPONICA, 10 (1964), 1-16.

1335 Yu, Beongcheon. NATSUME SŌSEKI. New York: Twayne, [1969].

1336 _____. "A Tragedy of Character: Sōseki's Kokoro." ORIENT/WEST, 9 (1963), 73-80.

TAKAGI, KYŌZŌ (1903-)

1337   Kirkup, James, and Michio Nakano, trans.   SELECTED POEMS.
        Cheadle [Engl.]: Carcanet Press, 1973.

        A slender volume of translations of a poet who writes of com-
        mon things in ordinary language.

TAKAHASHI, SHINKICHI (1901-)

1338   Stryk, Lucien, and Takashi Ikimoto, trans.   AFTERIMAGES: ZEN
        POEMS. New York: Anchor Books, 1972.

        Good selection in good translations of a poem at first much
        influenced by Western ideas but later turning to Zen. Dis-
        cussion by Zen poetics.

TAKEDA, TAIJUN (1912-)

1339   Shibuya, Yusaboro, and Sanford Goldstein, trans.   THIS OUTCAST
        GENERATION. LUMINOUS MOSS. Rutland, Vt.: Charles E.
        Tuttle Co., [1967].

        Two short novels. MAMUSHI NO SUE deals with Japanese
        Left in Shanghai at the end of World War II; HIKARIGOKE
        is about cannibalism in Hokkaido, northern Japan.

TAKEYAMA, MICHIO (1903-)

1340   Hibbett, Howard, trans.   HARP OF BURMA. Tokyo: Charles E.
        Tuttle Co., [1966].

        BIRUMA NO TATEGOTO is a moving novel of the horrors of
        war.

TANIZAKI, JUN'ICHIRO (1886-1965)

Collections

1341   Hibbett, Howard, trans.   SEVEN JAPANESE TALES. New York:
        Alfred A. Knopf, 1963.

        Includes both early and late works by one of the foremost
        writers of twentieth-century Japan, in excellent translations.

Fiction—Translations

ASHIKARI

1342   Humpherson, Roy, and Hajime Okita, trans.   ASHIKARI AND SHUNKIN,
        MODERN JAPANESE NOVELS. Tokyo: Hokuseido Press, [1936].

Two short novels. SHUNKIN illustrates Tanizaki's concern with dominant female characters and is important to his later work.

FŪTEN RŌJIN NO NIKKI

1343 Hibbett, Howard, trans. DIARY OF A MAD OLD MAN. New York: Alfred A. Knopf, 1965.

Beautifully translated novel of the passion of an old man for his daughter-in-law.

KAGI

1344 _____. THE KEY. New York: Alfred A. Knopf, 1961.

A novel of sexual passion in the form of diaries. Excellent translation.

OTSUYA KOROSHI

1345 Zenchi, Iwado, trans. A SPRING-TIME CASE. Tokyo: Japan Times, [1927].

SASAME YUKI

1346 Seidensticker, Edward G., trans. THE MAKIOKA SISTERS. New York: Alfred A. Knopf, 1957.

A family novel which focuses on three sisters in a world that is losing its values. Perhaps his greatest work. Excellent translation.

SHUNKIN SHŌ

1347 Humpherson, Roy, and Hajime Okita, trans. ASHIKARI AND SHUNKIN, MODERN JAPANESE NOVELS. See entry no. 1342.

TADE KUU MUSHI

1348 Seidensticker, Edward G., trans. SOME PREFER NETTLES. London: Secker and Warburg, 1955.

A characteristic work and perhaps the most popular novel among Western readers. A sensitive treatment of personal relations. Excellent translation.

Studies

1349   Keene, Donald. "Tanizaki Jun'ichiro." In LANDSCAPES AND
       PORTRAITS, pp. 171-85. See entry no. 797.

       Good critical introduction.

TOKUTOMI, KENJIRŌ [TOKUTOMI, ROKA] (1868-1927)

1350   Strong, Kenneth, trans. FOOTPRINTS IN THE SNOW. New York: Pega-
       sus, 1970.

       OMOIDE NO KI is the account of the life of an author who
       was converted to Christianity and much influenced by Western
       writers.

TŌSON, SHIMAZAKI (1872-1943)

Translations

1351   Morita, James R., trans. "Shimazaki Tōson: Four Collections of
       Poems." MONUMENTA NIPPONICA, 25 (1970), 325-69.

       A pioneer in modern poetry in Japan. Good historical sketch
       and fair translations.

Studies

1352   McClellan, Edwin. "The Novels of Tōson Shimazaki." HARVARD
       JOURNAL OF ASIATIC STUDIES, 24 (1962-63), 82-174.

1353   _____. "Tōson Shimazaki." In TWO JAPANESE NOVELISTS,
       pp. 73-163. See entry no. 1333.

       Two valuable studies of the works and the historical back-
       ground of an important early modern writer.

1354   Roggendorf, Joseph. "Shimazaki Tōson, a Maker of the Modern Japa-
       nese Novel." MONUMENTA NIPPONICA, 7 (1951), 40-66.

       Good study of the place of Tōson in the literary history of
       the early modern novel.

TSUBOUCHI, SHŌYŌ (1859-1935)

Translations

SHŌSETSU SHINZUI

1355   Keene, Donald, trans. "The Essence of the Novel." In MODERN

JAPANESE LITERATURE, pp. 55-58. See entry no. 1144.

Critical essay by this important Japanese dramatist and critic of the early modern period, who also made a contribution to realistic fiction based on Western models.

Studies

1356   Ryan, Marleigh, Grayer. THE DEVELOPMENT OF REALISM IN THE FICTION OF TSUBOUCHI SHŌYŌ. Seattle: Univ. of Washington Press, 1975.

Excellent critical study.

WAKAYAMA, BOKUSUI (1885-1928)

1357   Honda, Heihachiro, trans. THE POETRY OF WAKAYAMA BOKUSUI. Tokyo: Hokuseido Press, [1958].

An important transitional figure who is now little read. Well translated.

YAMAMOTO, YŪZŌ (1887-)

1358   Shaw, Glenn, trans. THREE PLAYS. Tokyo: Hokuseido Press, 1957.

Three historical tragedies.

YOSANO, AKIKO (1878-1941)

1359   Goldstein, Sanford, and Seishi Shinoda, trans. TANGLED HAIR: SELECTED TANKA FROM "MIDAREGAMI." Lafayette, Ind.: Purdue Univ. Studies, 1971.

1360   Honda, Heihachiro, trans. THE POETRY OF YOSANO AKITA. Tokyo: Hokuseido Press, 1957.

1361   Iwasaki, Yozan T., trans. "Thirty Poems by Akiko Yosano." NEW ORIENT, 3 (Jan. 1927), 19-22.

An important woman poet who tried to revive the short tanka form. The Goldstein-Shimoda translation is the best of the translations and has an introduction to the life and works. It contains the Japanese text.

YOSHIKAWA, EIJI (1892-)

1362   Uramatsu, Fuki Wooyenaka, trans. THE HEIKE STORY. New York: Alfred A. Knopf, 1956.

The SHIN HEIKE MONOGATARI, an imaginative reconstruction of the medieval HEIKE MONOGATARI. See entry nos. 1002-4. The story of the rise of the Taira general, Kiyomori.

12. Periodicals

1363 JAPAN QUARTERLY. Tokyo: Asahi Shimbun-Sha, 1954-- .

A general magazine devoted to all aspects of Japanese culture, including literature.

1364 MONUMENTA NIPPONICA: STUDIES IN JAPANESE CULTURE. Tokyo: Sophia University, 1938-- .

An essential scholarly journal with many translations and critical articles on Japanese literature.

1365 TRANSACTIONS OF THE ASIATIC SOCIETY OF JAPAN. Tokyo: Asiatic Society of Japan, 1922-- .

The grandfather of Western language journals on Japan. Many important early translations and historical studies of literature appear in this.

Chapter 4
KOREA

A. BIBLIOGRAPHY

1366 BIBLIOGRAPHY OF KOREAN STUDIES: A BIBLIOGRAPHICAL GUIDE
TO KOREAN PUBLICATIONS ON KOREAN STUDIES APPEARING
FROM 1945 TO 1958. Seoul: Asiatic Research Center, Korea Univ.,
1961.

1367 BIBLIOGRAPHY OF KOREAN STUDIES: VOL. II, 1959 TO 1962.
Seoul: Asiatic Research Center, Korea Univ., 1965.

   Annotations in English. Useful for seeing the scope of Korean
   studies in language and literature.

1368 BIBLIOGRAPHY OF THE JAPANESE EMPIRE. See entry no. 785.

   Some material on Korea.

1369 Courant, Maurice Auguste Louis Marie, comp. BIBLIOGRAPHY
CORÉENNE: TABLEAUX LITTÉRAIRE DE LA COREE. 3 vols. Paris:
Le Roux, 1894-1896; SUPPLEMENT À LA BIBLIOGRAPHIE CORÉENNE
(JUSQU'EN 1899). Paris: Le Roux, 1901; 4 vols. in 3. New York:
Burt Franklin, [1967].

   Pioneering work, but of little use to the general reader.

1370 Elrod, Jefferson McRae, comp. AN INDEX TO ENGLISH LANGUAGE
PERIODICAL LITERATURE PUBLISHED IN KOREA, 1890-1950. Seoul:
Korean National Assembly Library, 1965.

   Comprehensive. A fair amount of literary material.

1371 Gompertz, G. St. G., comp. "Bibliography of Western Literature on
Korea from Earliest Times until 1950." TRANSACTIONS OF THE
KOREAN BRANCH OF THE ROYAL ASIATIC SOCIETY, 40 (1963),
1-263.

1372   Harvard Univ. Library. CHINA, JAPAN AND KOREA: CLASSIFICA-
       TION SCHEDULE. Cambridge, Mass.: Harvard Univ. Press, 1968.

       Works in the Widener Library. Does not include the Asiatic
       collections.

1373   AN INDEX TO ENGLISH PERIODICAL LITERATURE PUBLISHED IN
       KOREA, 1945–66. Seoul: Korea Research Center, 1967.

1374   Jones, Helen D., and Robin L. Winkler, comps. KOREA: AN ANNO-
       TATED BIBLIOGRAPHY OF PUBLICATIONS IN WESTERN LANGUAGES.
       Washington, D.C.: Library of Congress, 1950.

       Especially useful for 1939–49.

1375   Lee, Soon Hi [Yi Sun-Hi], comp. KOREA: A SELECTED BIBLIOG-
       RAPHY IN WESTERN LANGUAGES 1950-1958. Washington, D.C.:
       n.p., 1959.

       Typescript of a M.A. thesis, Catholic University of America.

1376   McCune, Shannon, comp. BIBLIOGRAPHY OF WESTERN LANGUAGE
       MATERIAL ON KOREA. Rev. and enl. ed. New York: Institute
       of Pacific Relations, 1950.

       Both of these are useful brief bibliographies for the period
       covered.

1377   Marcus, Richard, et al. KOREAN STUDIES GUIDE. Berkeley: Univ.
       of California Press, 1954.

       A good descriptive bibliography. Includes literature.

1378   Silberman, Bernard S., comp. JAPAN AND KOREA, A CRITICAL
       BIBLIOGRAPHY. See entry no. 792.

1379   Underwood, Horace H., comp. "Occidental Literature on Korea: A
       Partial Bibliography." TRANSACTIONS OF THE KOREAN BRANCH
       OF THE ROYAL ASIATIC SOCIETY, 20 (1931), 1-185.

       An important very complete, early bibliography, with an index
       following page 185.

1380   Underwood, Horace H., Jr. "Korean Literature in English." TRANS-
       ACTIONS OF THE KOREAN BRANCH OF THE ROYAL ASIATIC
       SOCIETY, 41 (1976), 65-115.

       The best bibliography of Korean literature available. Criti-
       cally annotated.

1381 UNION CATALOGUE OF BOOKS ON KOREA IN ENGLISH, FRENCH, GERMAN, RUSSIAN, ETC. Tokyo: International House of Japan Library, 1971.

Brief but useful.

1382 Wood, Robert S., comp. "Korean Literature: A Comprehensive Bibliography in English." KOREA JOURNAL, 8 (March 1968), 30-34.

Useful for periodical material.

B. REFERENCE

1383 Gale, James S. A HISTORY OF THE KOREAN PEOPLE. Seoul: Christian Literature Society, 1927.

Good, if somewhat out-of-date. To 1919.

1384 Griffis, William E. COREA, THE HERMIT NATION. 9th rev. ed. New York: Charles Scribner's Sons, 1911.

Still useful. Written mostly from Japanese sources. To 1910. First published in 1897.

1385 Hae Tae-Hung. GUIDE TO KOREAN CULTURE. [Seoul]: Yonsei Univ. Press, [1968].

Not a history but a brief guide to culture. Contains some translations of poetry, legends, and folktales.

1386 Han U-Gŭn. HISTORY OF KOREA. Trans. Lee Kyung-Shik. Ed. Grafton K. Mintz. Seoul: Eul-Yoo Publishing Co., [1970]; rpt. Honolulu: East-West Center Press, 1971.

Lengthy history from the beginnings to the Republic. Some cultural history.

1387 Henderson, Gregory. "Korea through the Fall of the Lolang Colony." KOREANA QUARTERLY, 1 (1959), 147-68.

Useful brief survey of the earliest period.

1388 Henthorn, William E. A HISTORY OF KOREA. New York: Free Press, [1971].

An up-to-date, good history for the general reader.

1389 [Hulbert, Homer B.] HULBERT'S HISTORY OF KOREA. Ed. Clarence Norwood Weems. 2 vols. New York: Hillary House Publications, 1962.

First published in 1905 and for many years the standard account of traditional Korea. Still of value.

1390 Joe, Wanne J. [Cho Wan-Jai]. TRADITIONAL KOREA: A CULTURAL HISTORY. Seoul: Chung'ang Univ. Press, 1972.

A good cultural history with considerable attention to literature.

1391 Kazakevich, I.S. KOREAN STUDIES. Moscow: Nauka, 1967

Surveys fifty years of Soviet scholarship on Korea.

1392 Keith, Elizabeth, and Elspet Robertson-Scott. OLD KOREA, THE LAND OF THE MORNING CALM. New York: Philosophical Library, 1946. Description of the traditional culture and the customs.

A popular book with good illustrations.

1393 Kim Changson, ed. THE CULTURE OF KOREA. [Honolulu]: Korean American Cultural Association, [1946].

Reprints of articles on all aspects of the culture with a brief section on literature including some translations.

1394 KOREA: ITS LAND, PEOPLE AND CULTURE OF ALL AGES. Seoul: Hakwon-Sa, 1960.

Encyclopedia survey. The quality of the essays varies. Contains a good brief sketch of the literature.

1395 KOREA, PAST AND PRESENT. Seoul: Kwangmyong, 1972.

An official handbook of Korea. Some material on literature.

1396 Korean National Commission for UNESCO. UNESCO KOREAN SURVEY. Seoul: Dong-a Publishing Co., 1960.

All aspects of Korean civilization are included.

1397 McCune, Shannon. KOREA'S HERITAGE: A REGIONAL AND SOCIAL GEOGRAPHY. Rutland, Vt.: Charles E. Tuttle Co., 1956.

The first part of this work is an excellent survey of Korean historical and social development.

1398 Osgood, Cornelius. THE KOREANS AND THEIR CULTURE. New York: Ronald Press, [1951].

Good material on traditional social history.

1399   Yi Pyeng-Do. "The Impact of the Western World on Korea in the 19th
        Century." CAHIERS D'HISTOIRE MONDIALE, 5 (1960), 957-75.

        Important for the later half of the nineteenth century, a
        period of massive foreign intrusion into Korean culture.

C. ANTHOLOGIES

1400   Ha Tae Hung, comp. KOREAN CULTURAL READER. Seoul: Korean
        National Commission for UNESCO, 1962.

        Brief selections of poetry, tales, and other prose.

1401   International P.E.N., Asian Writers' Translation Bureau, comp.
        ASIAN LITERATURE: POETRY, SHORT STORIES AND ESSAYS. Seoul:
        International P.E.N., 1975.

1402   _____. SHORT STORIES AND PLAYS. Seoul: International P.E.N.,
        1975.

        Both P.E.N. volumes contain selections from Korean poetry
        and short stories.

1403   Solberg, S.E., trans. "Korean Literature Issue." LITERATURE EAST &
        WEST, 14 (1970), 309-461.

        Good selection in good translations of many short pieces from
        both classical and modern literature.

D. LITERARY HISTORY AND CRITICISM

1404   Chang Tok-Soon, et al. HUMOUR IN KOREAN LITERATURE. Seoul:
        International Cultural Foundation, 1970.

        Four articles on humor in English.

1405   CHOSON MUNHAK T'ONGSA [HISTORICAL SURVEY OF KOREAN
        LITERATURE]. 2 vols. Pyongyong: Publishing House of the Academy
        of Science, 1959.

        Text in English. Not seen.

1406   Jeon Kyu-Tae [Chŏn Kyu Tae]. KOREAN HERITAGE. Seoul: Jeong
        Eum Sa, 1975.

        Includes a number of articles on literature by a professor of
        Korean literature.

1407   Kim Sok-Ha. "Idea of Paradise in Korean Literature." KOREA JOUR-
        NAL, 14 (1974), 25-30.

1408   Kim Yong-Chul. "Literature for the Cultural Learner: Toward a
        Method of Korean Studies." KOREA JOURNAL, 16 (June 1976),
        10-26.

        Useful sociological approach to classical Korean literature.

1409   Kim Yung-Chung, trans. WOMEN OF KOREA: A HISTORY FROM
        ANCIENT TIMES TO 1945. Seoul: Ehwu Woman's Univ. Press for
        the Committee for the Compilation of the History of Korean Women,
        1976.

        Contains a good chapter on women writers as well as much
        useful background material.

1410   Korean Overseas Information Service. LITERATURE. Seoul: 1973.

        A brief introduction to the periods and types.

1411   KOREAN STUDIES TODAY; DEVELOPMENT OF THE FIELD. Seoul:
        National Univ., 1970.

        Chapters on the study of classical and modern literature.

1412   Lee, Peter H. [YI Hak-Su]. KOREAN LITERARY HISTORY. Washing-
        ton, D.C.: American Council of Learned Societies, 1961.

1413   _____. KOREAN LITERATURE, TOPICS AND THEMES. Tucson: Univ.
        of Arizona Press, 1965.

        This is substantially a revision of the entry above. An excel-
        lent introductory handbook on Korean literature, the best
        available at the present time.

1414   Lee Sang-Sup [Yi Sang-Sŏp]. "An Historical Survey of Korean Litera-
        ture." In ASPECTS OF KOREAN CULTURE. Seoul: Soodo Women's
        Teachers College Press, 1974, pp. 60-73.

        Good brief introduction.

1415   Mosler, David P. "Sources of Humor in Korean Literature." JOURNAL
        OF KOREAN STUDIES, 1 (1971), 123-30.

1416   National Academy of Arts. SURVEY OF KOREAN ARTS: LITERATURE.
        Seoul: 1970.

        Articles covering the literature from earliest times to the
        present. More historical than critical.

1417   Paik Chul. "Introduction to Korean Literature." LITERATURE EAST & WEST, 14 (1970), 320-36.

A very brief, but excellent introduction.

1418   Park Kyung-Soo. "Peasant Literature in Korea." EAST ASIAN REVIEW, 2 (1975), 62-72.

1419   Pihl, Marshall R. "Korean Literature, a Voice of Humanism." KOREA JOURNAL, 10 (June 1970), 24-25.

1420   _____. "Korean Literature in Translation." KOREA JOURNAL, 10 (June 1970), 28-30.

Two brief notes by an able critic.

1421   Rutt, Richard. "The Chinese Learning and Pleasures of a Country Scholar." TRANSACTIONS OF THE KOREAN BRANCH OF THE ROYAL ASIATIC SOCIETY, 36 (1960), 1-100.

In earlier times Koreans often wrote in Chinese, and the study of Chinese was as essential to education as Latin was in medieval and renaissance Europe. An able account of Chinese studies at the "grass roots" level.

1422   _____. "The Dual Cultural Background of Korean Literature." ASIAN PACIFIC QUARTERLY, 5, No. 3 (Winter 1973), 38-47.

Foreign influences have made the preservation of the native, national elements in their culture important to the modern generation of Koreans. Rutt argues that the substantial Chinese tradition must be preserved as well. See also the next entry.

1423   _____. "Old Korean Literature in Chinese Neglected." KOREA JOURNAL, 10 (January 1970), 8-9.

1424   Skillend, W.E. "Korean Literature." In GUIDE TO THE EASTERN LITERATURES. See entry no. 57.

An excellent brief survey, perhaps the first choice for the novice.

1425   Solberg, S.E. "Moulder and Moulded: Some Extra-Literary Forces in Korean Literature, an Observation." KOREAN AFFAIRS, 2 (Winter 1963), 61-83.

1426   Song Yo-In. TRANSLATION: THEORY AND PRACTICE. Seoul: Dongguk Univ. Press, 1975.

Useful scholarly account of the problems of translating Korean works into English.

1427   Suh Doo Soo [Sŏ-Tu-Su]. KOREAN LITERARY READER, WITH A SHORT HISTORY OF KOREAN LITERATURE. Seoul: Dong-A Publishing Co., 1965.

This is an anthology of Korean-language texts, with a very good one-hundred page history of the literature in English.

1428   Trollope, Mark Nupler. "Corean Books and their Authors." TRANS-ACTIONS OF THE KOREAN BRANCH OF THE ROYAL ASIATIC SOCIETY, 31 (1932), 1-104.

Valuable for its discussion of classical works in Chinese.

1429   Zong In-Sob [Chŏng in-Sŏp]. AN INTRODUCTION TO KOREAN LITERATURE. Seoul: Hyangnin-sa, 1970.

A collection of essays on various aspects of Korean literature.

E. POETRY—ANTHOLOGIES

1430   Chang Tŏk-Sun, trans. "Exceptional Poems on Non-Poetic Themes." KOREA JOURNAL, 13, No. 3 (March 1973), 24-29.

Translations of a particular form, the sasol sijo, of the sijo or traditional short form of poetry.

1431   Grigsby, Joan S., trans. THE ORCHID DOOR: ANCIENT KOREAN POEMS. Kobe: J.L. Thompson, [1935]; rpt. New York: Paragon Book Co., 1970.

Very free translations of old Korean poems, including those written in Chinese. Paraphrases of other translations in effective poetic renderings.

1432   Ha Tae Hung, trans. POETRY AND MUSIC OF THE CLASSICAL AGE. Seoul: Yonsei Univ. Press, 1960.

Translations of sijo poetry. A Victorian pseudo-poetic diction mars these translations.

1433   Hyun, Peter [Hyŏn Ung], trans. VOICES OF THE DAWN: A SELECTION OF KOREAN POETRY FROM THE SIXTH CENTURY TO THE PRESENT DAY. London: John Murray, [1960].

A good collection. Over fifty poets are represented.

1434   Lee, Peter H. [Yi Hak-Su], trans. ANTHOLOGY OF KOREAN POETRY FROM THE EARLIEST ERA TO THE PRESENT. New York: John Day Co., [1964].

1435   _____. POEMS FROM KOREA, AN HISTORICAL ANTHOLOGY. Honolulu: Univ. Press of Hawaii, 1974.

This second work is a revision of Lee's first. The best anthology presently available, by a major authority on Korean literature.

1436   _____. "Two Sijo Cycles from the Korean." ORIENT/WEST 7 (July 1962), 27-29.

1437   Pai, Inez Kong, trans. THE EVER WHITE MOUNTAIN: KOREAN LYRICS IN THE CLASSICAL SIJO FORM. Tokyo: John Weatherhill; Rutland, Vt.: Charles E. Tuttle, 1965.

Excellent translations.

1438   Rutt, Richard, trans. THE BAMBOO GROVE: AN INTRODUCTION TO SIJO. Berkeley: Univ. of California Press, 1971.

Superior selections and translations.

1439   _____. "An Introduction to Sijo, a Form of Short Korean Poem." TRANSACTIONS OF THE KOREAN BRANCH OF THE ROYAL ASIATIC SOCIETY, 34 (1958), 1-88.

Earlier versions of material presented in the preceding entry.

1440   Zong in-Sob [Chŏng In-Sŏp], trans. A PAGEANT OF KOREAN POETRY. Seoul: Hyangnin-sa, 1963.

Over two hundred are represented in adequate translations.

F. POETRY—HISTORY AND CRITICISM

1441   Chŏng Pyŏng-Uk. "Humor in Ancient Korean Poetry and Songs." KOREA JOURNAL, 10 (May 1970), 15-18, 10.

1442   _____. "A Study of Korean Sijo Vocabulary: Toward a Study of Korean Poetic Diction." In THE TRADITIONAL CULTURE AND SOCIETY OF KOREA. Honolulu: Center for Korean Studies, Univ. of Hawaii, 1975, pp. 33-66.

Languages analysis which attempts to separate Korean from Chinese elements in the poetry.

1443   Henthorn, William E. "The Kyonggi Ch'ega." ORIENS EXTREMUS,
        16 (1969), 75-84.

        Study of the Kyonggi-style poem, a long form.

1444   Kim T'ae-Gon. "Formal Genres of Shamanist Songs." KOREA JOUR-
        NAL, 15, No. 6 (April 1975), 18-25.

        An analysis of religious chants by structure and content.

1445   Lee, Peter H. [Yi Hak Su]. "Introduction to the Sijo: The Epigram."
        EAST AND WEST, 7 (1959), 61-66.

        Good brief analysis of the chief characteristics of the form.

1446   _____. "Korean Discursive Poetry." ORIENT/WEST, 8, No. 4 (July
        1963), 47-53.

1447   _____. "Popular Poems in the Koryo Dynasty as Described in the
        KORYO SA and AKCHANG KASA." ORIENS EXTREMUS, 5 (1958), 202-2
        202-27.

        The nature of early Korean poetry from the HISTORY OF
        KORYO (KORYO SA) and from an early anthology. A su-
        perior scholarly study.

1448   _____. STUDIES IN THE SAENAENNORAE: OLD KOREAN POETRY.
        Rome: Instituto Italiano per il Medio ed Estremo Oriente, 1959.

        An important scholarly study, with translations, of the oldest
        Korean language poems.

1449   McCann, David R. "Weighing the Balance: Form and Content in the
        Korean Kasa." KOREAN STUDIES FORUM, 1 (1976-77), 19-31.

        A structural analysis of a popular form of poetry.

1450   Pihl, Marshall R. "Landmark Poetic Forms of the Pre-Modern Era."
        KOREA JOURNAL, 10, No. 1 (January 1970), 4-7.

        A good brief survey of the poetic genres.

1451   Rutt, Richard. "Hanmun--Korean Literature in Chinese." KOREA
        JOURNAL, 13, No. 3 (March 1973), 30-36.

        A study of Korean poetry in Chinese, with some translations.

1452   _____. "An Introduction to Sijo, a Form of Short Korean Poem."
        TRANSACTIONS OF THE KOREAN BRANCH OF THE ROYAL ASIATIC
        SOCIETY, 34 (1953), 1-88.

Thorough analysis of this popular traditional poetic form which has been revived today, with some translations.

1453 _____. "Nature of Classic Sijo." KOREA JOURNAL, 4, No. 4 (April 1964), 7-11.

Brief introduction to the form.

1454 Wilson, Graeme. "The Korean Sijo." JAPAN QUARTERLY, 17 (1970), 183-90.

Good critical introduction to the form.

G. DRAMA—HISTORY AND CRITICISM

1455 Ch'oe Sang-Su. A STUDY OF THE KOREAN PUPPET PLAY. Seoul: Korean Books Publishing Co., 1961.

Good handbook on the puppet play, including its origins and importance. Well illustrated.

1456 _____. A STUDY OF THE MASK PLAY OF HA-HOE. Seoul: Korean Books Publishing Co., 1959.

General discussion of a type of folk drama. Illustrated.

1457 Kardoss, John. AN OUTLINE HISTORY OF KOREAN DRAMA. Greenvale, N.Y.: Long Island Univ. Press, 1966.

A brief study. Not seen.

1458 Kim Moon-Hwan. "Folk Drama and its Tradition." KOREA JOURNAL, 10, No. 5 (May 1970), 37-41.

1459 Kyrne, Douglas. "The Korean Theatre." KOREAN STUDIES, 7 (February 1958), 6-7, 10.

1460 Lee Doo-Hyun. "History of Korean Drama." KOREA JOURNAL, 4, No. 9 (June 1964), 4-7.

Both of these brief articles are illustrated.

1461 Pak Chin. "Sixty Years of New Drama in Korea." KOREA JOURNAL, No. 3 (March 1969), 13-23.

On actors and theatrical performances of modern drama since 1908.

1462 Sim Woo-Sung, and Kim Se-Chung. INTRODUCTION TO KOREAN

FOLK DRAMA. Trans. Margaret M. Moore. Seoul: Korean Folk
Theatre Troupe "Namsadang," 1970.

Brief treatment of the types of folk drama.

1463 Yi Tu-Hyon. "Korean Mask and Mask Dance Plays." TRANSACTIONS
OF THE KOREAN BRANCH OF THE ROYAL ASIATIC SOCIETY, 42
(1966), 49-67.

1464 _____. "Mask Dance Dramas." Trans. Alan C. Heyman. In TRADI-
TIONAL PERFORMING ARTS OF KOREA. Seoul: Korean National
Commission for UNESCO, 1975, pp. 35-80.

Both good studies of the folk drama. The second includes
color photographs.

1465 Yoh Suk-Kee. "Korean Mask Plays." DRAMA REVIEW, 15 (1971),
143-52.

Emphasizes the comic element. A good critical article with
Illustrations.

H. FICTION—ANTHOLOGIES

1466 Allen, Horace Newton, comp. KOREAN TALES, BEING A COLLEC-
TION OF STORIES TRANSLATED FROM THE KOREAN FOLK LORE.
New York: G.P. Putnam's Sons, 1889.

Retellings of folk tales and legends.

1467 Chang Duk-Soon [Chang Tŏk-Sun], comp. THE FOLK TREASURY OF
KOREA: SOURCES IN MYTH, LEGEND AND FOLKTALE. Trans. Kim
Tae-Sung. Seoul: National Univ., Society of Korean Oral Literature,
1970.

A large collection of folk materials which classifies myths,
legends, and folktales.

1468 Chu Yo-Sup, comp. THE FOREST OF THE WHITE COCK: TALES
AND LEGENDS OF THE SILLA PERIOD. [Seoul: Eom-mun-gag Publishing Co., 1962].

Retellings of stories based on early legends.

1469 Ehwa Women's Univ., English Student Association. LEGENDS FROM
THE HILLS AND VALLEYS OF KOREA. Seoul: Ehwa Women's Univ.,
1969.

1470 Griffis, William Elliot. THE UNMANNERLY TIGER AND OTHER

KOREAN TALES. New York: Thomas Y. Crowell, 1911.

Stories about fairies and animals presented in a simple style.

1471 Ha Tae Hung, trans. FOLK TALES OF OLD KOREA. Seoul: Yonsei Univ. Press, 1962.

Tales from both literary and folk sources.

1472 _____. THE KOREAN NIGHTS ENTERTAINMENTS: (COMIC STORIES). Seoul: Yonsei Univ. Press, 1969.

About one hundred humorous stories retold in dramatic form.

1473 _____. TALES FROM THE THREE KINGDOMS. Seoul: Yonsei Univ. Press, 1969.

Stories from the SAMGUK SAGI, SAMGUK YUSA, and other early sources, adapted for the modern reader. See also entry nos. 1526-28.

1474 Im Pang, and Yuk Yi, comps. KOREAN FOLK TALES: IMPS, GHOSTS AND FAIRIES. Trans. James S. Gale. New York: E.P. Dutton, 1913; rpt. Rutland, Vt.: Charles E. Tuttle Co., 1962.

Anecdotes and stories of court life, originally written in Chinese.

1475 Kim So-Un. THE STORY BAG: A COLLECTION OF FOLK TALES. Trans. Settsu Higashi. Rutland, Vt.: Charles E. Tuttle Co., 1955.

Stories heard by the author as a child in Korea and written down by him in Japanese.

1476 Metzger, Berta, comp. TALES TOLD IN KOREA. New York: Frederick A. Stokes, 1932.

A successful attempt to retell many of the significant stories, including SIM CH'ONG, CH'UNYANG, and HONG KILTONG. See also entry nos. 1503-7.

1477 Pak Tae-Yong. A KOREAN DECAMERON. 2 vols. Seoul: Korean Literature Editing Committee, 1961-62.

Retellings of stories of sexual adventure, a popular genre in Korea as elsewhere.

1478 Park Yonjun, comp. TRADITIONAL TALES OF OLD KOREA: A MIXTURE OF LEGEND AND HISTORY OF KOREA'S COLORFUL PAST. 5 vols. Seoul: Munhwa, 1974.

Over four hundred stories from oral tradition.

1479 Pyun, Y.T. [Pyŏn Tŏng-T'ae], trans. TALES FROM KOREA. Seoul: 11 Cho Kak, 1963.

First published about 1934. Some thirty-three stories.

1480 Rutt, Richard, and Chong-Un Kim, trans. VIRTUOUS WOMEN: THREE MASTERPIECES OF TRADITIONAL KOREAN FICTION. Seoul: Korean National Commission for UNESCO, 1974.

Three seventeenth-century novels. See also entry nos. 1506, 1513, 1515.

1481 Zong In-Sob [Chŏng In-Sŏp], trans. FOLK TALES FROM KOREA. New York: Grove Press, 1953.

About one hundred stories with a discussion of motifs and types. A good collection.

I. FICTION—HISTORY AND CRITICISM

1482 Korean National Commission for UNESCO. SYNOPSES OF KOREAN NOVELS: READER'S GUIDE TO KOREAN LITERATURE. Seoul: [1972].

Synopses of a large number of classical and modern works.

1483 Lee, Peter H. [Yi Hak-Su]. "Notes toward a History of Korean Fiction." ORIENS EXTREMUS, 8 (1961), 208-22.

Good study of the nature of early Korean fiction, in both Korean and Chinese, and its sources.

1484 Rutt, Richard. "Women in Yi Dynasty through Classical Novels." KOREA JOURNAL, 14, No. 1 (January 1974), 41-45.

1485 Skillend, W.E. KODAE SOSŎL: A SURVEY OF KOREAN TRADITIONAL POPULAR NOVELS. London: School of Oriental and African Studies, Univ. of London, 1968.

Major scholarly reference work on all known early works of fiction.

J. MISCELLANEOUS WRITINGS

1486 Ha Tae Hung. MAXIMS AND PROVERBS OF OLD KOREA. Seoul: Yonsei Univ. Press, 3rd ed., 1970.

Over one thousand proverbs with commentary.

1487 Lee, Peter H. [Yi Hak-Su]. KOREAN LITERARY BIOGRAPHIES. [Washington, D.C.]: American Council of Learned Societies, 1962.

1488   Levy, Howard Seymour, comp. KOREAN SEX JOKES IN TRADI-
        TIONAL TIMES. Washington, D.C.: Warm-Soft Village Press, 1972.

        Anecdotes from early collections, with commentary.

1489   McCune, George M. "The Yi Dynasty Annals of Korea." TRANSAC-
        TIONS OF THE KOREAN BRANCH OF THE ROYAL ASIATIC SOCIETY,
        29 (1939), 57-82.

        Scholarly study of an early historical work and comment on
        traditional history writing.

1490   Rutt, Richard. "Traditional Korean Poetry Criticism: Fifty Sihwa."
        TRANSACTIONS OF THE KOREAN BRANCH OF THE ROYAL ASIATIC
        SOCIETY, 42 (1972), 105-43.

        Good essay on traditional literary theory and on the relation-
        ship of the Korean-language tradition to the ever-present Chi-
        nese tradition.

K. COMPARATIVE STUDIES

1491   Jeon Kyu-Tao. "The Influence of Chinese Literature on Korean Litera-
        ture." TAMKANG REVIEW, 2-3 (1971-72), 101-15.

1492   Kim Joo-Hyon. "The Tudor Mask in Comparison with the Yi Dynasty
        Mask." KOREA JOURNAL, 15, No. 8 (August 1975), 25-31.

        The Elizabethan court masque compared with the early Korean
        court masque.

1493   Lee Chol. "Russian Literature in Korea." EAST ASIAN REVIEW, 2
        (1975), 188-99.

1494   McCann, David R. "Korea and American Literature, a Comparative
        Exploration." KOREA JOURNAL, 14, No. 3 (March 1974), 31-39.

1495   Rockhill, William Woodville. CHINA'S INTERCOURSE WITH KOREA
        FROM THE 15TH CENTURY TO 1895. London: Luzac and Co., 1905.

        Somewhat out of date, but still useful.

1496   Rutt, Richard. "Chinese Literature outside China: Traditional Litera-
        ture in Korea." CONTEMPORARY REVIEW, 224 (1974), 205-12.

1497   Yi Ha-Yun. "A Comparative Approach to Korean Literature." KOREA
        JOURNAL, 3, no. 6 (June 1963), 23-26.

1498   Yi Pyeng-Do. "The Impact of the Western World on Korea in the
        19th Century." CAHIERS D'HISTOIRE MONDIALE, 5 (1960), 957-75.

        Useful background for the period of rising Western influence
        on all aspects of Korean life.

1499   Zong In-Sob [Chŏng In-Sŏp]. "Western Literature and Modern Korean
        Literature." KOREANA QUARTERLY, 1 (1960), 93-99.

L. EARLIER AUTHORS AND WORKS

Ch'oe Ch'i-Wŏn (or Koun) (857-941)

1500   Chang Tŏk-Sun. "Ch'oe Ch'i-Wŏn and Legendary Literature." KOREA
        JOURNAL, 17, No. 8 (August 1977), 56-64.

        Legends about the writer in folklore and literature.

Ch'oe Pu (1454-1505)

1501   Meskill, John, trans. CH'OE PU'S DIARY: A RECORD OF DRIFTING
        ACROSS THE SEA. Tucson: Univ. of Arizona Press, 1965.

        The P'YOHAEROK (RECORD OF DRIFTING) was written at
        the royal command in 1488 to record Pu's journey to China.

Chŏng Ch'ŏl (1536-94)

1502   Lee, Peter H. [Yi Hak-Su]. "The SONGGANG KASA of Chŏng Ch'ŏl."
        T'OUNG PAO, 49 (1961), 149-93.

        Good introduction to the work of a medieval poet, with
        translations.

Ch'unhyang Jŏn (Tale of Ch'unyang) (eighteenth century)

1503   Chin In-Sook, trans. A CLASSICAL NOVEL "CH'UN-HYANG."
        Seoul: Korea Center, International P.E.N., 1970.

        Perhaps the most popular of all Korean novels. A romantic
        story of the tribulations of a faithful wife. There are many
        Korean versions. See also entry no. 1485. This is a less
        than adequate retelling.

1504   Gale, James S., trans. "Choon Yang." THE KOREAN MAGAZINE,
        1, No. 9 (September 1917), 392-403; No. 10 (October), 440-50;
        No. 11 (November), 496-506; No. 12 (December), 551-58; 2 No. 1

(January 1918), 21-28; No. 2 (February), 69-78; No. 3 (March), 122-30; No. 4 (April), 169-76; No. 5 (May), 213-23; No. 6 (June), 267-72; No. 7 (July), 326-36.

A good full-length version.

1505 Matsuhara, Iwao, trans. CHUN-HIANG: OPERA. Tokyo: n.p., 1947.
An operatic version of the story with English and Japanese parallel translations.

1506 Rutt, Richard, trans. "The Song of a Faithful Wife, Ch'un-Hyang." In VIRTUOUS WOMEN, pp. 235-333. See entry no. 1480.

Without question the best translation. Not a retelling.

1507 Sim Chai Hong, trans. FRAGANCE OF SPRING: THE STORY OF CHOON HYANG. Seoul: Korean Republic, 1956; rpt. 1962, 1970.

A well-written redaction of the story rather than a translation.

1508 Urquhart, Edward J., trans. THE FRAGRANCE OF SPRING. Seoul: Sijo-sa, 1929.

A now out-of-date retelling of the story in verse.

Hŏ Kyun (1569-1618)

TRANSLATIONS

1509 Pihl, Marshall R., trans. "The Tale of Hong Kil-Tong." KOREA JOURNAL, 8 No. 7 (July 1968), 4-17.

An excellent translation of the HONG KIL-TONG CHON (STORY OF HONG KIL-TONG), an adventure story about the dubious activities of a high official.

STUDIES

1510 Ku Cha-Gyun. "Early Modern Thinkers: Ho Kyun." KOREA JOURNAL, 10, No. 2 (February 1970), 14-20, 24.

1511 Pihl, Marshall R. "The Tale of Hong Kil-Tong, Korea's First Vernacular Novel." KOREA JOURNAL, 8, No. 7 (July 1968), 18-21.

Hyech'o (fl. eighth century)

1512 Jan Yun-Hua. "The Korean Record on Vārānasī and Sārnāth." KOREA

KOREA JOURNAL, 10, No. 9 (September 1970), 28-31.

Account of a journey to India (WANG-O-CH'ŎN-CH'UG-GUK-CH'ON) by a monk. This article is on the historical background.

Inhyŏn Wanghu Chŏn (Tale of Queen Inhyŏn) (late seventeenth-early eighteenth century)

1513   Kim Chong-Un, trans. "The True History of Queen Inhyŏn." In VIRTUOUS WOMEN, pp. 179-233. See entry no. 1480.

Excellent translation of a (partly fictional?) memoir of a court lady and court intrigues. Very popular.

Kim Man-Jung (1637-92)

TRANSLATIONS

1514   Gale, James S., trans. THE CLOUD DREAM OF THE NINE. London: Daniel O'Connor, 1922.

A good translation of the KUUNMONG, a somewhat scandalous tale of polygamy and intrigue.

1515   Rutt, Richard, trans. "A Nine Cloud Dream." In VIRTUOUS WOMEN, pp. 1-177. See entry no. 1480.

An essential work for the understanding of Korean literature here very well translated.

STUDIES

1516   Chung Kyu-Bok [Chong Kyu-Bok]. "A Comparative Study of the Fantasy Structure of KU-UNMONG." In KOREAN HERITAGE, pp. 251-62. See entry no. 1406.

1517   _____. "The Ideological Background of KUUNMONG." JOURNAL OF ASIATIC STUDIES, 10 (1968), 85-87.

1518   Sŏl Sŏng-Gyŏng. "A Structural Study of KUUNMONG." KOREA JOURNAL, 7, No. 10 (October 1977), 12-26.

A lengthy structural analysis, with charts.

Kim Sakkat (1807-63)

1519   Ha Tae-Hung. THE LIFE OF A RAINHAT POET: A DRAMA. Seoul:

Yonsei Univ. Press, 1969.

A fictionized biography of this wandering minstrel-poet.

1520   Rutt, Richard. "Kim Sakkat, Vagabond Poet." TRANSACTIONS OF THE KOREAN BRANCH OF THE ROYAL ASIATIC SOCIETY, 41 (1964), 59-87.

Excellent scholarly study of the poet and his works, with excellent translations.

Kim Si-Sŭp (1435-93)

1521   Mesler, David P., trans. "A Peep over the Wall with Master Lee." JOURNAL OF KOREAN STUDIES, 1 (1969), 190-27.

Fiction by a master writer who pioneered the use of Korean, rather than Chinese, locales in popular fiction.

Kŭmwŏn (early nineteenth century)

1522   Rutt, Richard, trans. "Footprints of the Wildgoose: HORAK HONGJO or HODONG SŎRAK KI." KOREA JOURNAL, 14, No. 5 (May 1974), 44-61; 14, No. 6 (June 1974), 41-49.

A travel diary by a young woman, interspersed with poems.

Kyunyŏ Chŏn (Life of Master Kyunyŏ) (1075)

TRANSLATIONS

1523   Lee, Peter H.,trans. [Yi Hak-Su]. "The Life of the Korean Poet Priest Kyunyŏ." ASIATISCHES STUDIEN, 11 (1957-58), 45-72.

Excellent complete translation of the life of a Buddhist monk who was also a poet. Annotated.

STUDIES

1524   _____. "The Importance of the KYUNYŎ CHŎN (1075) in Korean Buddhism and Literature--BHADRA-CARI-PRANIDHĀNA in Tenth Century Korea." JOURNAL OF THE AMERICAN ORIENTAL SOCIETY, 81 (1961), 409-14.

Pak In-No (1561-1643)

1525   Lee, Peter H. [Yi Hak-Su]. "The KASA Poems of Pak In-No, Their Place in the History of Korean Poetry." ORIENS EXTREMUS, 10 (1963), 217-59.

Poems by a gentleman-master of the kasa form on a variety of subjects from war to rural contentment.

Samguk-Sagi (completed 1145)

1526   Chu Yo-Sup, comp.   THE FOREST OF THE WHITE COCK.   See entry no. 1468.

1527   Ha Tae Hung, trans.   TALES FROM THE THREE KINGDOMS.   See entry no. 1473.

The HISTORICAL RECORD OF THE THREE KINGDOMS begins about 57 B.C. and was completed in the Koryo dynasty in 1145.   It is a major source of legends.   Some of the stories are retold in the collections above.

Samguk Yusa (thirteenth century)

1528   Ha Tae-Hung, and Grafton K. Mintz, trans.   SAMGUK YUSA: LEGENDS AND HISTORY OF THE THREE KINGDOMS OF ANCIENT KOREA.   Seoul: Yonsei Univ. Press, 1972.

An important source of legend and myth compiled by the monk Ilyŏn (or Iryŏn) [Kim Kyŏn-Myŏng], who died in 1289. A good translation.   Selections are in entry nos. 1526-27.

Sim Ch'ong (traditional)

TRANSLATIONS

1529   THE TALE OF SIM CHUNG.   Pyongyang: Foreign Languages Publishing House, 1958.

Not seen.

1530   Taylor, Charles M., trans.   WINNING BUDDHA'S SMILE, A KOREAN LEGEND.   Boston: Gorham Press, 1919.

A retranslation from the French.

STUDIES

1531   Pihl, Marshall R.   "A Legend Becomes a Story."   ASIAN PACIFIC QUARTERLY, 4, No. 1 (Summer 1972), 18-26.

A summary of the work and a good study of the development of the story.

Tripitaka (traditional)

1532   Paik Nak Choon. "TRIPITAKA KOREANA: Library of Wood Cuts of
Buddhist Classics at Haeinsa." TRANSACTIONS OF THE KOREAN
BRANCH OF THE ROYAL ASIATIC SOCIETY, 32 (1951), 62-78.

Description of editions of the famous journey to India by the
Chinese monk Hsuan Tsang (see entry nos. 1518-19). Impor-
tant for the transmission of Buddhism to China, Korea, and
Japan. Illustrated.

Yi Kyu-Bo (fourth century)

1533   Rutt, Richard, trans. "The LAY OF KING TONG-MYONG." KOREA
JOURNAL, 13, No. 7 (July 1973), 48-54.

Good translations of an important epic poem.

Yongbi Ŏch'ŏn-Ga (Songs of Dragons) (ca. 1445)

1534   Hoyt, James, trans. SONGS OF THE DRAGONS. Seoul: Korean
National Commission for UNESCO and the Royal Asiatic Society, 1971.

1535   Lee, Peter H. [Yi Hak-Su], trans. SONGS OF FLYING DRAGONS,
A CRITICAL READING. Cambridge, Mass.: Harvard Univ. Press, 1975.

An important collection of heroic poems incorporating the
myths of China and Korea presented to the throne in 1445.
Both of the above translations are excellent. Lee's work includes an extensive critical study and full apparatus.

Yun Sŏn-Do (1587-1671)

TRANSLATIONS

1536   Lee, Peter H. [Yi Hak-su], trans. "The ANGLER'S CALENDAR, from the
Korean of Yun Sŏn-Do." HUDSON REVIEW, 14 (1961), 247-55.

STUDIES

1537   _____. "The Life and Poetry of Yun Sŏn-Do, the Greatest Poet in
the Sijo Form." MONUMENTA SERICA, 22 (1963), 79-120.

The ANGLER'S CALENDAR (ŎBU SASI SA) is a sijo cycle of poems
comparing pastoral life with the court. The second article is
an important study of the poet, who is said to have discovered
the beauties of the Korean language.

M. MODERN LITERATURE

1. Anthologies

1538   International P.E.N., Korean Centre. MODERN KOREAN SHORT STORIES AND PLAYS. Seoul: 1970.

Large anthology--eighteenth stories and three plays.

1539   Pihl, Marshall R., ed. LISTENING TO KOREA, A KOREAN ANTHOL-OGY. New York: Praeger, 1973.

Excellent translations of stories and essays intended to illustrate modern Korean life.

2. Literary History and Criticism

1540   Chang Dŏk-Sun. "Living Myth in Modern Korean Literature." KOREA JOURNAL, 8, No. 9 (September 1968), 8-14.

On the uses of folktales and legends by modern writers.

1541   Cho Yon-Hyon. "Modern Korean Literature." KOREA JOURNAL, 7 (December 1967), 4-13.

Largely concerned with literary organizations and movements since 1945.

1542   Giuglaris, M.H. "Development of Contemporary Korean Literature." BOOKS ABROAD, 29 (1955), 36-40.

General survey of literature under Japanese domination and since the liberation.

1543   Kim, Kay T. "Korean Literature." In ENCYCLOPEDIA OF WORLD LITERATURE IN THE 20TH CENTURY. New York: Frederick Ungar, 1969, II, 227-32.

Covers a good deal of material for the space allotted.

1544   Kim Sang-Ok. "Sijo and Modern Korean Literature." KOREA JOURNAL, 4 (April 1964), 12-16.

On the use of the old sijo verse form by modern writers.

1545   Kim U-Chang. "The Situation of Writers under Japanese Colonialism." KOREA JOURNAL, 16, No. 5 (May 1976), 4-15.

Concerned with psychological and philosophical problems.

1546 Ku Chagyun. "The Modernization of Korean Literature." ASIATIC RESEARCH BULLETIN, 6, No. 4 (June 1963), 1-7.

1547 O'Rourke, Kevin. "Literature after the Korean War." KOREA JOURNAL, 17, No. 6 (June 1977), 4-12.

Sees many modern Korean writers as alienated from the life of the modern world.

1548 Paik Chul [or Baik Chul]. "The History and Development of Korean Modern Literature." KOREANA QUARTERLY, 4 (1962), 134-52.

1549 _____. "Post-War Korean Literature." SOLIDARITY, 5 (1970): 52-55.

Two brief surveys of recent trends.

1550 Suh Man-Il. "Current Trends in Korean Literature." NEW KOREA, No. 9 (September 1957), pp. 10-14.

An interesting view for the year in which it was written.

1551 Yoo Joo-Hyun. "Main Current of Postwar Korean Literature." KOREA JOURNAL, 4, No. 9 (September 1964), 12-17.

From 1945.

1552 Yu Pyong-Ch'on. "Korean Writers in America." KOREA JOURNAL, 7, No. 12 (December 1967), 17-19.

See also Younghill Kang, and Richard Kim, entry nos. 1601-04, 1606-08.

3. Poetry—Anthologies

1553 International P.E.N., Korean Centre. MODERN KOREAN POETRY. Seoul: 1970.

Almost one hundred poets in adequate translations. Many modern sijo poems.

1554 Kim, Joyce Jaihun, trans. THE IMMORTAL VOICE: AN ANTHOLOGY OF MODERN KOREAN POETRY. Seoul: Immun Publishing Co., 1974.

Over fifty poets represented in good translations. From the 1920s through the 1950s. A superior anthology.

1555 Ko Won, trans. CONTEMPORARY KOREAN POETRY. Iowa City: Univ. of Iowa Press, 1970.

A great number of poets, both major and minor, are represented in good translations. Many of the poems are of minor
interest. Covers the entire twentieth century.

1556   Korean Poets Association. KOREAN VERSES. Seoul: Mum Won Publishing Co., 1961.

    A good selection. Includes sijo poems.

1557   Rutt, Richard, trans. AN ANTHOLOGY OF KOREAN SIJO. Taejon:
Congja Sijo Society, 1970.

    Superior translations of poems in this revived older form.

1558   Zong In-Sob [Chŏng In-Sŏp], trans. AN ANTHOLOGY OF MODERN
POEMS IN KOREA. Seoul: Munhwa-Dang, 1948.

    About one hundred poets represented, usually by one poem each.

4. Poetry—History and Criticism

1559   Kim Jong-Gil. "Tragic Ecstasy in Modern Korean Poetry." ASIA
PACIFIC QUARTERLY, 6 (1974), 26-33.

    A good critical article beyond the mere survey.

1560   _____. "T.S. Eliot's Influence on Modern Korean Poetry." LITERA-
TURE EAST AND WEST, 13 (1969), 359-76.

    A good scholarly study.

1561   Kim Sang-Ok. "Sijo and Modern Korean Literature." KOREA JOUR-
NAL, 4, No. 4 (April 1964), 12-16.

1562   Kim U-Ch'ang. "Sorrow and Stillness: A View of Modern Korean
Poetry." LITERATURE EAST & WEST, 13 (1969), 141-66.

    A good critical essay on opposing psychological forces in
modern Korean poetry, with translated examples.

1563   Kim Yong-Jik. "Humor in Modern Korean Poems." KOREA JOURNAL,
10, No. 4 (April 1970), 8-10, 18.

1564   Koo Sang. "The Korean War as Seen through Korean Poetry." KOREAN
P.E.N., No. 7 (August 1973), pp. 45-61.

1565   Nahm, Andrew C. "Poetry and Sons of the Koreans as an Oppressed
People, 1910-1945." KOREA JOURNAL, 16, No. 10 (October 1976),
4-18.

Deals with the period of Japanese occupation.

1566   Rockstein, Edward D.   "Some Notes on the Founders of Modern Korean
       Poetry." KOREA JOURNAL, 9, No. 12 (December 1969), 14-18.

       Comments and good translations of some of the pre-World-War-
       II generation.

1567   Rutt, Richard.   "Sijo Verse in Korean." KOREA JOURNAL, 10, No.
       6 (1970), 4-11.

5. Drama—Anthologies

1568   Zong In-Sob [Chŏng In-Sŏb], trans. PLAYS FROM KOREA. Seoul:
       Chung-Ang Univ. Press, 1968.

       A collection of one-act plays.

6. Drama—History and Criticism

1569   Henthorn, William E.   "The Early Days of Western Inspired Drama in
       Korea." YEARBOOK OF COMPARATIVE AND GENERAL LITERATURE,
       15 (1966), 204-13.

       Through Western-type theater has been common in Korea in
       the twentieth century, there have been few great plays. This
       is a good account of developments from 1885 to 1940, the
       period of Japanese cultural domination.

1570   _____. HAN'GUK SHINGUKSA YON'GU [HISTORY OF MODERN
       KOREAN DRAMA]. Seoul: National Univ. Press, 1966.

       English synopsis, pp. 321-31. Not seen.

1571   Lee Doo-Hyun.   "History of Korean Drama." KOREA JOURNAL, 4,
       No. 6 (June 1964), 4-7.

       Deals with theater groups and plays performed.

1572   Yoh Suk-Kee.   "Problems of Korean Drama--Its Present and Future."
       KOREA JOURNAL, 2, No. 8 (August 1962), 17-18.

       On the influence of the modern Western drama and the activi-
       ties of the Drama Center.

7. Fiction—Anthologies

1573   Hong Myoung-Hee, trans. KOREAN SHORT STORIES. Seoul: Il Ji-
       Sa, 1975.

Eight good stories in excellent translations.

1574 International P.E.N., Korean Centre. COLLECTED SHORT STORIES FROM KOREA. Vol. I. Seoul: Eomung-gag, 1961.

A successful anthology of "best" short stories, well translated.

1575 Kim Chong-Un, trans. POSTWAR KOREAN SHORT STORIES, AN ANTHOLOGY. Seoul: National Univ. Press, 1974.

Adequate translations of eighteen stories.

1576 Lee, Peter H. [Yi Hak-Su], ed. FLOWERS OF FIRE: TWENTIETH-CENTURY KOREAN STORIES. Honolulu: Univ. Press of Hawaii, 1974.

An extensive collection, well translated. Perhaps the most successful modern collection.

1577 O'Rourke, Kevin, trans. TEN KOREAN SHORT STORIES. Seoul: Korean Studies Institute, Yonsei Univ., 1973.

A good selection, reasonably well translated.

1578 Zong In-Sob [Chŏng In-Sŏp], trans. MODERN SHORT STORIES FROM KOREA. Seoul: Munho-sa, 1958.

A good selection of stories in somewhat uneven translations.

8. Fiction—History and Criticism

1579 Chun Kwang-Yong. "Modern Korean Novels." KOREA JOURNAL, 10, No. 6 (1970), 42-44.

Brief descriptions of recent works.

1580 Hyun, Peter [Hyŏn Ung]. "Notes on Modern Korean Fiction." TRANS-ACTIONS OF THE KOREAN BRANCH OF THE ROYAL ASIATIC SO-CIETY, 42 (1966), 69-74.

Brief article on the earliest developments.

1581 Kang Hyeon-Jew. "Changing Image of America in Korean Popular Literature, with an Analysis of Short Stories betwen 1945-1975." KOREA JOURNAL, 16, No. 10 (October 1976), 19-33.

A good analysis of images, including cliches.

1582 Kim Chong-Ch'ul. "Humor in Modern Korean Novels." KOREA JOURNAL, 10, No. 4 (April 1970), 4-7, 18.

1583   Kim Young-Ch'ul. "Types of Allegory in Modern Korean Fiction, a Comparative View." KOREA JOURNAL, 15, No. 7 (July 1975), 4-16.

Begins with Dante, Spenser, and Bunyan to define allegory, and then applies this to modern works.

1584   O'Rourke, Kevin. "The Korean Short Story of the 1920's and Naturalism." KOREA JOURNAL, 17, No. 3 (March 1977), 48-63.

A good critical study touching on various writers who accepted Western views of the despair of the human spirit.

1585   Paik Chul. "Christian Influences on Modern Korean Novels." KOREAN AFFAIRS, 1 (1962), 196-203.

1586   _____. "Tides of Modern Korean Literature." KOREA JOURNAL, 2 No. 8 (August 1962), 8-12, 35.

1587   Underwood, Horace H., and Norman Thorpe, comps. "Modern Korean Fiction in English, a List." KOREA JOURNAL, 15, No. 9 (1975), 53-68.

A useful bibliography. Attempts to list all translations.

9. Modern Authors and Works

CHO BYUNG-HWA (1921-)

1588   Kim Dong Sung, trans. BEFORE LOVE FADES AWAY. Seoul: Chang Shim Munwhasa, 1957.

Cho is a very popular modern poet who conveys the sadness of the modern world to his readers. This is a translation of a volume published in 1955 (SARANGI KAGI CHONE). O'Rourke's translations (see next three entries) are more successful.

1589   O'Rourke, Kevin, trans. TWENTY POEMS. Seoul: Kyung-Hee Univ. 1976.

1590   _____. WHERE CLOUDS PASS BY: SELECTED POEMS OF CHO BYUNG-HWA. Seoul: Chungang, 1974.

1591   O' Rourke, Kevin, and Norman Thorpe, trans. FOURTEEN POEMS NU CHO BYUNG-HWA. Seoul: Kyung-Hee Univ., 1973.

There is some overlapping in these three collections, and Thorpe, a talented young scholar, has done some translations

of his own in FOURTEEN POEMS. Good translations of a
poet who is subtle and difficult to translate.

CHOI OK-KA [CH'OE OK-KA] (1906-)

1592　Ko Won, ed. IN THE VINEYARD: THIRTY POEMS. Seoul: Soo-do
Women's Teacher's College, 1961.

Poems on Christian themes translated into a rather old-
fashioned idiom.

HAHN MOO SOOK [HAN MOO-SOOK] (1919-)

1593　Chong Chong-Wa, trans. MOO-SOOK HAHN'S THE RUNNING
WATER HERMITAGE. Seoul: Moonwang, 1967.

Collections of short stories

1594　IN THE DEPTHS. Seoul: Hwimoon, 1962.

HAN YONG-UN [HAN YOUNG-UN] (1879-1944)

Translations

1595　Kang, Younghill, and Francis Keely, trans. MEDITATIONS OF A
LOVER. Seoul: Yonsei Univ. Press, 1970.

This 1926 book (NIM-UI CH'IMMUK) is a major work in
modern Korean poetry, the work of a very original poet who
combines romantic images and Buddhist symbolism. Free but
very readable translations.

Studies

1596　Rockstein, Edward D. "Your Silence--Doubt in Faith: Han Yongun
and Ingmar Bergman." ASIAN PACIFIC QUARTERLY, 6, No. 2 (Autumn 1974), 1-16.

Excellent translations of fourteen poems and a discussion of
Han's modernity.

HWANG SUN-WŎN [HWANG SOONWON] (1915-)

1597　Chang Youngsook, and Robert P. Miller, trans. THE CRY OF THE
CUCKOO. Seoul: Pan Korea Books, 1975.

1598　Kim Chong-Un, trans. "The Drizzle." KOREA JOURNAL, 8, No. 1
(January 1968), 28-30.

A good novel (K'AIN-UI HUYE--"THE SONS OF CAIN"),
in entry no. 1597 and a short story in this entry in satisfactory translations.

HYŎN CHIN-GŎN (1900-1943)

1599   Shin Tong-Uk. "Hyŏn Chin-Gŏn." KOREA JOURNAL, 10, No. 9
(September 1970), 32-40, 31.

1600   _____. "Hyŏn Chin-Gŏn and his Literature." KOREA JOURNAL,
16, No. 5 (May 1976), 16-27.

Studies of a novelist who writes realistically of social problems.

KANG, YOUNGHILL (1903-)

1601   EAST GOES WEST: THE MAKING OF AN ORIENTAL YANKEE.
New York: Charles Scribner's Sons, 1937.

A memoir by the Korean who more than any other expressed
the feelings of Koreans who made America their home.
Kang's works listed in this and the next two entries were
originally written in English.

1602   THE GRASS ROOF. New York: Charles Scribner's Sons, 1931.

Memoir of Kang's early years in Korea and his decision to
migrate to America.

1603   THE HAPPY GROVE. New York: Charles Scribner's Sons, 1933.

A children's book about growing up in Korea. This is a
partial revision of THE GRASS ROOF.

Studies

1604   Kim, Elaine A. "Searching for a Door to America: Yonghill Kang,
Korean-American Writer." KOREA JOURNAL, 17, No. 4 (April 1977),
38-47.

KIM CHI HA (1941-)

1605   CRY OF THE PEOPLE AND OTHER POEMS. Hayama, Japan: Autumn
Press, 1974.

Poems by an important modern poet.

KIM, RICHARD E. (1932-)

1606   THE INNOCENT. New York: Ballantine, 1969.

1607 LOST NAMES: SCENES FROM A KOREAN BOYHOOD. New York: Praeger, 1970.

1608 THE MARTYRED. New York: George Braziller, 1964; rpt. New York: Pocket Books, 1965.

All originally in well-written English. Novels about Korea during the war years by a writer who has gained a reputation in the West.

KIM SOWOL [KIM CHONG-SIK] (1903-34)

Translations

1609 Kim [Joyce] Jaihuin, trans. AZALEAS: POEMS BY SOWOL KIM. Seoul: Hankuk Univ. of Foreign Studies Press, 1973.

1610 _____. LOST LOVE: 99 POEMS BY SOWOL KIM, KOREA'S GREATEST LYRIC POET. Seoul: Pan Korea Books, 1975.

An important poet who wrote of nature and the folk tradition. This second entry is an enlarged and improved version of the preceding one. Good translations.

1611 Kim Dong Sung, trans. SELECTED POEMS OF KIM SO-WOL. Seoul: Sung Moon Gak, 1959.

Serviceable translations, but not as good as those in the two preceding entries.

Studies

1612 Cho Chung Sook. "Sowol and Western Poetry." YEARBOOK OF COMPARATIVE AND GENERAL LITERATURE, 11 (1962), 154-58.

Concerned with Western influences on the poet, but also discusses the general characteristics of Korean poetry.

1613 Lee, M. Claudia. "A Comparative Analysis of Selected Nature Poetry of Emily Dickinson and So Wol Kim." ST. LOUIS UNIVERSITY RE-SEARCH JOURNAL, 6 (1975), 333-73.

A good comparative study which sheds much light on Kim.

KIM TON-IN (1900-1951)

1614 Kim Song-Hyeon. "Kim Ton-In: World of Naturalism." KOREA JOURNAL, 10, No. 6 (1970), 31-33.

Brief account of a writer who wrote over one hundred short stories which are heavily psychological and pessimistic.

KIM YONG-IK [KIM YOUNG-IK] (1920-)

1615   BLUE IS THE SEED. Boston: Little, Brown, 1964.

1616   THE DIVING GOURD. New York: Alfred A. Knopf, 1962.

1617   THE HAPPY DAYS. Boston: Little, Brown, 1960; rpt. as THE DAYS OF HAPPINESS, London: Hutchinson, 1962.

1618   LOVE IN WINTER. Garden City, N.Y.: Doubleday, 1969.

1619   THE SHOES FROM YANG SAN VALLEY. Garden City, N.Y.: Doubleday, 1970.

> All titles by Kim Yong-Ik listed here were originally written in English. He is a good writer who has been moderately successful in his adopted language. The DIVING GOURD is a novel, LOVE IN WINTER a collection of short stories, and the others children's books.

KIM YU-JŎNG (1908-37)

1620   Chin In-Sook. "Cynic Kim Yu-Jong and his Works." KOREA JOURNAL, 10, No. 6 (June 1970), 38-41.

> Brief account of a writer who deals in local color and satire.

LI KI-YUNG (1895-)

1621   Yun Jang-Ryul. "Li Ki Yung and his Literature." NEW KOREA, No. 6 (June 1958): pp. 19-22.

> About a writer who depicts village life and social change.

LI MIROK [YI MIRYOK] (1899-1950)

1622   Hammelmann, H.A., trans. THE YALU FLOWS, A KOREAN CHILD-HOOD. London: Harvill Press, 1954; rpt. East Lansing: Michigan State Univ. Press, 1956.

> This work was originally written in German and attained considerable popularity in Europe and America. A memoir of the problems of a Korean adjusting to Western society. A sequel was supposed to have existed, but it has not been published and may have disappeared.

Korea

MOH YOUN SOOK

1623   Kim, Joyce Jaihun, trans. TWENTY THREE POEMS. Seoul: Pioneer Press, 1976.

Well-translated selection of poems by Korea's foremost woman poet.

O YŎNG-JIN

1624   Song Yo-In, trans. "Wedding Day." KOREA JOURNAL, 11, No. 12 (December 1971), 36-50; 12, No. 1 (January 1972), 39-47.

A modern comedy, well translated.

PAK TU-JIN (1916-)

1625   Poitras, Edward W., trans. SEA OF TOMORROW: FORTY POEMS OF PAK TU-JIN. Seoul: Il Cho Gak, 1971.

Excellent translations of a major poet who uses the love of the countryside to express patriotic sentiments.

PI, C.D. [P'I CH'ON-DUK] (1910-)

Translations

1626   A FLUTE PLAYER: POEMS AND ESSAYS. Seoul: Samhwa, 1968.

Personal essays apparently written originally in English and poems translated by the poet from Korean. The author is a well-know essayist and translator.

Studies

1627   Kim U-Ch'ang. "C.D. Pi, a Poet of 'Little, Beautiful Things of Life.'" KOREA JOURNAL, 8, No. 11 (November 1968), 16-19.

YI IN-JIK (1854-1915?)

1628   Skillend, W.E. "The Texts of the First New Novel in Korean." ASIA MAJOR, 14 (1968), 21-62.

The novel TEARS OF BLOOD by Yi In-Jik (1906) marks the beginning of a new, modern kind of fiction in Korea. This scholarly study compares the 1940 and 1955 editions of the work and also adds useful information about the author and his times.

YI Ŏ-NYŎNG [LEE O-YOUNG] (1932-)

1629   Steinberg, David I., trans. IN THIS EARTH AND IN THAT WIND: THIS IS KOREA. Seoul: Hollym Corp., [1967].

YI PYŎNG-GI [YI YONG-GI] (1891-1968)

1630   Kim Che-Hyŏn. "Yi Yong-Gi, the Renovater of Modern Sijo." KOREA JOURNAL, 10, No. 6 (1970), 45-47.

An innovator in adapting the ancient sijo form to modern poetry which is to be read, but not necessarily sung (as the older poetry was).

YI SANG [KIM HAE-GYŎNG] (1912-39)

1631   Kim Mun-Jik. "Yi Sang and his Works." KOREA JOURNAL, 10, No. 6 (1970), 34-37.

Brief study of a modern writer whose characters exemplify the modern intellectual in a world without purpose.

YŎM SANG-SŎP (1897-1963)

1632   Sin Tong-Uk. "Thematic Development in Yon Sang-Sop's Novels." Trans. Nun Sang-Duk. KOREA JOURNAL, 10, No. 7 (1970), 21-25.

A study of a psychological novelist.

10. Periodicals

(All of the following are scholarly journals which regularly publish materials on literature, unless otherwise noted.)

1633   JOURNAL OF KOREAN STUDIES. Seattle: Korean Studies Society, 1969-- .

1634   KOREA JOURNAL. Seoul: Korea National Commission for UNESCO, 1961-- .

Many translations and short articles on Korean literature intended for the general reader.

1635   KOREANA QUARTERLY. Seoul: International Research Centre, 1959-- . A popular journal.

1636   KOREAN STUDIES FORUM. Pittsburgh: Univ. of Pittsburgh, 1976-- . On all aspects of Korea, including literature.

1637　TRANSACTIONS OF THE KOREAN BRANCH OF THE ROYAL ASIATIC
SOCIEY.　Seoul:　Royal Asiatic Society of Great Britain and Ireland,
Korea branch, 1900-- .

Chapter 5

SOUTHEAST ASIA

(This includes Burma, Cambodia, Indonesia, Laos, Malaysia, Thailand, and Vietnam. Works relating to more than one area are listed in this section.)

A. BIBLIOGRAPHY

1638   Bixler, Paul, comp. SOUTHEAST ASIA: BIBLIOGRAPHICAL DIREC-
       TIONS IN A COMPLEX AREA. [Middletown, Conn.]: CHOICE,
       [1974].

> An excellent series of bibliographical essays on the basic his-
> torical material for the area, revised from a series in CHOICE.
> Little literary material.

1639   BOOKS ON SOUTHEAST ASIA, A SELECT BIBLIOGRAPHY. New York:
       Institute of Pacific Relations, 1959.

> A useful brief list, now out of date.

1640   Boudet, Paul, and Remy Bourgeois, comps. BIBLIOGRAPHIE DE L'INDO-
       CHINE FRANÇAISE, 1913-1934. 4 vols. Hanoi: Imprimerie d'Estreme
       Orient, 1929-34; rpt. New York: Burt Franklin, n.d.

> Mostly books and articles in French. Continues Cordier, be-
> low.

1641   Cordier, Henri. BIBLIOTECA INDOSINICA, DICTIONNAIRE BIBLIOG-
       RAPHIQUE DES OUVRAGES RELATIFS À LA PENINSULE INDOCHINOISE.
       5 vols. Paris: Imprimerie National, E. Leroux, 1912-32; rpt. 5 vols.
       in 3, New York: Burt Franklin, 1967.

> Some sixty thousand entries. A basic work, but mostly of use
> to the expert. See also Boudet, above.

1642   Cornell University. Library. SOUTHEAST ASIA CATALOGUE. Comp. Giok Po Oey. 7 vols. Boston: G.K. Hall, 1976.

A valuable work, but difficult for the nonspecialist to use.

1643   Embree, John F., and Lillian Ota Dotson, comps. BIBLIOGRAPHY OF THE PEOPLES OF MAINLAND SOUTHEAST ASIA. New Haven: Yale Univ., Southeast Asia Studies Program, 1950; rpt. New York: Russell and Russell, 1972.

Still useful. Good sections on literature and folklore.

1644   Iluy, Stephen N., and Margaret H. Case, comps. SOUTHEAST ASIAN HISTORY, A BIBLIOGRAPHIC GUIDE. New York: Praeger, [1962].

Selective and useful for background. Little cultural material.

1645   Hobbs, Cecil, comp. INDOCHINA, A BIBLIOGRAPHY OF THE LAND AND PEOPLE. Washington, D.C.: Library of Congress, 1956; rpt. Westport, Conn.: Greenwood Press, 1968.

1646   _____. SOUTHEAST ASIA: AN ANNOTATED BIBLIOGRAPHY OF SELECTED REFERENCE SOURCES IN WESTERN LANGUAGES. Rev. and enl. ed. Washington, D.C.: Library of Congress, 1964.

1647   _____. SOUTHEAST ASIA SUBJECT CATALOGUE. 6 vols. Boston: G.K. Hall, 1972.

Three very useful lists by the former head of the Southeast Asia section of the Library of Congress. The preceding entry is perhaps of most use to the general reader.

1648   Jenner, Philip N., comp. SOUTHEAST ASIAN LITERATURE IN TRANS-LATION, A PRELIMINARY BIBLIOGRAPHY. Honolulu: Univ. of Hawaii Press, 1973.

The major bibliography for literature of the area. Very complete, despite the "preliminary." Revises his briefer A PRE-LIMINARY BIBLIOGRAPHY OF SOUTHEAST ASIAN LITERA-TURE IN TRANSLATION, 1970. Jenner analyzes the contents of journals, making it possible to find translations of authors in periodical sources.

1649   Johnson, Donald Clay, comp. A GUIDE TO REFERENCE MATERIALS ON SOUTHEAST ASIA BASED ON THE COLLECTIONS IN THE YALE AND CORNELL UNIVERSITY LIBRARIES. New Haven: Yale Univ. Press, 1970.

1650   _____. INDEX TO SOUTHEAST ASIAN JOURNALS, 1960-1974, A

GUIDE TO ARTICLES, BOOK REVIEWS, AND COMPOSITE WORKS.
Boston: G.K. Hall, 1977.

Very detailed. One hopes that it will be continued.

1651 _____. SOUTHEAST ASIA, A BIBLIOGRAPHY FOR UNDERGRADUATE
LIBRARIES. Williamsport, Pa.: Bro-Dart, 1970.

This brief item is valuable because of its selectivity. Little
literary material in either this or entry no. 1649.

1652 Tregonning, Kennedy G., comp. SOUTH EAST ASIA, A CRITICAL
BIBLIOGRAPHY. Tucson: Univ. of Arizona Press, 1969.

Good annotations on about two thousand entries.

B. REFERENCE

1653 Bastin, John, ed. THE EMERGENCE OF MODERN SOUTHEAST ASIA,
1511-1957. Englewood Cliffs: Prentice-Hall, 1967.

Some thirty selections from mostly Western observers.

1654 Cady, John Frank. SOUTHEAST ASIA, ITS HISTORICAL DEVELOP-
MENT. New York: McGraw-Hill, [1964].

A lengthy readable history of the area.

1655 Cowan, C.D., and O.W. Wolters, eds. SOUTHEAST ASIAN HISTORY
AND HISTORIOGRAPHY. ESSAYS PRESENTED TO D.G.E. HALL.
Ithaca: Cornell Univ. Press, 1976.

Valuable collection of specialized studies by experts.

1656 Hall, D[aniel] G.E. A HISTORY OF SOUTH-EAST ASIA. 3d ed.
New York: St. Martin's Press, 1968.

Considered by many to be the standard history.

1657 _____, ed. HISTORIANS OF SOUTHEAST ASIA. London: Oxford
Univ. Press, 1961.

Valuable studies of history (including legendary history) by
native authors. Sections are noted below.

1658 Harrison, Brian. SOUTHEAST-ASIA, A SHORT HISTORY. 3d ed.
New York: St. Martin's Press, 1966.

An excellent short history.

1659   Steinberg, David, et al. IN SEARCH OF SOUTHEAST ASIA, A
        MODERN HISTORY. New York: Praeger, 1971.

        More difficult for the beginner than the preceding entry, but
        more adequate for the complexities of the subject.

1660   Williams, Lea E. SOUTHEAST ASIA, A HISTORY. Oxford: Oxford
        Univ. Press, 1976.

        Another useful short history.

C. LITERARY HISTORY AND CRITICISM

1661   Benda, Harry J., and John A. Larkin, eds. THE WORLD OF SOUTH-
        EAST ASIA, SELECTED HISTORICAL READINGS. New York: Harper
        and Row, 1967.

        Useful because it includes a number of prose pieces by native
        writers, as well as some by Westerners.

1662   Benedict, Paul K. "Languages and Literatures of Indochina." FAR
        EASTERN QUARTERLY, 6 (1947), 379-89.

        Excellent brief overview of the subject.

1663   Buck, Marry M. "An Introduction to the Study of the RĀMĀYANA in
        South and South-East Asia." In PROCEEDINGS OF THE FIRST INTER-
        NATIONAL CONFERENCE OF TAMIL STUDIES. Kuala Lumpur: 1968,
        pp. 72-88. See also entry 1668.

        The Indian epic, the RĀMĀYANA, has been redacted all over
        Southeast Asia, in both art and literature.

1664   Echols, John. "The Background of Literatures in Southeast Asia and
        the Philippines." In SIX PERSPECTIVES ON THE PHILIPPINES. Ed.
        George M. Guthrie. Manila: Bookmark, 1968, pp. 113-64.

        Valuable article by one of the leading experts on Southeast-
        Asian literature. Essential reading.

1665   Gonzalez, N.V.M. "The Artist in Southeast Asia." BOOKS ABROAD,
        30 (1956), 301-06.

        Considers writers in Ceylon, Thailand, Indonesia, and Malaysia.

1666   Hla Nai Pan. "Mon Literature and Culture over Thailand and Burma."
        JOURNAL OF THE BURMA RESEARCH SOCIETY, 41 (1958), 65-75.

        Literature in the Mon language has managed to preserve its
        identity against competing and larger language families.

1667   Sebeok, Thomas A. "The Languages of Southeast Asia." FAR
       EASTERN QUARTERLY, 2 (1943), 349-56.

       Valuable article by a distinguished linguist on the complex
       language situation, which affects the literature of the area.

1668   Singaravelu, S. "A Comparative Study of the Story of Rama, in
       South India and South-East Asia." In PROCEEDINGS OF THE FIRST
       INTERNATIONAL CONFERENCE OF TAMIL STUDIES. Kuala Lumpur:
       1968, pp. 89-140.

       See also entry 1663.

1669   Thompson, Stith, and Jonas Balys. THE ORAL TALES OF INDIA.
       Bloomington: Indiana Univ. Press, 1958.

1670   Thompson, Stith, and Warren E. Roberts. TYPES OF INDIC ORAL
       TALES: INDIA, PAKISTAN, AND CEYLON. Helsinki: Suomalainen
       Tiedeakatemia, 1960.

       This and the preceding volumes classify folktale motifs and
       story types. Though they are concerned with India, story
       migrations make them useful for Southeast Asia. See entry
       no. 63.

Chapter 6
BURMA

A. BIBLIOGRAPHY

1671 Bernot, Denise, comp. BIBLIOGRAPHIE BIRMANE, ANNÉES 1950-
1960. Paris: Edition du Centre National de la Recherche Scientifique,
1968.

Books and periodicals arranged by subject. Includes Burmese
material. Brief annotations.

1672 Jenner, Philip N., comp. SOUTHEAST ASIAN LITERATURE IN TRANS-
LATION. See entry no. 1648.

1673 Trager, Frank N., ed. BURMA, A SELECTED AND ANNOTATED
BIBLIOGRAPHY. New Haven: Human Relations Area Files, 1973.

About two thousand entries, mostly English. Good annotations.
Revises his ANNOTATED BIBLIOGRAPHY OF BURMA, 1956.

B. REFERENCE

1674 Cady, John F. HISTORY OF MODERN BURMA. Ithaca: Cornell Univ.
Press, 1958.

Covers the last 150 years, through colonialism to the present
national state. A good modern history.

1675 Harvey, Godfrey E. HISTORY OF BURMA FROM THE EARLIEST
TIMES TO 10 MARCH 1824: THE BEGINNINGS OF THE BRITISH
CONQUEST. London: Frank Cass, 1925; rept. New York: Octagon,
1967.

Pioneering work on the early period. Some material on literature and culture.

1676   Htin Aung, U. A HISTORY OF BURMA. New York: Columbia Univ. Press, 1967.

        Valuable on early history. Uses mostly Burmese sources and corrects Western interpretations.

1677   Scott, James G. [pseud., Shway Yoe]. THE BURMAN, HIS LIFE AND NOTIONS. New York: W.W. Norton and Co., 1963.

        First published in 1882. A major work on the social life and customs of the Burmese, which are probably not much different now, at least in rural areas. Some selections from literature, pp. 566-76.

1678   Trager, Frank N. BURMA, FROM KINGDOM TO REPUBLIC, A HISTORICAL AND POLITICAL ANALYSIS. New York: Praeger, 1966.

        Good study of the dynamics of the society. Little cultural material.

C. LITERARY HISTORY AND CRITICISM

1679   Allott, Anna. "Burmese Literature." In GUIDE TO THE EASTERN LITERATURES, pp. 387-401. See entry no. 57.

        Good historical sketch with brief biographies of the major writers.

1680   Ba Thein, U. "A Dictionary of Burmese Authors." Trans. Ba Kye and Gordon H. Luce. JOURNAL OF THE BURMA RESEARCH SOCIETY, 10 (1920), 137-54.

        Useful notes on authors and works.

1681   Bode, Mabel Haynes. THE PALI LITERATURE OF BURMA. London: Royal Asiatic Society of Great Britain and Ireland, 1909.

        A good specialized study of the literature of formal Burmese Buddhism, which has little connection with the court and popular literature of the country.

1682   Donne, C.W., Hla Pe, and J.A. Stewart. "Country Life in Burmese Literature." BULLETIN OF THE SCHOOL OF ORIENTAL AND AFRICAN STUDIES, 12 (1948), 703-12.

        Important article on a major mode of the literature.

1683   H[la] P[e]. "Burmese Literature." In CASSELL'S ENCYCLOPEDIA OF WORLD LITERATURE, London: Cassell, 1973, I, p. 85.

        Another good brief sketch.

1684 Minn Latt. "Mainstreams in Burmese Literature." EASTERN HORIZON, 2 (1962), 27-35.

A good survey of major developments.

1685 Nu, U. "Burma's World of Letters." GUARDIAN, 4 February 1957, pp. 14-16.

Brief appreciation by the famous writer-diplomat.

1686 "Perspective of Burma." ATLANTIC MONTHLY, 201, No. 2 (February 1958), supp.

Valuable. Constitutes a good introduction to Burmese life and includes translations of literary works.

1687 Pew Saya. "Burmese Literary Art." JOURNAL OF THE BURMA RESEARCH SOCIETY, 9 (1919), 83-96.

An interesting essay (English translation, pp. 92-96), on styles of literary discourse, placed in a historical perspective.

1688 Win, U. "Cultural Aspects of Burmese Literature." In ASIA AND THE HUMAÑITIES, pp. 176-82. See entry no. 52.

D. POETRY—STUDIES AND ANTHOLOGIES

1689 Hle Pe, Anna J. Allott, and John Okell, trans. "Three 'Immortal' Burmese Songs." BULLETIN OF THE SCHOOL OF ORIENTAL AND AFRICAN STUDIES, 26 (1963), 559-71.

Translation and commentary on three of the five poems considered immortal and because they reflect a great crisis in the author's life. Two of the poets composed their poems faced with execution (Anatathuriya and U Pon Nya), and the third in exile (Let-we Thon-dara). For the latter two parts see below.

1690 Lustig, Friedrich V., trans. BURMESE CLASSICAL POEMS. Rangoon: Rangoon Gazette, [1966].

Nearly thirty poems are translated with brief biographical sketches. The best collection available. Bilingual.

1691 _____. "Some Thoughts about Burmese Poetry." ARYAN PATH, 42 (1971), 309-12.

Brief appreciations of some major poets, mostly the traditional ones.

1692 Scott, J.G. BURMA: A HANDBOOK OF PRACTICAL INFORMATION.
3d rev. ed. London: Daniel O'Connor, 1921.

Translations of poetry are included, pp. 426-59.

1693 Stewart, J.A. "The Greek Anthology--Burmese Parallels." JOURNAL
OF THE BURMA RESEARCH SOCIETY, 18 (1928), 12-15.

Comparisons between Burmese poetry and the great ancient
Greek collection of short lyrics.

1694 _____. "A Mon Song of the Seasons, with Translations and Notes."
JOURNAL OF THE BURMA RESEARCH SOCIETY, 22 (1932), 18-22.

A seventeenth- or eighteenth-century "shepherd's calendar,"
describing the seasons of the year.

1695 Williams, H. Allen. "Translating Burmese Poetry." GUARDIAN, No.
10 (March 1964), p. 44.

1696 Zan Aung, Shwe. "The Probable Origin of Burmese Poetry." JOUR-
NAL OF THE BURMA RESEARCH SOCIETY, 8 (1918), 9-14.

Traces the origin to Sanskrit poetic forms.

E. DRAMA—STUDIES AND TRANSLATIONS

1697 Ba Cho Deroke, U. "The Burmese Marionette Stage." ASIAN HORI-
ZON, 1 (1948), 51-58.

On the popular puppet plays, which use romantic and sometimes historical subjects.

1698 Htin Aung, Maung. BURMESE DRAMA, A STUDY, WITH TRANSLA-
TIONS OF BURMESE PLAYS. London: Oxford Univ. Press, 1957.

Four plays translated in full and extracts from others. Traditional plays down to the nineteenth century.

1699 _____. "Tragedy and the Burmese Drama." JOURNAL OF THE
BURMA RESEARCH SOCIETY, 29 (1939), 157-65.

Comparisons with European ideas of tragedy.

1700 Maung, E. "The Burmese Drama." JOURNAL OF THE BURMA
RESEARCH SOCIETY, 8 (1918), 33-38.

Studies the plots of dramas in relationship to contemporary life.

1701 Stewart, J.A. "The Burmese Drama." JOURNAL OF THE BURMA

RESEARCH SOCIETY, 2 (1912), 30–37.

A synopsis of SAWYABALA, THE OUTLAW, a popular play,
from a recent performance. Notes on the staging and acting.

F. MISCELLANEOUS WRITINGS—STUDIES AND TRANSLATIONS

1702 Gray, James. ANCIENT PROVERBS AND MAXIMS FROM BURMESE
SOURCES, OR THE NITI LITERATURE OF BURMA. London: Trubner,
1886.

Good collection of folk and literary proverbs with introduction
and notes.

1703 Hle Pe, U., trans. BURMESE PROVERBS. London: John Murray,
[1962].

Perhaps the best-translated collection of proverbs.

1704 Htin Aung, Maung. BURMESE FOLK-TALES. Calcutta: Oxford Univ.
Press, 1948.

A good collection of oral tales, with Thompson motif-numbers.
See also entry nos. 63, 1669–70.

1705 _____. BURMESE LAW TALES: THE LEGAL ELEMENTS IN BURMESE
FOLKLORE. London: Oxford Univ. Press, 1962.

1706 Maung Tin. "The Burmese Novel." JOURNAL OF THE BURMA RE-
SEARCH SOCIETY, 7 (1917), 175–80.

Discusses the traditional novel in relationship to the the plots
of popular dramas.

1707 Stewart, J.A. "Burmese Prose Style." JOURNAL OF THE BURMA
RESEARCH SOCIETY, 12 (1922), 102–06.

On varieties of traditional style in literature and other writing.

1708 Taylor, L.F. "Folklore and Legends of Burma." JOURNAL OF THE
BURMA RESEARCH SOCIETY, 10 (1920), 93–103.

Discusses legends under various standard headings: flood myths,
bird myths, love songs, and others.

1709 Tet Htoot, U. "The Nature of the Burmese Chronicles." In HISTORI-
ANS OF SOUTHEAST ASIA, pp. 50–62. See entry no. 1657.

On the moralistic nature of Burmese traditional history.

1710   Tin Ohn. "Modern Historical Writing in Burmese 1724-1942." In
        HISTORIANS OF SOUTHEAST ASIA, pp. 85-93. See entry no. 1657.

> A good sketch, mostly pre-twentieth-century, of the effect of
> the West on traditional historical writing.

1711   Tin Pe Maung. "The Burmese Novel." JOURNAL OF THE BURMA
        RESEARCH SOCIETY, 7 (1917), 175-80.

> Comments on the traditional novel, as yet largely unaffected
> by the West.

1712   Iin Swe. "Survey of Children's Literature of Burma." GUARDIAN,
        No. 7 (July 1964), pp. 41-44.

G. EARLIER AUTHORS AND WORKS

Alangdaw Dhamma Wizaya Thagyin (traditional)

1713   M.K. "An Old Arakanese Romance." JOURNAL OF THE BURMA RE-
        SEARCH SOCIETY, 18 (1928), 44-50.

> A love story of a beautiful princess amidst the intrigues of the
> court. This kind of song was recited by rhapsodists.

Chronicle of the City of Tagaung (date unknown)

1714   Maung Tin, and Gordon H. Luce, trans. "Chronicle of the City of
        Tagaung." JOURNAL OF THE BURMA RESEARCH SOCIETY, 11 (1921),
        29-54.

Hliang Teik Khaung Tin (1833-75)

1715   Ohn Maung, Kyaiklat U, trans. "A Famous Poetess and her Famous
        Song." GUARDIAN, No. 10 (September 1963), p. 37.

> A poem by a princess who suffered the infidelity of her hus-
> band, the execution of her mother, and other indignities.

Jātakas

1716   Okell, J. "Translation and Embellishment of an Early Burmese JĀTAKA."
        JOURNAL OF THE ROYAL ASIATIC SOCIETY, Pts. 3 & 4 (1967),
        pp. 133-48.

> The JĀTAKA stories of the Buddha have been popular in Burma.
> A good general account of the type with translated extracts.

Kon-Baung-Zet (Glass Palace Chronicle) (eighteenth century)

TRANSLATIONS

1717 Pe Maung Tin, and G.H. Luce, trans. THE GLASS PALACE CHRO-
NICLE OF THE KINGS OF BURMA. Oxford: Clarendon Press, 1923.

Part of the official history of Burma from earliest times down
to 1752, and a source for literature.

STUDIES

1718 Htin Aung, U. BURMESE HISTORY BEFORE 1287: A DEFENSE OF
THE CHRONICLES. London: Asoka Society, 1970.

A criticism of Pe Maung Tin and Luce, above, and other
commentators.

Let-We Thon-dara [Maung Myat San] (fl. 1752-65)

1719 Byo Po. "A Study of Letwe-Thondara's Poem Written During his Exile."
JOURNAL OF THE BURMA RESEARCH SOCIETY, 7 (1917), 45-54.

The text of the poem with a free translation. A poem of
lament from exile, perhaps the most admired of all Burmese
poems for both content and style.

1720 Han Kyin. "Letwe Thondara's Poem." JOURNAL OF THE BURMA
RESEARCH SOCIETY, 12 (1922), 35-38, 152.

1721 Hla Pe, et al. "Three 'Immortal' Burmese Songs." See entry no. 1689.

1722 Khin Zaw, U, trans. "A New Translation of Let-We-Thon-Dara's
Famous RATU." JOURNAL OF THE BURMA RESEARCH SOCIETY, 25
(1935), 129-35.

1723 Luce, Gordon H. "English Poetical Translations of the YADUS of Let-we-
Thondara." JOURNAL OF THE BURMA RESEARCH SOCIETY, 6 (1916),
13-17.

All of these articles contain translation and commentary. The
one by Hle Pe and others is the best (entry no. 1689).

1724 Zan Aung, Shwe. "Ratus or Lyrical Poems of Letwethondara." JOUR-
NAL OF THE BURMA RESEARCH SOCIETY, 11 (1921), 98-102.

Critical comment on previous scholarship and translation.

Obhāsa, U (1758?-98?)

1725   White, O., trans. A TRANSLATION OF WETHANDAYA (VESSANTARA JĀTAKA) OF U OBHĀSA. Rangoon, 1906.

The work of a scholarly monk who gave his life to translating the ten Jātaka birth stories from the Pali. He created an ornate and elegant style, a model for later Burmese writers.

Pok Ni, U (1849-?)

1726   Hle Pe, trans. KONMARA PYA-ZAT, AN EXAMPLE OF POPULAR BURMESE DRAMA. London: Luzac, 1952.

A palace-intrigue play of 1875, with Buddhist philosophical overtones. Good introduction on the stage and the nature of the drama.

Pôn Nya (1807-66)

1727   Ba Han. "U Ponnya's PADUMA." JOURNAL OF THE BURMA RESEARCH SOCIETY, 7 (1917), 137-39.

A violent and romantic play on the treachery of women.

1728   . "U Ponnya's WIZAYA." JOURNAL OF THE BURMA RE-SEARCH SOCIETY, 6 (1916), 139-43.

Summary and appreciation of a play in which a king is forced to exile his lawless sons.

1729   Hle Pe. "Three Immortal Burmese Songs." See entry no. 1689.

Rājādhirāja Vilāsinī (nineteenth century)

1730   Maung Tin, trans. "RADJADHIRAJA VILASINI: The Manifestation of the KING OF KINGS, a Pali Historical Novel." JOURNAL OF THE BURMA RESEARCH SOCIETY, 4 (1914), 7-21.

An account of King Bodawpaya (1781-1819), by a monk.

Rāmāyana (traditional)

1731   Connor, J.P. "The RAMAYANA in Burma." JOURNAL OF THE BURMA RESEARCH SOCIETY, 15 (1925), 80-81.

The Indian epic, The RAMAYANA, is popular in various redactions all over Southeast Asia. A brief summary of the Burmese versions.

Seindakyawthu [U Aw] (1736-71)

1732   Ban Han.   "Seindakyawthu, Man and Poet." JOURNAL OF THE
       BURMA RESEARCH SOCIETY, 8 (1918), 107-11.

       A child prodigy, this poet became famous for short lyrics on
       various subjects.

Slapat Rajawan Datow Smin Ron (traditional)

1733   Halliday, R., ed. and trans. "SLAPAT RAJAWAN DATOW SMIN RON, a
       History of Kings." JOURNAL OF THE BURMA RESEARCH SOCIETY,
       12 (1922), 1-67.

       Text, translation, and notes to a Mon historical work filled
       with legend and ethical thoughts.

Ugga Byan (ca. 1595)

1734   Collis, M.S. "An Arakanese Poem of the 16th Century." JOURNAL
       OF THE BURMA RESEARCH SOCIETY, 13 (1923), 221-31.

       An anonymous poem in which a wife narrates a picture of the
       social scene and her longing for her traveling husband.

Uttamagyaw (or Urramagyaw) (1453-1542)

1735   Ba Han, trans. "Shin Uttamagyaw and his TAWLA: a Nature Poem."
       JOURNAL OF THE BURMA RESEARCH SOCIETY, 7 (1917), 172-73;
       261-62; 8 (1918), 29-31, 150-51, 261-62; 9 (1919), 25-26, 107-08,
       149-50; 10 (1920), 14.

1736   Byo Po. "Shin Uttamagyaw and his TAWLA, a Nature Poem." JOUR-
       NAL OF THE BURMA RESEARCH SOCIETY, 7 (1917), 159-71, 255-61;
       8 (1918), 21-29, 143-50, 255-61; 9 (1919) 15-25, 103-07, 145-49;
       10 (1930), 13-14.

       A tawla is a poem about a journey through the forest. This
       is a Buddhist devotional poem by a monk-poet.

H. MODERN LITERATURE

1. History and Criticism

1737   Htin Maung. "Burmese New Writing." GUARDIAN, No. 10 (August
       1954), pp. 13-14.

       A plea for the support of modern literature against the classi-
       cal tradition.

1738   Pe On, U. "Modern Burmese Literature." ASIAN REVIEW, 56 (1960), 226-32.

On late nineteenth- and twentieth-century writers and scholars.

1739   Tin Htway, U. "The Role of Literature in Nation Building." In SOUTHEAST ASIA IN THE MODERN WORLD. Ed. Bernhard Grossman. Wiesbaden: Harrassowitz, [1972], pp. 35-60.

Discusses all kinds of writing, not only literature, as it concerns the Burmese struggle for freedom.

2. Authors and Works

MIN THU WUN [U WUN] (1909-)

1740   MINTHUWUN, A SELECTION OF HIS POEMS WITH ENGLISH TRANS-LATIONS PRINTED ON THE OCCASION OF HIS LEAVING FOR ENGLAND AS A STATE SCHOLAR. Rangoon: Pinya Hall Social Club, 1936.

Ten poems and one short story by a leading stylist and critic.

MYINT THEIN PE (1914-)

1741   Milne, Patricia M., trans. SELECTED SHORT STORIES OF THEIN PE MYINT. Itaca: Cornell Univ. Press, 1974.

Generous selection of stories by a popular modern writer and political official, with a sketch of the author and his place in the literary scence.

NU, U (1907-)

1742   THE PEOPLE WIN THROUGH, A PLAY. New York: Taplinger, 1957.

Patriotic play by a former prime minister of Burma, originally written in English.

PO SEIN (1880-1952)

1743   Sein, Kenneth, and J.A. Withey. THE GREAT PO SEIN: CHRONICLE OF THE BURMESE THEATER. Bloomington: Indiana Univ. Press, 1966.

Biography of the leading figure in the Burmese theater in the twentieth century.

ZAW GYI [U THEIN HAN] (1907-)

1744   SELECTION: POEM AND FOUR SHORT STORIES. Rangoon: n.p., 1960.

By a philosophical poet and essayist.

I. PERIODICALS

1745   GUARDIAN. Rangoon: n.p., 1953-- .

A newspapers, with occasional brief comments on Burmese
literary life and reviews of books. Available only in major
libraries. Also on microfilm.

1746   JOURNAL OF THE BURMA RESEARCH SOCIETY. Rangoon: B.R.S.,
1911-- .

The major source for scholarship on Burmese literature. Available on microfilm and microfiche.

Chapter 7
CAMBODIA

A. BIBLIOGRAPHY

1747 Dik Keam, comp. CATALOGUE DES AUTEURS KHMER ET ETRANGERES. Phnom Penh: Association des Ecrivains Khmers, 1966.

   Mostly Cambodian works, but some Western authors are included.

1748 Fisher, Mary L., comp. CAMBODIA, AN ANNOTATED BIBLIOGRAPHY OF ITS HISTORY, GEOGRAPHY, POLITICS AND ECONOMICS SINCE 1954. Cambridge: MIT Press, 1967.

   Very useful list of mostly English titles. Little cultural material.

1749 United Nations. E.C.A.F.E. Library, McKong Documentation Centre. CAMBODIA, A SELECT BIBLIOGRAPHY. Bangkok: E.C.A.F.E. Library, 1967.

   Lists about one thousand books and articles, mostly on the modern period.

B. REFERENCE

1750 American University. AREA HANDBOOK FOR CAMBODIA. Washington, D.C.: Government Printing Office, 1968.

   Much useful general information on recent events.

1751 Briggs, Lawrence P. ANCIENT KHMER EMPIRE. Philadelphia: American Philosophical Society, 1951.

   Very good on the early history of Cambodia (called Khmer in ancient times) to the fall of Angkor in 1432. Illustrated.

1752   Ghosh, Manomohan. A HISTORY OF CAMBODIA FROM THE EARLIEST
        TIMES TO THE END OF THE FRENCH PROTECTORATE. Saigon: J.K.
        Gupta, 1960.

        A fairly detailed history of the area.

1753   Steinberg, David J., et al. CAMBODIA: ITS PEOPLE, ITS SOCIETY,
        ITS CULTURE. New Haven: Human Relations Area Files Press, 1959.

        Good collection of articles, half in English and half in French,
        by specialists.

C. LITERARY HISTORY AND CRITICISM

1754   Cuisinier, Jeanne. "The Gestures in the Cambodian Ballet: Their
        Traditional Symbolic Significance." INDIAN ARTS AND LETTERS, 1
        (1927), 93-103.

        On the traditional Cambodian dance-drama.

1755   Jacob, Judith. "Some Features of Khmer Versification." In IN
        MEMORY OF J.R. FIRTH. Ed. Charles Ernest Bazell. London:
        Longmans, 1966, pp. 227-41.

        Excellent article on metrics with specimens of the poetry.
        Highly technical.

1756   Karpeles, Suzanne. "The Influence of Indian Civilization in Further
        India (The Expression of the RAMAYANA in the Cambodian Version."
        INDIAN ARTS AND LETTERS, 1 (1927), 30-39.

        As in Burma and Thailand and elsewhere in Southeast Asia,
        the Indian epic, the RAMAYANA, has been altered to appeal
        to another culture.

1757   L[oofs], H.H.E. "Cambodian Literature." In CASSELL'S ENCYCLO-
        PEDIA OF WORLD LITERATURE. London: Cassell, 1973, I, pp. 88-89.

        A good brief survey of the literature.

1758   Makhali-Phail. THE YOUNG CONCUBINE. Trans. W. Weismuller,
        New York: Random House, 1942.

        Mystical novel about the life of a princess of mixed Cambodian-
        European blood. Written originally in French.

1759   Pym, Christopher. "Literary Taste." In his THE ANCIENT CIVILIZA-
        TION OF ANGKOR. New York: New American Library, 1968,
        pp. 103-09.

An attempt to demonstrate what literature contributed to life in early Cambodia. Speculative, but intelligent and valuable.

1760 Sheppard, Dato Haji Mubin. "The Khmer Shadow Play and its Links with Ancient India: A Possible Source for the Malay Shadow Play of Kelantan and Trengganu." JOURNAL OF THE MALAY BRANCH OF THE ROYAL ASIATIC SOCIETY, 41 (1968), 199-204.

A popular form of drama in which two-dimensional puppet figures are projected on a screen. The figures are of great artistic value. The subject matter is legendary.

Chapter 8
INDONESIA

A. BIBLIOGRAPHY

1761   Kennedy, Raymond, comp. BIBLIOGRAPHY OF INDONESIAN PEOPLES AND CULTURES. Rev. and ed. Thomas U. Maretzki and H.T. Fischer. 2d rev. ed. New Haven: Yale Univ., Southeast Asian Studies Program, 1962.

> Over ten thousand books and articles listed by regional languages. No subject index and hence difficult to use. Material mostly in Dutch and English.

1762   U.S. Library of Congress. General Reference and Bibliography Division. NETHERLANDS EAST INDIES, A BIBLIOGRAPHY OF BOOKS PUBLISHED AFTER 1930 AND PERIODICAL ARTICLES PUBLISHED AFTER 1932, AVAILABLE IN U.S. LIBRARIES. Washington, D.C.: Library of Congress, 1945.

> About three thousand titles in Dutch and English.

B. REFERENCE

1763   Bastin, John, ed. MALAYAN AND INDONESIAN STUDIES. Oxford: Oxford Univ. Press, 1964.

> Series of studies by experts on a variety of topics.

1764   Christie, Anthony Herbert. "Indonesia: Culture in Historic Times." ENCYCLOPEDIA BRITANNICA, 1962 ed., pp. 274a-276b.

> A good brief survey.

1765   Friederich, Rudolf Th. THE CIVILIZATION AND CULTURE OF BALI. Ed. Ernst R. Rost. Calcutta: Susil Gupta, 1959.

> A useful volume concerned with the atypical island of Bali, where Hinduism remains while the rest of Indonesia is Moslem.

1766   Grant, Brice. INDONESIA. Melbourne: Univ. of Melbourne Press, 1966.

    A good concise history.

1767   Henderson, John W., et al. AREA HANDBOOK FOR INDONESIA. Washington, D.C.: Government Printing Office, 1970.

    An all-purpose handbook on the area, largely but not entirely devoted to social and political matters.

1768   McVey, Ruth T., ed. INDONESIA. New Haven: Human Relations Area Files, 1962.

    A good collection of studies on all aspects of Indonesian life. Some parts listed below.

1769   Vlekke, Bernard H.M. NUSANTARA: A HISTORY OF INDONESIA. The Hague: W. Van Hoeve, 1959.

    The chief chronological history to 1941. Detailed.

1770   Zainu'ddin, Ailsa. A SHORT HISTORY OF INDONESIA. New York: Praeger, 1970.

    An elementary but good brief history.

C. ANTHOLOGIES

1771   Echols, John M., ed. INDONESIAN WRITING IN TRANSLATION. Ithaca: Cornell Univ., Department of Far Eastern Studies, [1956?].

    The best anthology available.

1772   "Perspective of Indonesia." ATLANTIC MONTHLY, 199 (June 1956), supp.

    Valuable collection of articles and translations.

1773   Rubenstein, Carol, ed. and trans. "Poems of the Indigenous Peoples of Sarawak: Some of the Songs and Chants, Parts I and II." SARAWAK MUSEUM JOURNAL, 21 (1973), 1-721.

    Large collection of songs, chants, folktales, with texts, translations, and commentary.

1774   Shimer, Dorothy Blair, ed. THE MENTOR BOOK OF MODERN ASIAN LITERATURE. See entry no. 35.

    Contains one poem each from seven Indonesian poets.

D. LITERARY HISTORY AND CRITICISM

1775 Alisjahbana, Sutan Takdir. INDONESIAN LANGUAGE AND LITERA-
TURE: TWO ESSAYS. New Haven: Yale Univ., Southeast Asian
Program, 1962.

> Two essays, "The Modernization of the Indonesian Languages"
> and "Development of the Indonesian Language and Literature,"
> that study the effect of national identity of the development
> of the modern language, comparing this to the simultaneous
> rise of nationalism and the modern languages in Renaissance
> Europe.

1776 Barnouw, Adriaan J. "Cross Currents of Culture in Indonesia." FAR
EASTERN QUARTERLY, 5 (1946), 143-51.

> Touches on many aspects of modern culture in an age of great
> change.

1777 Barrett, E.C.G. "Indonesian and Malaysian Literature." In GUIDE
TO THE EASTERN LITERATURES, pp. 267-78. See entry no. 57.

> Useful brief sketch of both the background and the major
> writers.

1778 Harrisson, Tom, and Benedict Sandin. "Borneo Writing Boards."
SARAWAK MUSEUM JOURNAL, 13 (1966), 32-286.

> On primitive writing devices and their use in recording legends
> and myths. Much material on myths and some translations of
> short poems.

1779 J[ohns], A[nthony] H. "Indonesian and Malaysian Literature." CASSELL'S
ENCYCLOPEDIA OF WORLD LITERATURE. London: Cassell, 1973, I,
pp. 306-09.

> A good account with more emphasis on modern works than
> earlier. Includes writings in Dutch.

1780 _____. "Sufism as a Category in Indonesian Literature." JOURNAL
OF SOUTHEAST ASIAN HISTORY, 2 (1961), 10-23.

> Analysis of some Moslem elements.

1781 Pigeaud, T. LITERATURE OF JAVA: CATALOGUE RAISONNÉ OF
JAVANESE MANUSCRIPTS. 3 vols. The Hague: Martinus Nijhoff,
1967-69.

> Though mostly a catalog, includes a good synopsis of the
> literature of Java (A.D. 900-1900) in volume 1.

Indonesia

E. DRAMA—STUDIES AND TRANSLATIONS

1782   Bloch, S., and A.K. Coomaraswamy. "Javanese Theatre." ASIA [Saigon], (July 1929), pp. 536–39.

1783   Brandon, James R., ed. ON THRONES OF GOLD: THREE JAVA-NESE SHADOW PLAYS. Cambridge: Harvard Univ. Press, 1970.

     Three plays from the wagang, the puppet–shadow–play theater, with an excellent introduction and a glossary of terms.

1784   Holt, Claire. ART IN INDONESIA, CONTINUITIES AND CHANGE. Ithaca: Cornell Univ. Press, 1967.

     Includes material on the shadow plays and extracts from old Javanese epics.

1785   Kleen, Tyra af. WAYANG (JAVANESE THEATRE). Stockholm: Ethnological Museum of Sweden, 1947.

     Brief sketch of the shadow theater.

1786   Mangkunagara VII of Surakarta. ON THE WAYANG KULIT (PURWA) AND ITS SYMBOLIC AND MYSTICAL ELEMENTS. Trans. Claire Holt. Ithaca: Cornell Univ. Press, 1957.

     On the puppet plays as they embody both Islamic and Indian themes.

1787   Peacock, James L. "Comedy and Characterization in Java: The LUDRAK Plays." JOURNAL OF AMERICAN FOLKLORE, 80 (1967), 345–56.

1788   _____. RITES OF MODERNIZATION: SYMBOLIC AND SOCIAL ASPECTS OF INDONESIAN PROLETARIAN DRAMA. Chicago: Univ. of Chicago Press, [1968].

     Two excellent scholarly studies by Peacock of lower–class (not Marxist) popular traditional drama as it adapts to modern social themes. An anthropological study.

1789   Rassers, W[illem] H. PANJI, THE CULTURE HERO: A STRUCTURAL STUDY OF RELIGION IN JAVA. The Hague: Martinus Nijhoff, 1959.

     Two excellent critical articles on the drama are included in this work: "On the Meaning of Javanese Drama" and "The Javanese Theatre."

1790   Zoete, Beryl, and Walter Spies. DANCE AND DRAMA IN BALI. New York: Charles Harper and Sons, 1939.

A good study of the drama in Bali, which has a different tradition from that of the rest of Indonesia.

F. MISCELLANEOUS WRITINGS—STUDIES

1791 Hooykaas, Jacoba. "The Changling in Balinese Folklore and Religion." BIJDRAGEN TOT DE TAAL-, LAND-, EN VOLKENKUNDE, 116 (1960), 424-36.

1792 _____. "A Journey into the Realm of Death: Balinese Folktales with Translations." BIJDRAGEN TOT DE TAAL-, LAND-, EN VOLKEN-KUNDE, 115 (1959), 176-91.

Two studies of folk legends.

1793 Johns, Anthony H. "The Role of Structural Organization and Myth in Javanese Historiography." JOURNAL OF ASIAN STUDIES, 24 (1964), 91-99.

Traditional Javanese history is a compendium of myth and legend. This essay studies the patterns of myth in the history.

1794 Lohuizen–de Leeuw, J.E. van. "The Beginnings of Old Javanese Historical Literature." BIJDRAGEN TOT DE TAAL-, LAND-, EN VOLKENKUNDE, 112 (1956), 383-94.

1795 Soedjatmoko, et al. INTRODUCTION TO INDONESIAN HISTORIOG-RAPHY. Ithaca: Cornell Univ. Press, [1965].

Emphasizes the difficult and fragmentary nature of early historical documentation in Indonesia.

G. EARLIER AUTHORS AND WORKS

Bagus Umbara (traditional)

1796 Hooykaas, C[hristiaan], trans. BAGUS UMBARA, PRINCE OF KORI-PAN: THE STORY OF A PRINCE OF BALI AND A PRINCESS OF JAVA. London: British Museum, 1968.

Translation of one episode of a traditional epic. Good illustrations.

Dipanagara, Pangeran Arga (ca. 1785-1855)

1797 Kumar, Ann, trans. "Dipanagara (ca. 1785-1855)." INDONESIA, 13 (1972), 69-118.

231

Translation of a long poem of the early religious experiences of a prince of Java. With commentary.

1798   Rickless, M.C. "Dipanagara's Early Inspirational Experiences." BIJDRAGEN TOT DE TAAL-, LAND-, EN VOLKENKUNDE, 130 (1974), 227-58.

Lengthy essay on the poet-priest-mystic, with a translation of one of his poems.

I La Galigo (traditional)

1799   Abidin, Andi Zainal. "The I LA GALIGO Epic Cycle of South Celebes and its Diffusion." INDONESIA, 17 (1974), 161-69.

Discusses this traditional folk epic, which begins with the creation as to plot and background.

Kaba Tjindua (traditional)

1800   Taufik, Abdullah. "Some Notes on the KABA TJINDUA MATO: An Example of Minangkabau Traditional Literature." INDONESIA, 9 (1970), 1-22.

Discussion of a historical epic of royalty, wars, and dynastic problems.

Mahābhārata (traditional)

1801   Chandra, Lokesh. "A New Indonesian Episode of the MAHĀBHĀRATA-CYCLES." ARCHIV ORIENTÁLNÍ, 4 (1959), 565-71.

Both of the great Indian epics, the MAHĀBHĀRATA and the RĀMĀYANA, are popular in local versions in Indonesia and elsewhere in Southeast Asia.

1802   Resink, C.J. "From the Old MAHĀBHĀRATA to the New RĀMĀYANA Order." BIJDRAGEN TOT DE TAAL-, LAND-, EN VOLKENKUNDE, 131 (1975), 214-35.

On the vitality of these myths in Indonesia life down to modern times.

Mangkunagara IV, King of Surakarta (ca. 1857-81)

1803   Suranto Atmosaputo, and Martin F. Hatch, trans. "SERAT WÉDATAMA, a Translation." INDONESIA, 14 (1972), 157-81.

A traditionally minded philosophical poem stressing Javanese

values against Islamic ones, it has retained its popularity to
modern times.

Prapañca of Majapahit (fl. 1366)

1804   Pigeaud, Theodore G. T., trans. JAVA IN THE 14TH CENTURY: A
STUDY IN CULTURAL HISTORY. 5 vols. The Hague: Martinus
Nijhoff, 1960-63.

Vol. 3 includes a complete translation of the NARARA KERTA
GAMA (BOOK OF LEARNING OF THE ORDER OF THE
REALM), a court epic embodying historical and legendary
material. Other volumes include the text, the historical
background, and an elaborate commentary.

Rāmāyana (traditional)

1805   Hooykaas, C[hristiaan]. "Bharata's Departure: A Passage on Artha-
sastra in the Old Javanese RĀMĀYANA KAKAWIN." JOURNAL OF THE
ORIENTAL INSTITUTE OF BARODA, 5 (1955), 187-92.

1806   "Four Line Yamaka in the Old Javanese RĀMĀYANA." JOURNAL OF
THE ROYAL ASIATIC SOCIETY, Nos. 1-2 (1958), pp. 58-71; Nos. 3-
4, pp. 122-38.

1807   _____. THE OLD JAVANESE RĀMĀYANA, AN EXEMPLARY
KAKAWIN AS TO FORM AND CONTENT. Amsterdam: Noord-
Hollandsche Uitg., 1959.

1808   _____. "Sanskrit KAVYA and the Old Javanese KAKAWIN (New
Light on the RĀMĀYANA)." JOURNAL OF THE ORIENTAL INSTI-
TUTE OF BARODA, 4 (1954-55), 143-48.

1809   _____. "Stylistic Figures in the Old Javanese RĀMĀYANA KAKAWIN."
JOURNAL OF THE ORIENTAL INSTITUTE OF BARODA, 7 (1958),
135-57.

The Hooykoos entries represent a series of studies and translations by a major authority on the literature of Java of versions
of the popular Indian epic, the story of Prince Rama and his
quest for his lost wife.

1810   Kats, J. "The RĀMĀYANA in Indonesia." BULLETIN OF THE SCHOOL
OF ORIENTAL AND AFRICAN STUDIES, 4 (1926-28), 579-85.

Comparison of the Indonesia version with other Southeast Asian
versions.

Indonesia

1811   Noorduyn, J.   "Traces of an Old Sundanese RAMAYANA Tradition."
      INDONESIA, 12 (1971), 151-57.

> Brief discussion of an independent, pre-Moslem tradition of
> the legend.

1812   Resink, G.J.   "From the Old MAHABHARATA to the New RAMAYANA
      Order."   See entry no. 1802.

Rantjak DiLabueh (traditional)

1813   Johns, Anthony H., ed. and trans.   RANTJAK diLABUEH, A
      MINANGKABAU KABA, A SPECIMEN OF THE TRADITIONAL LITERA-
      TURE OF CENTRAL SUMATRA, BASED ON THE VERSION OF DATUK
      PADUKO ALAM AND SUTAN PAMUNTJAK. . . . Ithaca: Cornell
      Univ., Department of Far Eastern Studies, 1958.

> A folk epic. Introduction, translation, and notes.

Sutasoma Kakavin (traditional)

1814   Ensink, J., trans.   "Sutasoma's Teaching to Gajavaktra: The Snake
      and the Tigress." BIJDRAGEN TOT DE TAAL-, LAND-, EN VOLKEN-
      KUNDE, 130 (1974), 195-226.

> A mystical poem concerning yoga and man's relation with na-
> ture. Text, translation, and commentary.

H. MODERN LITERATURE—ANTHOLOGIES

1815   Aveling, Harry, trans.   CONTEMPORARY INDONESIAN POETRY.
      St. Lucia: Univ. of Queensland Press, 1975.

> Well-translated collection of poems in English. A good
> sampling of modern work.

1816   _____. GESTAPU: INDONESIAN SHORT STORIES OF THE ABORTIVE
      COMMUNIST COUP OF 30TH SEPTEMBER 1965. [Honolulu: Univ. of
      Hawaii, Southeast Asian Studies Program, 1975.]

1817   Courlander, Harold, trans.   KANTCHIL'S LIME PIT AND OTHER
      STORIES FROM INDONESIA. New York: Harcourt, Brace, [1950].

> Collection of folktales, retold.

1818   Hendon, Rufus S., ed.   SIX INDONESIAN SHORT STORIES. New
      Haven: Yale Univ., Southeast Asian Studies Program, [1968].

> A good selection, well translated.

1819   QUADRANT [Sydney], 13, No. 5 (September–October 1969).

An issue devoted to criticism, poetry, and essays from
Indonesia.

1820   Raffel, Burton, trans. ANTHOLOGY OF MODERN INDONESIAN
POETRY. Berkeley: Univ. of California Press, 1964.

A good selection from the beginning of the twentieth century.

1821   _____. THE DEVELOPMENT OF MODERN INDONESIAN POETRY.
Albany: State Univ. of New York, [1967].

Not a history but a series of translations with comments.

1822   Suradi, Bintang, ed. and trans. CONTEMPORARY PROGRESSIVE
INDONESIAN POETRY. [Djakarta: League of People's Culture, 1962].

Not seen.

1823   WESTERLY [Nedlands, Australia], No. 2 (October 1966).

An issue devoted to Indonesia: a background article, poems
by Chairil Anwar, and four short stories by Pramoedya Ananta
Toer.

1824   Wigmore, Lionel, ed. SPAN. See entry no. 39.

Prose and poetry from ten modern authors.

1. History and Criticism

1825   Aveling, Harry. "The Thorny Rose and the Avoidance of Passion in
Modern Indonesian Literature." INDONESIA, 7 (1969), 67–76.

Notes the lack of realistic female characters and the avoidance of erotic material in modern literature in contrast with
that in the literature of the past.

1826   Holmes, James S. "A Quarter Century of Indonesian Literature."
BOOKS ABROAD, 29 (1955), 31–35.

A good survey of main currents against the shifting social
scene.

1827   Johns, Anthony H. "Genesis of a Modern Literature." In INDONESIA,
pp. 410–37. See entry no. 1768.

An excellent article on the problems of developing a national
literature in Indonesia.

1828   _____. "The Novel as a Guide to Indonesian Social History."
BIJDRAGEN TOT DE TAAL-, LAND-, EN VOLKENKUNDE, 115
(1959), 232-48.

1829   _____. "Toward a Modern Literature in Indonesia." MEANJIN, 19
(1960), 380-87.

   The modern movement may be said to begin in 1922, but only
   in locations and by literary journals encouraged by the Dutch.
   Both articles (entry nos. 1828-29) deal with the great impact
   of the troubled political scene on the writer.

1830   Kroef, Justus M. van der. "The Colonial Novel in Indonesia."
COMPARATIVE LITERATURE, 10 (1958), 215-31.

   On nineteenth- and twentieth-century European writers,
   mostly Dutch, who have written on the Indonesian scene.

1831   Mohamad, Goenawan. "Contemporary Indonesian Literature." SOLI-
DARITY, 3, No. 9 (1968), 22-28.

   On recent writers and the political scene.

1832   Raffel, Burton. "The Beginnings of Modern Indonesian Poetry." ASIA,
No. 2 (August 1964), pp. 67-79.

   Mostly on the introduction of Western classics and popular
   literature through the Dutch administration beginning in 1917.

1833   Teeuw, A[driaan]. MODERN INDONESIAN LITERATURE. The Hague:
Martinus Nijhoff, 1967.

   The major historical and critical account. Includes some
   translations.

1834   _____. "Modern Indonesian Literature Abroad." BIJDRAGEN TOT DE
TAAL-, LAND-, EN VOLKENKUNDE, 127 (1971), 256-63.

   Brief survey of Western criticism and scholarship with critical
   remarks about some recent translations.

1835   Vlach, Robert. "Indonesian Poetry, Where does it Stand?" LITERA-
TURE EAST & WEST, 9 (1965), 284-85.

1836   Watson, C.W. "Some Preliminary Remarks on the Antecedents of
Modern Indonesian Literature." BIJDRAGEN TOT DE TAAL-, LAND-,
EN VOLKENKUNDE, 127 (1971), 417-33.

   Discusses early forms of popular literature in the modern mode
   (beginning about 1920), which include translations from Chinese and Western writings and writing in Malay.

2. Authors and Works

ACHDIAT KARTA, MIHARDJA (1911-)

1837   Johns, Anthony H., trans. "Sensation at Top of Coconut Palm." MEANJIN, 4 (1960), 389-99.

> A short story about a devout country youth who is changed by the life of the big city.

1838   Maguire, R.J., trans. ATHEIS. St. Lucia: Univ. of Queensland Press, 1972.

> An important philosophical novel.

ANWAR, CHAIRIL (1922-49)

1839   Raffel, Burton. "Chairil Anwar, Indonesian Poet." LITERARY REVIEW, 10 (1967), 133-57.

> Good introduction to the most respected poet of modern Indo- nesia. Despite his short life and small output, Anwar had great influence on his contemporaries.

1840   _____, ed. THE COMPLETE POETRY AND PROSE OF CHAIRIL ANWAR. Albany: State Univ. of New York Press, 1970.

> About seventy poems and some prose selections.

JAYA PRANA (ca. 1949-)

1841   Hooykaas, C[hristiaan]. THE LAY OF JAYA PRANA, THE BALINESE URIAH. London: Luzac and Co., 1958.

> A ballad in traditional form associated with the decision in 1949 to cremate the remains of the sage Jaya Prana. Text, translation, and notes.

KARTINI, RADEN ADJENG (1879-1904)

1842   Symmers, Agnes Louise, trans. LETTERS OF A JAVANESE PRINCESS. Ed. Hildred Geertz. Pref. Eleanor Roosevelt. New York: W.W. Norton, [1964].

> Sensitive letters about the role of women in the modern world. Originally written in Dutch.

LUBIS, MOCHTAR (1919-)

1843   Holt, Claire, trans. TWILIGHT IN JAKARTA. London: Hutchinson, [1963].

1844   Johns, Anthony H., trans. A ROAD WITH NO END. London: Hutchinson, [1968].

        Entries 1843 and 1844 are two good modern novels about the plight of modern Indonesia.

SITUMORANG, SITOR (1923-)

1845   "The Rites of the Bal Aga, Poems." INDONESIA, 23 (1977), 113-28.

        Poems originally written in English by a poet who was jailed in the 1965 revolution.

TUR, PRAMUDYA ANANTA (1925-)

1846   Johns, Anthony H., trans. "Inem." MEANJIN, 22 (1963), 365-74.

        A short story about childhood.

1847   _____. "Pramudya Ananta Tur: The Writer as Outsider, an Indonesian Example." MEANJIN, 22 (1963), 354-63.

        Discusses the ideas of this important prose writer and intellectual, especially his alienation from the modern world.

I. PERIODICALS

1848   BIJDRAGEN TOT DE TAAL-, LAND-, EN VOLKENKUNDE. The Hague: Martinus Nijhoff [and others], 1852-- .

        Major scholarly journal on Indonesia and related areas. Articles in Dutch and English.

1849   INDONESIA. Ithaca: Cornell Univ., Indonesia Project, 1966--.

        Social, cultural, and literary studies and translations.

1850   SARAWAK MUSEUM JOURNAL. Kuching: Sarawak Government Printing Office, 1911-- .

        Mostly concerned with archaeology and ethnographic studies, but occasionally includes articles on language, literature, and folktales.

Chapter 9
LAOS

A. BIBLIOGRAPHY

1851   Halpern, Joel M., and James A. Hafner, comps. A PRELIMINARY
AND PARTIAL BIBLIOGRAPHY OF MISCELLANEOUS RESEARCH MATE-
RIALS ON LAOS. Brussels: Centre d'Étude du sud-east asiatique et
l'extrême Orient, 1971.

Contains a brief section on language and literature, pp. 58-59.

1852   Kené, Thao, comp. BIBLIOGRAPHIE DU LAOS. [Vientiane: Editions
du Comité Littéraire], 1958.

A good brief bibliography. All entries in French.

1853   Lafont, Pierre Bernard, comp. BIBLIOGRAPHIE DU LAOS. Paris:
L'École française d'Extrême-Orient, 1964.

The best bibliography for the area. Literature listed on
pp. 120-23. All titles in French.

1854   Mogenet, Luc, comp. BIBLIOGRAPHIE COMPLEMENTAIRE DU LAOS
(1962-1973). Vientiane: Bibliothèque Nationale, 1973.

Mostly material in French. No subject classification.

B. REFERENCE

1855   AREA HANDBOOK FOR LAOS. Washington, D.C.: Government
Printing Office, 1967.

Very useful guide with good brief surveys of "artistic and
intellectual expression," pp. 119-26.

1856   Berval, René de, et al. KINGDOM OF LAOS: THE LAND OF THE

ELEPHANTS AND OF THE WHITE PARASOL. Saigon: France-Asie, [1959].

Some fifty-five essays and notes. Translation of PRÉSENCE DU ROYAUME LAO (Saigon: 1956), which appeared as a separate issue of FRANCE-ASIE. Relevant articles are noted below.

1857 Lebar, Frank M., and Adrienne Suddard, eds. LAOS, ITS PEOPLE, ITS SOCIETY, ITS CULTURE. New Haven: Human Relations Area Files Press, 1960.

A good survey of various aspects of the culture.

1858 Manich Jumsai, M.L. HISTORY OF LAOS (INCLUDING THE HISTORY OF LANNATHAI, CHIENGMAI). Bangkok: Nai Vitaya Rujiravanichathep, 1967.

An attempt to write a history of early Laos from its legends.

1859 Viravong, Maha Sila. HISTORY OF LAOS. Trans. U.S. Joint Publications Research Service. New York: Paragon Books, 1964.

Originally published in 1957 on microfilm. From the beginnings to the mid-nineteenth century. Much use of legendary material for the early period.

C. LITERARY HISTORY, CRITICISM, AND COLLECTIONS

1860 Abhay, Thao Nhouy. "The Court of Love and Poetry in Laos." ASIA [Saigon], 2 (1952), 219-22.

1861 _____. "Versification." In KINGDOM OF LAOS, pp. 335-58. See entry no. 1856.

These two articles by Abhay present the best available material on the traditional poetry.

1862 Finot, Louis. "Laotian Writings." In KINGDOM OF LAOS, pp. 307-27. See entry no. 1856.

On the development of the script.

1863 Martini, François. "Language." In KINGDOM OF LAOS, pp. 328-35. See entry no. 1856.

A brief nontechnical account of the Lao language.

1864 Perry, Ronald L., trans. "Translations from the Lao." HUDSON REVIEW, 13, (1960), 74-86.

Traditional songs from oral tradition, plus three prose fables, translated into English.

1865 Phimmasone, Phouvong. "Literature." In KINGDOM OF LAOS, pp. 336-44. See entry no. 1856.

1866 S[nellgrove], D.L. "Laotian Literature." In CASSELL'S ENCYCLO-PEDIA OF WORLD LITERATURE. London: Cassell, 1973, I, p. 554.

This article and the one preceding complement one another. Snellgrove's is perhaps the better introductory sketch.

D. EARLIER AUTHORS AND WORKS

Pannasjātaka (traditional)

1867 Terral-Martini, G. "Velāmajātaka." BULLETIN OF THE SCHOOL OF ORIENTAL AND AFRICAN STUDIES, 49 (1959), 609-16.

An analysis of one of the tales from the Lao recension of the Jātaka stories imported from India.

Ramayana (traditional)

1868 Dhana, Prince. "The Rama JĀTAKA (a Lao Version of the Story of Rāma)." JOURNAL OF THE SIAM SOCIETY, 36 (1946), 1-22.

Another Southeast-Asian version of adventures of the hero of the Indian epic, the RĀMĀYANA.

Sin Xǎy (date unknown)

1869 Abhay, Thao Nhouy. "SĬN XǍY." In KINGDOM OF LAOS, pp. 359-75. See entry no. 1856.

1870 Perry, Ronald. "The SĬN XǍI, after the Lao of Pang Kham." HUDSON REVIEW, 20 (1967), 11-48.

This is the most famous work of Laotian literature, famed for its philosophical content and literary excellence and known by every educated person. It is based on the Hindu PANNASAJĀTAKA (see above). Abhay's article (entry no. 1869) is a summary, discussion, and partial translation; Perry presents a very readable translation.

E. MODERN LITERATURE

1871 RAINS IN THE JUNGLE. [Hanoi]: Neo Lao Haksat Publications, 1967.

1872   THE WOOD GROUSE. [Hanoi]:   Neo Lao Haksat Publications, 1968.

Two collections of translations of Pathet Lao short stories
celebrating the leftist movement.

Chapter 10
MALAYA AND SINGAPORE

A. BIBLIOGRAPHY

1873   Cheeseman, Harold A.R., comp. BIBLIOGRAPHY OF MALAYA, BEING
       A CLASSIFIED LIST OF BOOKS WHOLLY OR PARTLY IN ENGLISH
       RELATING TO THE FEDERATION OF MALAYA AND SINGAPORE.
       London: Longsman, Green, 1959.

       About one thousand books and articles arranged by subject.
       Includes a list of fiction, mostly Western, about Malaya,
       pp. 66-72, and a list of poems about Malaya and Singapore,
       pp. 156-59.

1874   Hussein, Ismail, comp. "A Selected Bibliography of Traditional Malay
       Literature." TENGARRA, 4 (1969), 94-115.

       A useful basic list.

1875   Lim, Beda, comp. "Malaya, a Background Bibliography." JOURNAL
       OF THE MALAY BRANCH OF THE ROYAL ASIATIC SOCIETY, 35
       (1962), 1-199.

       Over three thousand book and periodical references, mostly
       concerned with social science and history. Mostly in English.

1876   Pelzer, Karl, comp. WEST MALAYSIA AND SINGAPORE, A SELECTED
       BIBLIOGRAPHY. New Haven: Human Relations Area Files, 1971.

       About four thousand items, mostly in sociology and history.

1877   Teeuw, Adries. A CRITICAL SURVEY OF STUDIES IN MALAY AND
       BAHASA INDONESIAN. The Hague: Martinus Nijhoff, 1961.

       A lengthy bibliographical essay. Very useful.

B. REFERENCE

1878 Kennedy, Joseph. A HISTORY OF MALAYA, A.D. 1400-1959. New York: St. Martin's Press, 1962.

> A good modern history. Little cultural material.

1879 Tregonning, K.G., ed. MALAYSIAN HISTORICAL STUDIES. Singapore: Univ. of Singapore Press, 1962.

> Series of studies by specialists on various phases of Malaysian history, emphasizing sources: Chinese, Arab and Persian, and Malay. See also entry no. 1892.

1880 Winstedt, Richard. A HISTORY OF MALAYA. Rev. and enl. ed. Singapore: Marican and Sons, [1962].

> A detailed early history by the leading Western expert. Up to the end of the colonial period.

1881 _____. MALAYA AND ITS HISTORY. 6th ed. London: Hutchinson, 1962.

> Perhaps the best brief history. Mostly on the colonial period up to modern times.

1882 _____. THE MALAYS, A CULTURAL HISTORY. 6th rev. ed. London: Routledge and Kegan Paul, [1966].

> The best cultural history. Arranged by topics. Includes a chapter on literature.

C. ANTHOLOGIES

1883 Brown, C.S. MALAY SAYINGS. London: Routledge and Kegan Paul, [1951].

> A large collection of short sayings in Malay and English.

1884 Hamilton, Arthur W.H., ed. and trans. MALAY PANTUNS: PANTUN MELAYU. 4th ed. Singapore: D. Moore, [1956].

> Translations of popular verse meant to be sung.

1885 _____. MALAY PROVERBS. BIDAL MELAYU. Singapore: D. Moore for Eastern Universities Press, [1955].

1886 MALAYAN LITERATURE. Rev. ed. New York: Colonial Press, 1901.

> A large and useful anthology of Malay literature in somewhat old-fashioned translations.

1887   Ryan, N.J., ed. MALAYA THROUGH FOUR CENTURIES, AN
       ANTHOLOGY 1500-1900. London: Oxford Univ. Press, 1959.

       Collection of various writings about Malaya illustrating its
       history.

1888   Wigmore, Lionel, ed. SPAN. See entry no. 39.

       Includes selections from two writers from Malaya and three
       from Singapore.

1889   Winstedt, Richard, trans. MALAY PROVERBS. London: John Murray,
       [1950].

       A brief, representative collection of standard proverbs.

D. LITERARY HISTORY AND CRITICISM

1890   Altmann, Gabriel, and Robert Stukovsky. "The Climax in Malay Pan-
       tun." ASIAN AND AFRICAN STUDIES [Bratislava], 1 (1965), 13-20.

       On the popular Malay lyric form.

1891   Barrett, E.C.G. "Indonesian and Malaysian Literature." In GUIDE
       TO THE EASTERN LITERATURES, pp. 267-78. See entry no. 57.

       A valuable brief sketch.

1892   Berg, C.C. "Javanese Historiography--A Synopsis of its Evolution."
       In HISTORIANS OF SOUTHEAST ASIA, pp. 13-23. See entry no.
       1657.

       On the intermixing of magic and legends with historical mate-
       rial and the Javanese attitude towards history. Includes poetic
       materials.

1893   Bottoms, J.C. "Malay Historical Works." In MALAYSIAN HISTORI-
       CAL STUDIES, pp. 36-62. See entry no. 1879.

       Good survey of the mixture of myth, legend, and historical
       fact that constitutes traditional Malay history.

1894   Brewster, Paul G. "Metrical, Stanzaic, and Stylistic Resemblances
       between Malayan and Western Poetry." REVUE DE LITTERATURE COM-
       PAREE, 32 (1958), 214-22.

       A far-ranging article on general resemblances between Malay
       lyric poetry and Western.

Malaya and Singapore

1895   Hussein, Ismail. "The Study of Traditional Malay Literature." JOUR-
       NAL OF THE MALAY BRANCH OF THE ROYAL ASIATIC SOCIETY,
       39, No. 2 (1966), 1-22.

       A survey of studies by both Western scholars and Malays.

1896   Iskandar, T. "Three Malay Historical Writings in the First Half of
       the 17th Century." JOURNAL OF THE MALAY BRANCH OF THE
       ROYAL ASIATIC SOCIETY, 40, No. 2 (1967), 38-53.

       Discusses the authorship of SEJARAH MĔLAYU (see below),
       HIKAYAT ACHEH, and BUSTANUS-SALATIN, all legendary
       histories.

1897   Johns, Anthony H. "Indonesian and Malaysian Literature." In
       CASSELL'S ENCYCLOPEDIA OF WORLD LITERATURE. See entry no.
       1779.

1898   Marrison, G.E. "Persian Influence in Malay Literature." JOURNAL
       OF THE MALAY BRANCH OF THE ROYAL ASIATIC SOCIETY, 28,
       No. 1 (1955), 52-69.

       Discusses romances, books of instruction for princes, theology,
       and history which came into Malay literature from Persia.

1899   Osman, Mohammad Taib. "Mythical Elements in Malay Historiography."
       TENGGARA, 2 (1968), 80-89.

       Brief article about this important component of Malay history.

1900   Rentse, Anker. "The Kelantan Shadow-Play (Wayang Kulit)." JOUR-
       NAL OF THE MALAY BRANCH OF THE ROYAL ASIATIC SOCIETY, 14,
       No. 3 (1936), 284-301.

       Description of the traditional drama staged in modern times,
       with plots of plays and drawings of shadow puppets.

1901   _____. "The Origin of the Wayang Theatre (Shadow Play)." JOURNAL
       OF THE MALAY BRANCH OF THE ROYAL ASIATIC SOCIETY, 20,
       No. 1 (1947), 12-15.

       Notes on the origins of the shadow puppets.

1902   Sheppard, Mubin. "Ma'yong, the Malay Dance Drama." TENGGARA,
       5 (1969), 107-13.

       On the romantic court drama. Short summaries of plays.

1903   Sweeney, Pil Amin. "The Pak Pandar Cycle of Tales." JOURNAL
       OF THE MALAY BRANCH OF THE ROYAL ASIATIC SOCIETY, 49,
       No. 1 (1976), 15-88.

Pak Pandar is a comic character from Malay folk literature,
now appearing in the general literature. Based on field
work and somewhat technical. Includes summaries of stories.

1904 _____. "Professional Malay Story Telling: Part I: Some Questions
of Style and Presentation." JOURNAL OF THE MALAY BRANCH OF
THE ROYAL ASIATIC SOCIETY, 46, No. 2 (1973), 1-53.

On oral tales--"folk romances"--often adapted into literary
Malay. Includes photographs of informants.

1905 _____. "The Shadow Play of Kelantan. Report on a Period of Field
Research." JOURNAL OF THE MALAY BRANCH OF THE ROYAL
ASIATIC SOCIETY, 43, No. 2 (1970), 53-80.

Important survey covering the background, form of the drama,
acting and actor's training, and other matters.

1906 Winstedt, Richard. A HISTORY OF CLASSICAL MALAY LITERATURE.
Oxford: Oxford Univ. Press, 1969.

The standard work on Malay literature from earliest times by
the greatest Western expert.

1907 _____. "Malay Literature." ASIAN REVIEW, 57 (1961), 201-11.

An interesting summary of Islamic, Indian, and Dutch influence
on Malay literature up to modern times.

1908 _____. "A Panji Tale from Kelantan." JOURNAL OF THE MALAY
BRANCH OF THE ROYAL ASIATIC SOCIETY, 22, No. 1 (1949), 53-60.

Lengthy summary of a bloody tale of court intrigue.

1909 Zoetmuller, Petrus J. KALANGWAN: A SURVEY OF OLD JAVANESE
LITERATURE. The Hague: Martinus Nijhoff, 1974.

A langthy survey with summaries and descriptions of many works
from 804 A.D. Includes illustrations of sculptured scenes from
traditional works.

E. EARLIER AUTHORS AND WORKS

Hikajat Bandjar

1910 Ras, Johannes J., ed. HIKAJAT BANDJAR: A STUDY IN MALAY
HISTORIOGRAPHY. The Hague: Martinus Nijhoff, 1968.

A chronicle of the Malay kingdom which existed in South

Borneo until 1860. A realistic view of palace intrigues.
Summary, parallel text and translation, introduction, and
notes.

Hikayat Hang Tuah (eleventh century)

1911   Ahmad, Kassim bin. CHARACTERIZATION IN HIKAYAT HANG TUAH:
       A GENERAL SURVEY OF METHODS OF CHARACTER-PORTRAYAL AND
       ANALYSIS AND INTERPRETATION OF THE CHARACTERS OF HANG
       TUAH AND HANG JEBAT. Kuala Lumpur: Dewan Bahasa dan Pustaka, 1966.

1912   Iskandar, T. "Some Historical Sources used by the Author of Hikayat
       Hang Tuah." JOURNAL OF THE MALAY BRANCH OF THE ROYAL
       ASIATIC SOCIETY, 43, No. 1 (1970), 35-47.

1913   Parnickel, B.B. "An Epic Hero and an 'Epic Traitor.'" BIJDRAGEN
       TOT DE TAAL-, LAND-, EN VOLKENKUNDE, 132 (1976), 403-17.

       A Malayo-Javenese romance derived from the oral tradition
       of the quest for a beautiful princess. A story of court intrigue
       in the kingdom of Java.

Hikayat Iskandar (fourteenth-fifteenth centuries)

1914   Winstedt, Richard. "The Date, Authorship and Some New MSS of the
       Malay Romance of Alexander the Great." JOURNAL OF THE MALAY
       BRANCH OF THE ROYAL ASIATIC SOCIETY, 16, No. 1 (1938), 1-23.

       On the Malay version of the Alexander romance, which begins
       in Greece and migrates through Persia into other Islamic
       countries.

HIKAYAT MAHARAJA RAVANA. See HIKAYAT SERI RAMA

Hikayat Muhammad Hanafiah (before 1511)

1915   Brakel, L.F., trans. THE STORY OF MUHAMMAD HANAFIYYAH, A
       MEDIEVAL MOSLEM ROMANCE. The Hague: Martinus Nijhoff, 1977.

       Romance about Mohammad and his early years and associates.
       A good translation somewhat abridged.

Hikayat Muhammad Mukabil

1916   Drews, G.W.J. "HIKAYAT MUHAMMAD MUKABIL (The Story of the Kadi
       and the Learned Brigand)." BIJDRAGEN TOT DE TAAL-, LAND-, EN
       VOLKENKUNDE, 126 (1970), 309-31.

A story based on Islamic tradition (like the tales of the
ARABIAN NIGHTS). Discussion of the background and a
lengthy summary of the plot.

Hikayat Pantini (early eighteenth century)

1917   Teeuw, Andries, ed. and trans. "HIKAYAT PANTINI," THE STORY OF
PANTINI. 2 vols. The Hague: Martinus Nijhoff, 1970.

A dynastic history of palace intrigue centered in the once-
important city of Pantini on the west coast of Thailand.
Text, translation, and notes.

Hikayat Raja-Raja Pasai (ca. 1350-1511)

1918   Sweeney, P.L. Amin. "The Connection between the Hikayat Raja
Pasai and the Sejarah Mẽlayu." JOURNAL OF THE MALAY BRANCH
OF THE ROYAL ASIATIC SOCIETY, 40, No. 2 (1967), 94-105.

1919   Winstedt, Richard. "The Chronicles of Pasai." JOURNAL OF THE
MALAY BRANCH OF THE ROYAL ASIATIC SOCIETY, 16, No. 1
(1938), 23-40.

1920   _____. "Malay Chronicles from Sumatra and Malaya." In HISTORIANS
OF SOUTHEAST ASIA, pp. 24-28. See entry no. 1657.

Studies of the oldest Malay chronicle and a source for the
SEJARAH MĒLAYU (see below). Uses material from the
Indian MAHĀBHĀRATA and RĀMĀYANA and other sources for
stories attached to historical personages.

Hikayat Seri Rāma (traditional)

1921   Barrett, E.C.G. "Further Light on Sir Richard Winstedt's 'Undescribed
Malay Version of the RĀMĀYANA.'" BULLETIN OF THE SCHOOL OF
ORIENTAL AND AFRICAN STUDIES, 26 (1963), 531-43.

On the first version in Malay of the Hindu epic, which was
in Malaya as early as the tenth century. The Hindu story
underwent Islamic adjustments later.

1922   Francisco, Juan R. "The Rāma Story in the post-Muslim Malay Literature of Southeast Asia." SARAWAK MUSUEM JOURNAL, 10 (1962),
468-85.

Comparisons of late versions, including folk versions, of the
epic.

1923   Overbeck H. "HIKAYAT MAHARAJA RAVANA." JOURNAL OF THE MALAY BRANCH OF THE ROYAL ASIATIC SOCIETY, 11, No. 2 (1933), 111-32.

On a late Malay version of the RĀMĀYANA.

1924   Zieseniss, Alexander. THE RĀMA SAGE IN MALAYSIA, ITS ORIGIN AND DEVELOPMENT. Trans. P.W. Burch. Singapore: Malaysian Sociological Research Institute, 1963.

Includes a lengthy summary of the Malay version, notes, and comparisons with the Sanskrit original.

1925   Zoetmuller, Petrus J. "Rāmāyana Kakawin." In KALANGWAN, pp. 217-33. See entry no. 1909.

Lengthy summary of the Malay version of the story.

Hikayat Sultan Bustaman

1926   Overbeck, H. "Hikayat Sultan Bustaman." JOURNAL OF THE MALAY BRANCH OF THE ROYAL ASIATIC SOCIETY, 9, No. 2, 33-122.

Malay version of the story of the famous Arab sultan which reflects the glory of the Moslem conquest of India.

Kedah Annals

1927   Winstedt, Richard. "The Kedah Annals." JOURNAL OF THE MALAY BRANCH OF THE ROYAL ASIATIC SOCIETY, 16, No. 2 (1938), 31-35.

A chronicle of adventure which makes reference to Rum (Rome) and China, with characters from the RĀMĀYANA but written by a Moslem.

Misa Melayu (eighteenth century)

1928   Maxwell, W.E., trans. "The Dutch in Perak." JOURNAL OF THE MALAY BRANCH OF THE ROYAL ASIATIC SOCIETY, 9, No. 2 (1882), 258-66.

Extracts from a verse chronicle depicting life at the court of Perak by a contemporary author.

Munshi Abdullah (1797-1854)

1929   Hill, A.H., trans. "The HIKYAT ABDULLAH, an Annotated Translation."

Malaya and Singapore

JOURNAL OF THE MALAY BRANCH OF THE ROYAL ASIATIC SOCIETY, 44, No. 2, (1971), 79-107.

Written in 1849, by a clerk to the Raffles embassy, this account records the British conquest of Malaya and the personalities involved from the inside. An index follows the pages of translation.

Peran Hutan

1930 Sweeney, Pil Amin. "PERAN HUTAN, a Malay WAYANG Drama." JOURNAL OF THE MALAY BRANCH OF THE ROYAL ASIATIC SOCIETY, 44, No. 2 (1971), 79-107.

A brief description of a popular play concerning a clownish jungle hunter. Illustrated. Text, but no translation.

Sejarah Mĕlayu (Malay Chronicle) (fifteenth-sixteenth centuries)

TRANSLATIONS

1931 Brown, C.C., trans. "The Malay Annals." JOURNAL OF THE MALAY BRANCH OF THE ROYAL ASIATIC SOCIETY, 25, Nos. 2-3 (1952), 1-276.

Often considered to be the finest work in Malay. Stories of the rulers and the courts at Malacca.

STUDIES

1932 Abdul Wahid, Zainal Abidin Bin." "SEJARAH MĔLAYU." ASIAN STUDIES, 4 (1966), 445-51.

Attempts to place the problem of dating the work and its legendary material into a Malayan perspective.

1933 Brown, C.C. "A Malay Herodotus." BULLETIN OF THE SCHOOL OF ORIENTAL AND AFRICAN STUDIES, 12 (1948), 730-36.

On the style and content--the author is compared with the anecdotal stories of the historian.

1934 Winstedt, Richard. "The Malay Annals or SEJARAH MĔLAYU." JOURNAL OF THE MALAY BRANCH OF THE ROYAL ASIATIC SOCIETY, 16, No. 1 (1938), 1-226.

Includes the Malay text and a chapter-by-chapter summary of the chronicle in English.

F. MODERN LITERATURE

1. Anthologies

1935   Rice, Oliver, and Abdallah Majid, eds. and trans. MODERN MALAY VERSE, 1946-1961. Kuala Lumpur: Oxford Univ. Press, 1963.

        A good anthology--six modern poets with about eight poems each translated with Malay parallel texts.

1936   Wignesan, T., ed. BUNGA EMAS: AN ANTHOLOGY OF CON-TEMPORARY MALAYSIAN LITERATURE, 1930-1963. [Kuala Lumpur]: A. Blong, [1964].

        A large, well-selected collection of poems and short stories originally written in English, Chinese, Tamil, and Malay. Includes an essay, "The Malayan Short Story in English," pp. 234-39, by T. Wignesan.

2. History and Criticism

1937   Ang Tien Se. "Modern Chinese Drama in Malaysia and Singapore." TENGGARA, 6 (1973), 140-53.

        Notes the rapid rise in the number of plays produced since 1925 with brief notes on many plays.

1938   Fernando, Lloyd. "The Relation of Sectional Literatures to the National Literature." TENGGARA, 6 (1973), 121-27.

        Concerns the development of a national consciousness in litera-ture by authors who write in Malay, Chinese, Indian languages, English, and other languages.

1939   Hamid, A. Baker. "Malay Novels of 1971." TENGGARA, 6 (1973), 154-59.

        List with brief comments.

1940   Han Suyin. "The Creation of a Malay Literature." EASTERN WORLD, 11, No. 5 (May 1957), 20-21.

        Brief discussion of the recent attempts to unite the various language traditions of Malaya into a national literature.

1941   Ismail, Yahya. "Malay Literary Guide for 1967." TENGGARA, 2 (1967), 127-31.

1942   _____. "Malay Literary Guide for 1966 and 1967." TENGGARA, 2 (1968), 90-97.

1943   Li Chuan-Siu. A BIRD'S-EYE VIEW OF THE DEVELOPMENT OF MOD-
ERN MALAY LITERATURE, 1921-1941. Kuala Lumpur: Penerbitan
Pustaka, 1970.

   Brief account beginning with literary societies and government
   support of literature. Discusses twelve authors and their works.

1944   _____. AN INTRODUCTION TO THE PROMOTION AND DEVELOP-
MENT OF MODERN MALAY LITERATURE, 1942-1962. [Kuala Lumpur]:
Penerbitan Yayasan Kanisius, 1975.

   Useful. Mostly about "promotion": Societies, official language reform, education, congresses, publishing, and others.

1945   Osman, Mohammad Taib. AN INTRODUCTION TO THE DEVELOPMENT
OF MODERN MALAY LANGUAGE AND LITERATURE. Singapore:
Eastern Universities Press, 1961.

1946   _____. MODERN MALAY LITERATURE. Kuala Lumpur: Dewan
Bahasa dan Pustaka for the Ministry of Education, 1965.

1947   _____. "Towards the Development of Malaysia's National Literature."
TENGGARA, 6 (1973), 105-20.

   Three useful brief works. The problem of developing national
   consciousness in a multilanguage culture is a central theme.

1948   _____. "Trends in Modern Malay Literature." In MALAYSIA. Ed.
Gungwu Wang. New York: Praeger, [1964], pp. 210-24.

1949   REPORT OF THE MALAYAN WRITERS' CONFERENCE, SINGAPORE,
1962. [Singapore: Dewan Bahasa dan Kebudayaan Kebangsaan, n.d.]

   Reports and summaries of papers on a great many literary subjects.

1950   Roff, William R. "The Mystery of the First Malay Novel (and Who
Was Rokambul?)." BIJDRAGEN TOT DE TAAL-, LAND, EN VOLKEN-
KUNDE, 130 (1974), 450-64.

   The first modern novel is said to have been FARIDAH HANUM
   (1925-26) but KECHURIAN LIMA MILLION RINGGIT (TALE OF
   THE THEFT OF FIVE MILLION DOLLARS) was published in 1922.
   Concerned with popular fiction of the "Nick Carter" variety.

1951   Salleh, Muhammad Haji. "Tradition and Innovation in Contemporary
Malayan-Indonesian Poetry." TENGGARA, 7 (1975), 36-83.

   Excellent study of modern trends with many translated examples.

1952 Wang Gung-Wu. "A Short Introduction to Chinese Writing in Malaya." In BUNGA EMAS, pp. 254-56. See entry no. 1936.

Surveys Chinese writing from the beginnings of the twentieth century, and notes a new generation who have not had an English education since 1945.

1953 Wignesan, T. "A Brief Survey of Contemporary Malay Literature." In BUNGA EMAS, pp. 243-48. See entry no. 1936.

1954 _____. "The Malayan Short Story in English." In BUNGA EMAS, pp. 234-39. See entry no. 1936.

1955 _____. "Origin and Scope of Tamil Literature in Malaysia." In BUNGA EMAS, pp. 240-42. See entry no. 1936.

Three useful articles. The Tamil literary contributions appear mostly in newspapers and in radio broadcasts.

1956 Za'ba [Zain al-'Abidin bin Ahmad]. "Recent Malay Literature." JOURNAL OF THE MALAY BRANCH OF THE ROYAL ASIATIC SOCIETY, 19, No. 1 (1941), 1-20.

Lists many works and authors, including periodical materials.

3. Authors and Works

SHANNON, AHMAD (1933-)

1957 Johns, Anthony H. "Man in a Merciless Universe: The Work of Shannon Ahmad." TENGGARA, 6 (1973), 128-39.

Discussion of the works of a realistic modern novelist.

SONTANI, UTUY TATANG (1920-)

1958 Aveling, H.G. "Seventeenth Century Bandanese Society in Fact and Fiction: TAMBERA Assessed." BIJDRAGEN TOT DE TAAL-, LAND-, EN VOLKENKUNDE, 123 (1967), 347-65.

Discussion of a novel about an adolescent boy named Tambera in a Moloccan village. By a major dramatist and writer of fiction.

G. PERIODICALS

1959 JOURNAL OF THE MALAY BRANCH OF THE ROYAL ASIATIC SOCIETY. Singapore: Royal Asiatic Society of Great Britain and Ireland, Malay Branch, 1923-- .

The major scholarly journal of Malay studies in all fields.
Articles mostly in English. Preceded by the JOURNAL OF
THE STRAITS BRANCH OF THE ROYAL ASIATIC SOCIETY
(nos. 1-86; July 1878-November 1922).

1960 TENGGARA. Kuala Lumpur: Raybooks Magazine. 1967-- .

A superior literary journal. Many articles and translations
of modern literature and some material on early literature.

Chapter 11
THAILAND (SIAM)

A. BIBLIOGRAPHY

1961   BIBLIOGRAPHY OF MATERIALS ABOUT THAILAND IN WESTERN
        LANGUAGES. Bangkok: Chulalongkorn Mahawitthayalai Hong Samut
        [Chulalongkorn Univ. Library], 1960.

      A comprehensive bibliography of about four thousand books
      and articles arranged by subject. No annotations.

1962   Bitz, Ira, comp. A BIBLIOGRAPHY OF CONTEMPORARY ENGLISH-
        LANGUAGE SOURCE MATERIALS ON THAILAND IN THE HUMANI-
        TIES, SOCIAL SCIENCES, AND PHYSICAL SCIENCES. Washington,
        D.C.: American Univ., 1968.

      A large bibliography but difficult to use for literary references.

1963   Brown, John M., and H. Carroll Parish, comps. THAILAND BIBLIOG-
        RAPHY. Gainesville: Univ. of Florida Libraries, 1958.

      Over two thousand books and articles. Still useful, but out-
      dated.

1964   Nagelkerke, G.A., comp. BIBLIOGRAPHICAL SURVEY OF THAILAND
        BASED ON BOOKS IN THE LIBRARY OF THE ROYAL INSTITUTE OF
        LINGUISTICS AND ANTHROPOLOGY AND ON ARTICLES IN THE
        JOURNAL OF THE SIAM SOCIETY. Leiden: Royal Institute of
        Linguistics and Antrhopology, 1974.

      A brief bibliography. Supplements Jenner (entry no. 1648)
      in listing the JOURNAL OF THE SIAM SOCIETY materials.

1965   Sharp, Lauriston, comp. BIBLIOGRAPHY OF THAILAND, A SELECTED
        LIST OF BOOKS AND ARTICLES. Ithaca: Cornell Univ., 1956.

      Brief. About thirty-three books and articles. Good
      selection but now outdated.

1966   Simmonds, E.H.S., comp. "Tai Literatures: A Bibliography of Works in Foreign Languages." BULLETIN OF THE ASSOCIATION OF BRITISH ORIENTALISTS, 3 (1965), 5-60.

        Very complete. Over five hundred items with author index.

1967   Thrombley, Woodward G., and William J. Siffin, comps. THAILAND: POLITICS, ECONOMIC AND SOCIO-POLITICAL SETTING, A SELECTIVE GUIDE TO THE LITERATURE. Bloomington: Indiana Univ. Press, 1972.

        Annotated. A good brief selection.

B. REFERENCE

1968   Busch, Noel Fairchild. THAILAND, AN INTRODUCTION TO MODERN SIAM. Princeton: Van Nostrand, 1959.

        A good introduction with enough reference to traditional history and culture to serve as a general guide. Some material on literature (including the RAMAKIEN), pp. 130-46.

1969   Chula Chakrabongse. LORDS OF LIFE: THE PATERNAL MONARCHY OF BANGKOK 1782-1902, WITH THE EARLIER AND MORE RECENT HISTORY OF THAILAND. New York: Taplinger, 1961.

        Detailed history, especially useful for the eighteenth century.

1970   Darling, Frank C., and Ann Darling. THAILAND, THE MODERN KINGDOM. Singapore: Donald Moore for Asia Pacific Press, 1971.

        Contains a good section on culture and some material on literature.

1971   Graham, W[alter] A. SIAM. 2 vols. London: Alexander Moring, 1924.

        Perhaps the best introduction to Thai culture for the general reader. Topically arranged. Art, music, dance, and drama in volume 2.

1972   Wood, William A.R. A HISTORY OF SIAM FROM THE EARLIEST TIMES TO THE YEAR A.D. 1781. Bangkok: Sam Bannakich Press, 1933; rpt. New York: AMS Press, 1972.

        A major work now in need of correction. It has not been superseded as a general picture of early Siam.

C. LITERARY HISTORY AND CRITICISM

1973   Anuman Radjadhon, Phraya. THE NATURE AND DEVELOPMENT OF

THAI LANGUAGE. Bangkok: Department of Fine Arts, [1961].

Brief, useful essay on the nature of the language.

1974 _____. THAI LITERATURE AND "SWASDI RAKSA." 4th ed. Bangkok: National Cultural Institute, 1956.

A useful summary of the main types. The SWASDI RAKSA is by Sunthorn Bhu (see below).

1975 _____. THAI LITERATURE IN RELATION TO THE DIFFUSION OF HER CULTURE. 3d ed. Bangkok: Department of Fine Arts, 1963.

Brief essay on the literature in a wider Southeast-Asian perspective.

1976 Bhakdi, Saiyude. "Siamese Literature." In ENCYCLOPEDIA OF WORLD LITERATURE. Ed. Joseph T. Shipley. New York: Philosophical Library, [1946], II, pp. 843-46.

An excellent introductory sketch.

1977 Hla Nai Pan. "Mon Literature and Culture over Thailand and Burma." JOURNAL OF THE BURMA RESEARCH SOCIETY, 41 (1958), 65-75.

A sketch of one of the sub-literatures of Thailand and Burma.

1978 Manich Jumsai, M.L. HISTORY OF THAI LITERATURE (INCLUDING LAOS, SHAN, KHAMTI, AHORN AND YUNNAN-NANCHAO). Bangkok: Chalermnit Press, [1973?].

A lengthy account covering the whole area. A popular history with lengthy retellings of plots.

1979 Prem Purachatra, Prince [Prem Chaya]. INTRODUCTION TO THAI LITERATURE. [Bangkok?: n.p., n.d.]

A good brief sketch of Thai literature by a literary specialist who was also a distinguished diplomat. This printing was apparently private and intended for distribution at a conference. It may have appeared elsewhere.

1980 _____. "Thailand and her Literature." DILIMAN REVIEW [Quezon City], 6 (1958), 251-66.

Touches on the highlights from the earliest times, with special attention to the PRA LAW (see below, entry nos. 2015-16).

1981 Siwasariyanon, Nai Witt. "Trends and High-Lights of Thai Literature." ASIAN REVIEW, 57 (1961), 295-303.

A very general sketch ranging from folk literature to romances. with some discussion of analogies with Western literature.

1982   S[nellgrove], D.L.   "Thai Literature."   In CASSELL'S ENCYCLOPEDIA OF WORLD LITERATURE.   London: Cassell, 1973, I, pp. 553-56.

Perhaps the best introductory sketch.

D. POETRY

1983   Bidyalankarana, <u>Prince.</u>   "The Pastime of Rhyme-Making and Singing in Rural Siam."   JOURNAL OF THE SIAM SOCIETY, 20, No. 2 (1926), 101-27.

On the nature and technique of popular poetry.

1984   Chitakasem, Manas.   "The Emergence and Development of the Nirat Genre in Thai Poetry."   JOURNAL OF THE SIAM SOCIETY, 60, No. 2 (1972), 135-68.

A comprehensive article on a type of poetry traditionally composed on long journeys away from home.

1985   Mosel, James N.   A SURVEY OF CLASSICAL THAI POETRY.   Bangkok: W. Areekul for the BANGKOK WORLD, 1959.

A commentary and the Thai text to accompany a tape recording of Thai poetry.

1986   Pramoj, M.R. Seni.   "A Poetic Translation from the Siamese: A Lokaniti Verse."   JOURNAL OF THE SIAM SOCIETY, 47, No. 2 (1959), 179.

A short selection of sacred poetry carved in stone on the Wat Phra Setuphon.

1987   Simmonds, E.H.S.   "Epic-Romance Poetry in Thailand."   SANGHHOM-SAT PARITHAT (SOCIAL SCIENCE REVIEW), 1, No. 2 (October 1963), 100-106.

A sketch of a major genre of traditional Thai poetry.

1988   Soonsawad, Thong-In.   THE THAI POETS: A GUIDE TO THE COLLECTED POETRY OF THAILAND AND THE WORKS OF THE MAJOR THAI POETS.   Bangkok: Poetry Society of Thailand and Office of Panorama of Thailand, 1968.

There is much useful information in this, but the translated material is poor.

E. DRAMA

1989   Dhaninivat Sonakul, Prince. "The DALANG." JOURNAL OF THE
SIAM SOCIETY, 43, No. 2 (1956), 113-35.

Historical background and summary of the plot of a Thai
drama based on the Panji cycle of romance.

1990   _____. THE KHON (MASKED PLAY). Bangkok: National Cultural
Institute, [1955].

Brief essay on a traditional dramatic genre.

1991   _____. THE NANG (SHADOW PLAY). Bangkok: National Cultural
Institute, [1955].

Brief sketch of this popular Southeast-Asian puppet play as it
is presented in Thailand.

1992   _____. The Shadow-Play as a Possible Origin of the Masked Play."
JOURNAL OF THE SIAM SOCIETY, 37, No. 1 (1948), 26-32.

On the early history of these two forms, with summaries of
plots.

1993   Ginsberg, Harry D. "The Manora Dance-Drama, an Introduction."
JOURNAL OF THE SIAM SOCIETY, 60, No. 2 (1972), 169-81.

A dance drama associated with the shadow play. The tale of
a heavenly bird-maiden and a prince from the Indian JATAKA
tales.

1994   Rutnin, Mattani. THE SIAMESE THEATRE, A COLLECTION OF RE-
PRINTS FROM THE JOURNAL OF THE SIAM SOCIETY. Bangkok:
[S. Chaicharoen], 1975.

An extensive and excellent collection of articles in a printing
superior to the originals. Most articles in English. Good
illustrations.

1995   Simmonds, E.H.S. "Some Evidence on Thai Shadow-Play Invocations."
BULLETIN OF THE SCHOOL OF ORIENTAL AND AFRICAN STUDIES,
24 (1961), 542-59.

A technical textual study suggesting a link between Thai,
Cambodian, Javanese, and Balinese ceremonial usages.

1996   Singaravelu, S. "Invocation to Nataraja in the Southeast Asian Shadow
Plays." JOURNAL OF THE SIAM SOCIETY, 58, No. 2 (1970), 43-54.

On invocations to the god Shiva, as transplanted to Southeast
Asia including Thailand.

1997 Smithies, Michael, and Euayporn Kerdchouay. "Nang Talung: The Shadow Theatre of Southern Thailand." JOURNAL OF THE SIAM SOCIETY, 60, No. 1 (1972), 377-90.

> A good description of all aspects of performance--theaters, actors, audience, and plays.

1998 Vajirāvudh, Mahā. "Notes of the Siamese Theatre." JOURNAL OF THE SIAM SOCIETY, 55, No. 1 (1967), 1-30.

> Notes on traditional types of theatrical performances followed by a classified list of characters in the RAMAYANA (see below, entries nos. 2017-23).

1999 Yuphō Dhanit. THE KHON AND LAKON: DANCE DRAMAS PRE-SENTED BY THE DEPARTMENT OF FINE ARTS. Bangkok: Department of Fine Arts, 1963.

> Lengthy study of traditional theater. Illustrated. Contains librettos, historical background, and notes.

2000 _____. THE PRELIMINARY COURSE OF TRAINING IN THE THEATRI-CAL ART. 2d rev. ed. Bangkok: Department of Fine Arts, [1954].

> A good brief essay on the training of the actor for the traditional theater.

F. FICTION

2001 Anuman, Rajadhon, Phraya. "A Study on the Thai Folk Tale." JOUR-NAL OF THE SIAM SOCIETY, 53, No. 2 (1968), 133-37.

> Brief account of a folk fantasy with connections with Mon history and Indian legend.

2002 Feinstein, Alan S., ed. FOLK TALES FROM SIAM. South Brunswick, N.J.: A.S. Barnes, 1969.

> Eighteen tales, mostly about animals and spirits.

2003 Ginsberg, Harry D. "The Thai Tale of Nang Tantrai and the Pisaca Tales." JOURNAL OF THE SIAM SOCIETY, 63, No. 1 (1975), 279-314.

> Summary of a folk tale derived from the Indian collection of animal tales, the PANCHATANTRA.

2004 Le May, Reginald, trans. SIAMESE TALES OLD AND NEW: THE FOUR RIDDLES AND OTHER STORIES. 2d rev. ed. London: Arthur Probsthain, 1958.

> A good selection of folk tales and popular stories.

2005   Seidenfaden, E. "Fairy Tales of Common Origin." JOURNAL OF
THE SIAM SOCIETY, 33, No. 1 (1941), 143-45.

2006   ____. "Further Notes on Fairy Tales of Common Origin." JOURNAL
OF THE SIAM SOCIETY, 34, No. 1 (1943), 59-62.

Connections between Siamese fairy tales and world-wide story
complexes.

G. EARLIER AUTHORS AND WORKS

Chronicle of the Emerald Buddha

2007   Notton, Camile, trans. THE CHRONICLE OF THE EMERALD BUDDHA.
[Bangkok: Bangkok Times Press], 1933.

Translation of a metrical chronicle on a palm leaf manuscript
in Pali and northern Thai.

Damrong, Prince (fl. 1893)

2008   Mosel, James N., trans. "A Poetic Translation from the Siamese:
Prince Damrong's Reply in Verse to Rama V." JOURNAL OF THE
SIAM SOCIETY, 47, No. 1 (1959), 103-11.

After the French invasion, King Chulalongkorn, seriously ill
and in despair, composed a poem saying goodbye to the royal
family. Prince Damrong's reply (1893) restored the king's
spirits. Translation and parallel Thai text.

Jātakas (traditional)

2009   Martini, Ginette, trans. "Pañcabuddabyākarapa." BULLETIN DE
L'ÉCOLE FRANÇAISE D'EXTRÊME-ORIENT, 45 (1969), 125-44.

Translation of a metrical Thai version of an Indian story with
commentary. Plates accompany the texts.

Khun Chāng Khun Phāēn (eighteenth century)

2010   Bidya, Prince. "Sebhā Recitation and the Story of Khun Chāng Khun
Pham." JOURNAL OF THE SIAM SOCIETY, 33, No. 1 (1941), 1-42.

This work is the great national epic of Thailand, redacted
and modified by various literary figures from King Rama II
(1763-1824) to Sunthorn Bhu (1786-1856). This article deals
with the rural tradition of reciting the story in rhyme.

2011   Prem Purachatra, Prince [Prem Chaya]. THE STORY OF KUNG
CHANG KUNG PHAN, TOLD IN ENGLISH. 2 vols. Bangkok:
Chatra Books, 1955.

> Books 1 and 2 retold in English. An account of court in-
> trigue in the early eighteenth century and a good picture of
> social life.

2012   Simmonds, D.H.S. "Thai Narrative Poetry: Palace and Provincial
Texts of an Episode from KUNG CHANG KHUN PHAEN." ASIA
MINOR, 10 (1963), 279-99.

> Compares a local version of the story with the main tradition.

Paksi Pakaranam (Book of the Birds)

2013   Crosby, J., trans. "A Translation of THE BOOK OF THE BIRDS."
JOURNAL OF THE SIAM SOCIETY, 7, No. 1 (1911), 1-90.

> A work of fantasy with religious overtones.

Phayaphrom (1802-87)

2014   Egerod, Søren, ed. and trans. PHAYAPHROM: THE POEM IN FOUR
SONGS, A NORTHERN THAI TETRAOLOGY. Lund, Sweden: Student-
litteratur, [1971].

> An important philosophical poem.

Pra Law (Phra Lo) (fifteenth century)

2015   Dhaninivat Sonakul, Prince. "The Date and Authorship of the Romance
of PHRA LO." JOURNAL OF THE SIAM SOCIETY, 41, No. 2 (1954),
179-83.

> A drama of court intrigue. This essay concerns itself with the
> historical background.

2016   Prem Purchatra, Prince [Phrem Chaya]. MAGIC LOTUS: A ROMANTIC
FANTASY. AN ADAPTATION FOR THE ENGLISH STAGE OF THE
FIFTEENTH-CENTURY SIAMESE CLASSIC PLAY "PRA LAW." 3d ed.
Bangkok: Chatra Books, 1949.

> The best introduction to the story for the general reader.

Rāmāyana (Ramakien) (traditional)

2017   Attagara, Kingkeo. "The RĀMĀYANA Epic in Thailand and Southeast

Asia." JOURNAL OF THE ASSAM RESEARCH SOCIETY, 15 (1961), 3-21.

> General survey of the varieties of the Hindu epic of Prince Rāma in Southeast Asia.

2018 Bocles, J.J. "A RĀMĀYANA Relief from the Khmer Sandung at Pimai in North-East Thailand." JOURNAL OF THE SIAM SOCIETY, 57, No. 1 (1969), 163-69.

> Illustrative of the varieties of the story in sculpture. Good plates.

2019 Cadet, J.M. THE RĀMAKĪEN: THE THAI EPIC, ILLUSTRATED WITH THE BAS RELIEF OF WAT PHRA JETUBON. Tokyo: Kodansha International, [1971].

> A handsome edition integrating the literary versions with a long series of bas reliefs. Excellent illustrations.

2020 Dhaninivat, Kromamum, Prince. "Hide Figures of the RĀMAKĪEN at the Ledermuseum in Offenback, Germany." JOURNAL OF THE SIAM SOCIETY, 53, No. 1 (1965), 60-66.

> Contains good illustrations of the leather, two-dimensional, articulated puppets used in the shadow plays.

2021 _____. "The RĀMAKĪEN: A Siamese Version of the Story of Rāma." In BURMA RESEARCH SOCIETY, FIFTIETH ANNIVERSARY PUBLICATIONS NO. 1. Rangoon: Burma Research Society, 1961, pp. 33-45.

> Summary and commentary on the story.

2022 Singaravelu, S. "A Comparative Study of the Sanskrit, Tamil, Thai, and Malay Versions of the Story of Rāma with Special Reference to the Process of Acculturation in Southeast Asian Versions." JOURNAL OF THE SIAM SOCIETY, 41, No. 2 (1968), 137-85.

> Extensive study of the migrations of the story with an analysis of the motifs.

2023 Velder, Christian. "Notes on the Saga of Rāma in Thailand." JOURNAL OF THE SIAM SOCIETY, 56, No. 1 (1956), 33-46.

> Traces the story from 1283 and follows its transformation into the RĀMAKĪEN version of 1797.

Sunthōn Phū [Sunthorn Bhu] (1786-1855)

2024 Anuman Radjadhon, Phraya. THAI LITERATURE AND "SWASDI RAKSA." See entry no. 1974.

Thailand (Siam)

An analysis of the story is included in this work, and a free prose translation.

2025   Prem Purachatra, Prince [Prem Chaya]. THE STORY OF PHRA ABHAI MANI, SUNTHORN BHU'S FAMOUS SIAMESE CLASSIC, TOLD IN ENGLISH BY PREM CHAYA. [Bangkok]: Chatra Books, 1952.

A long imaginative romance of two brothers who are heroes in a world of magic. A very popular Thai classic.

H. MODERN LITERATURE

1. History, Criticism, Anthologies

2026   Fels, Jacqueline de. "Popular Literature in Thailand." JOURNAL OF THE SIAM SOCIETY, 63, No. 1 (1975), 219-38.

On modern fiction, including "best sellers," and how they differ from traditional works.

2027   Mosel, James N. "Contemporary Thai Poetry." UNITED ASIA, 12 (1960), 159-65.

Surveys the scene back to the nineteenth century--a good survey of essentials. Some translations.

2028   _____. TRENDS AND STRUCTURE IN CONTEMPORARY THAI POETRY. Ithaca: Cornell Univ. Press, 1961.

The best general introduction, with a substantial essay on Thai poetry and translations of eleven poems with Thai and English texts.

2029   Siwasariyanon, Witt, ed. THAI SHORT STORIES. Bangkok: International P.E.N., Thailand Centre, 1971.

A good collection of modern short stories.

2. Authors and Works

KHUKRIT PRĀMŌT [PRAMOJ KUKRIT]

2030   RED BAMBOO. Bangkok: Progress Bookstore, [1961].

A modern novel which is a political allegory.

PRAMUANMARG, V. NA [WIPHĀWADĪ RANGSIT]

2031   Tulachandra, trans. PRISNA. [Bangkok]: Chatra Books, 1961.

This is part 1 on a long modern novel. No more published.

RAMA VI, KING OF THAILAND [VAJIRAVUDH] (1881-1925)

2032   Dhaninivat Sonaku, Prince. "King Rama VI's Last Work." JOURNAL OF THE SIAM SOCIETY, 39, No. 2 (1952), 181-89.

MADANABĀDHĀ or "The Romance of the Rose" (1923) is a play mixing modern and traditional themes by one of Thailand's most prolific early twentieth-century writers. This article includes a summary of the work and correspondence about it.

2033   _____. MADANBĀDHĀ, OR THE ROMANCE OF A ROSE, A PLAY IN FIVE ACTS. Bangkok: Aksaraniti, 1925.

A retelling of the story for the modern stage.

2034   Pin Malakul, M.L. "Dramatic Achievement of King Rama VI." JOURNAL OF THE SIAM SOCIETY, 63, No. 1 (1975), 260-78.

A general assessment of his contribution. Illustrated, with plates.

I. PERIODICALS

2035   JOURNAL OF THE SIAM SOCIETY. Bangkok: Siam Society, 1904-- .

The major scholarly organ for Siamese studies. Includes translations and literary studies as well as articles on other disciplines.

Chapter 12
VIETNAM

A. BIBLIOGRAPHY

2036 Chen, John H.M., comp. VIETNAM, A COMPREHENSIVE BIBLIOG-
RAPHY. Metuchen, N.J.: Scarecrow Press, 1973.

A list of over two thousand items with cross-references to
subjects.

2037 Cong-Huyen-Ton-Nu, Nha-Trang. VIETNAMESE FOLKLORE, AN
INTRODUCTION AND ANNOTATED BIBLIOGRAPHY. Berkeley:
Center for South and Southeast Asia Studies, 1970.

A brief introduction to the subject.

2038 Keynes, Jane Godfrey, comp. A BIBLIOGRAPHY OF WESTERN-
LANGUAGE PUBLICATIONS CONCERNING NORTH VIETNAM IN
THE CORNELL UNIVERSITY LIBRARY. Ithaca: Cornell Univ., South-
east Asia Program, 1966.

A useful, subject-classified list. Little literary material.

2039 Nguyễn Khắc Khan, comp. "Bibliography on the Acceptance of Western Cultures in Vietnam from the Sixteenth to the Twentieth Centuries."
EAST ASIA CULTURAL STUDIES, 6 (1967), 228–49.

Lists about 280 books and articles in Vietnamese and in
European languages.

2040 Ross, Marion W., comp. BIBLIOGRAPHY OF VIETNAMESE LITERATURES
IN THE WASON COLLECTION AT CORNELL UNIVERSITY. Ithaca:
Cornell Univ., Southeast Asia Program, 1973.

About 2,800 items, with subject indexes, including works in
English and French.

2041 Tran-Thi-Kim-Sa, comp. BIBLIOGRAPHY ON VIETNAM, 1954–1964.

Saigon: National Institute of Administration, 1965.

Includes about three thousand items, mostly in English and French.

B. REFERENCE

2042 AREA HANDBOOK FOR VIETNAM. Washington, D.C.: Government Printing Office, 1967.

A good general reference work done by a group at American University.

2043 Buttinger, Joseph. A DRAGON DEFIANT: A SHORT HISTORY OF VIETNAM. New York: Praeger, [1972].

Useful, especially on the pre-modern period, where little material is available.

2044 Nguyễn Dinh-Hoà, et al. SOME ASPECTS OF VIETNAMESE CULTURE. Carbondale: Southern Illinois Univ. Center for Vietnamese Studies, 1972.

Relevant articles are noted below.

2045 Smith, Ralph B. VIET-NAM AND THE WEST. Ithaca: Cornell Univ. Press, [1971].

Covers 1858-1907. A good cultural history. The first chapter is a good brief account of the historical tradition.

2046 Thai-Van-Kiem. VIETNAM PAST AND PRESENT. [Paris and Saigon: Vietnam Department of Education and National Commission for UNESCO, 1957].

A useful popular guide to all aspects of Vietnamese life. Profusely illustrated.

C. LITERARY HISTORY AND CRITICISM

2047 Aimy, B.D. "The Moon in the Literature of Viet-Nam." ASIA, 1 (1951), 394-402.

2048 Doan-Van-An. "Brief History of Vietnamese Literature." ASIAN CULTURE, 3, No. 2 (1961), 31-40.

2049 THE EVOLUTION OF VIETNAMESE LITERATURE FROM "NOM" TO ROMANIZED CHARACTER. Saigon: Horizons, [1957].

This and the preceding entry are two useful brief sketches
of the history of the literature (see also entry no. 2051).

2050   Lien Ahn. "Pessimism in Vietnamese Poetry." ASIA, 3 (1953), 397–
        400.

2051   L[oofs], H.H.E. "Vietnamese Literature." CASSELL'S ENCYCLOPEDIA
        OF WORLD LITERATURE. London: Cassell, 1963, I, pp. 577–79.

        Perhaps the best brief sketch of all aspects.

2052   Nguyên Dinh-Hoà. "Vietnamese Language and Literature." In SOME
        ASPECTS OF VIETNAMESE CULTURE, pp. 1–18. See entry no. 2044.

        A brief sketch of the nature of the language and an essay on
        the literature.

2053   Schultz, George F. "The Vietnamese Language." VIET-MY [Saigon],
        3, No. 1 (March 1958), 37–43.

        Includes some useful notes on the script.

2054   Shaffer, H.L., Jr. "Literary Examination in Old Vietnam." VIET-MY,
        8, No. 1 (March 1963), 38–45.

        Interesting brief account of the use in early Vietnam of the
        Chinese system of examinations on the Confucian classics for
        qualification to government posts.

2055   Song-Ban. THE VIETNAMESE THEATRE. Hanoi: Foreign Languages
        Publishing House, 1960.

        Brief account of the theater of social protest.

D. POETRY

2056   Burton, Eva. "Communication in Vietnamese Poetry." VAN-HOA
        NGUYETSAN [Saigon], 13, No. 9 (September 1964), 1265–73.

        Technical analysis of "tender" and "aggressive" consonants as
        a stylistic device, based on the method of Ivan Fonagy.

2057   Ly-Chanh-Trung. INTRODUCTION TO VIETNAMESE POETRY. Trans.
        Kenneth Kilshire. [Saigon: Department of National Education, 1960].

        A good introductory sketch of the general nature of Vietnam-
        ese poetry.

2058   Nguyên Ngoe Bích. "The Poetic Tradition of Vietnam." In SOME

ASPECTS OF VIETNAMESE CULTURE, pp. 19-38. See entry no. 2044.

A critical essay with prose translations of both early and modern poetry.

2059 _____, trans. A THOUSAND YEARS OF VIETNAMESE POETRY. With Burton Raffel and W.S. Merwin. New York: Alfred A. Knopf, 1975.

A large selection of poetry from 987 to modern times, with some historical and critical comment. The best introduction available.

2060 Raffel, Burton, trans. FROM THE VIETNAMESE: TEN CENTURIES OF POETRY. New York: October House, [1968].

A good brief collection of superior translations.

2061 Shimer, Dorothy Blair, ed. VOICES OF MODERN ASIA. See entry no. 36.

Contains one poem each by eleven Vietnamese poets.

2062 V.-L. "Vietnamese Poetry in the 16th Century." ASIA, 4 (1953), 566-74.

Provides a fuller coverage of the early period than other accounts.

2064 Vu-Huy-Chan. "Singing--From the Rice Field to the Vietnamese Theatre." VIET-MY, 3, No. 3 (June 1958), 12-21.

A good essay tracing the development of popular song from its folk origins to its use in the theater. Some translations included.

E. FICTION

2065 Chivas-Baron, Cl. STORIES AND LEGENDS OF ANNAM. Trans. from French by E.M. Smith-Dampier. New York: A. Melrose, 1920.

Large collection of Vietnamese folk tales, retold.

2066 THE FIRST MOSQUITO AND OTHER STORIES. Hanoi: Foreign Languages Publishing House, 1958.

2067 Hoa-Mai. THE PEASANT, THE BUFFALO, AND THE TIGER: VIETNAMESE LEGENDS. Hanoi: Foreign Languages Publishing House, [1958].

This and the preceding entries are collections containing popular tales and legends.

2068   Schultz, George F. VIETNAMESE LEGENDS. Rutland, Vt.: Charles E. Tuttle Co., 1965.

Vietnamese legends retold for young readers.

2069   Vo-Dinh. THE TOAD IS THE EMPEROR'S UNCLE: ANIMAL FOLK-TALES FROM VIET-NAM. Garden City, N.Y.: Doubleday, [1970].

Eighteen traditional animal tales.

F. EARLIER AUTHORS AND WORKS

Dang-Trân-Côn (fl. 1740)

2070   Alley, Rewi, trans. LAMENT OF THE SOLDIER'S WIFE. Hanoi: Foreign Languages Publishing House, [1959?].

2071   Burrowes, William D., trans. "CHINH PHU NGAM, or Lament of a Warrior's Wife." ASIATISCHE STUDIEN, 1 (1955), 70-94.

A very popular love lament written about the year 1740. Alley's translation is highly readable and freer than Burrowes', which is scholarly and annotated.

Nguyên Dinh Chieu (1822-88)

2072   Vu Dinh Lien. "Nguyên Dinh Chieu, the Bard of South Vietnam." VIETNAMESE STUDIES, 1 (1964), 263-78.

Account of a patriotic poet who fought the French and produced the LAC-VAN-TIEN, a moralizing epic.

Nguyên Du (1765-1820)

TRANSLATIONS

2073   Le-Xuan-Thuy, trans. KIM-VÂN-KIÊU. 2d ed. Saigon: Khai-Tri, 1968.

The KIM-VÂN-KIÊU (named after its heroine) is considered the greatest poem in Vietnamese. Containing over three thousand lines, it depicts the emotions and inner life of a talented young woman. Translations with notes and commentary.

Vietnam

2074 Negherbon, William, trans. "The Story of Lady Kiều." In SOME
ASPECTS OF VIETNAMESE CULTURE, pp. 39-58. See entry no. 2044.

An appreciation and retelling, with translations of selected
passages.

2075 "Nguyễn Du and 'Kiều.'" VIETNAMESE STUDIES, 4 (1965), 2-111.

An essay on Du and his times, and translations from the KIM-
VĂN-KIỀU and other works. Important.

2076 Nguyễn Phuroc Thien. "KIM VĂN KIỀU." VIET-MY, 8, No. 2 (June
1963), 6-15.

a retelling of the story with comments.

STUDIES

2077 Thai-Văn-Kieu. "A Literary, Philosophical and Scientific Study of the
KIM-VĂN-KIỀU." In VIETNAM PAST AND PRESENT, pp. 107-27.
See entry no. 2046.

A summary of the work with comments.

2078 Tran-Quang-Thuan. ESTHETIC PSYCHOLOGY OF "KIM-VĂN-KIỀU"
OR KIEU'S REAL AND DREAM WORLD. [Saigon: Dat-Tu, 1966].

An interesting attempt to bring modern psychology to bear on
the work.

G. MODERN LITERATURE

1. Anthologies

2079 THE FIRE BLAZES. Hanoi: Foreign Languages Publishing House, 1965.
Modern short stories concerned with the resistance.

2080 GUNNERS WITHOUT INSIGNIA. Hanoi: Foreign Languages Publishing
House, 1966.

Short stories by Xuan Vu, Bui Hien, and others concerning the
war years.

2081 Mai Huu, et al. THE BEACON BANNER: SHORT STORIES ABOUT
THE WAR OF RESISTANCE IN VIETNAM. Hanoi: Foreign Languages
Publishing House, 1964.

2082 THE MOUNTAIN TRAIL: STORIES. Hanoi: Viet Nam Women's Union,
1970.

274

Seven short stories about women heroes in the war.

2083   P.E.N. Vietnam Center. POEMS AND SHORT STORIES. Saigon: Tin Sach, [1966].

Good representative selection of modern material.

2084   RETURN TO DIEN BIEN PHU AND OTHER STORIES. Hanoi: Foreign Languages Publishing House, 1961.

War stories, the title story referring to the decisive defeat of the French at Dien Bien Phu.

2085   Xuan Thieu, et al. THE WHITE BUFFALO: SHORT STORIES. Hanoi: Foreign Languages Publishing House, 1962.

A generous selection of modern stories.

2. History and Criticism

2086   Lan Bang Ba. "Some Remarks on Contemporary Vietnamese Poetry." VIETNAM BULLETIN, 13 (1971), 2-13.

Brief sketch which includes some translation.

2087   Nguyên Cung Giu. "Contemporary Vietnamese Writing." BOOKS A-BROAD, 29 (1955), 19-25.

A brief but well-balanced account.

2088   Nguyên Ngoc Bich. "War Poems from the Vietnamese." HUDSON REVIEW, 20 (1967), 361-68.

Discussion of the treatment of war. Includes some translations and reference to pre-modern poetry.

2089   Thê Phong. A BRIEF GLIMPSE AT THE VIETNAMESE LITERARY SCENE 1900-1956. Trans. Dam Xun Cam. Saigon: Dai Nam Van Hien Book Co., [1974].

Brief sketch. Useful for the early modern scene.

2090   Thong Pham-Huy. "Vietnamese Literature since 1939." ASIAN HORI-ZONS, 1 (1948), 57-74.

2091   Weiss, Peter. NOTES ON THE CULTURAL LIFE OF THE DEMOCRATIC REPUBLIC OF VIETNAM. New York: Dell Publishing Co., [1970].

Impressions by a European journalist of Vietnamese literature during the war. Includes some material from the South. Translated from the German.

3. Authors and Works

AHN-DỨC

2092   [Friend, Robert C., trans.] HON DAT. NOVEL. Hanoi: Foreign Languages Publishing House, 1969.

A prize-winning Socialist novel.

BUC-DUC-AI

2093   THE YOUNG WOMAN OF SAO BEACH. Hanoi: Foreign Languages Publishing House, 1962.

HỒ CHÍ MINH [NGUYỄN-TAT-THANH] (1890-1969)

2094   Palmer, Aileen, trans. PRISON DIARY. Hanoi: Foreign Languages Publishing House, 1967.

Poems and aphorisms by the late revolutionary leader of North Vietnam.

NAM CAO [TRAN-HUU-TRI] (1917-51)

2095   CHI PHEO AND OTHER STORIES. Hanoi: Foreign Languages Publishing House, 1961.

The author wrote many stories and novels and was active against the French government in the 1930s and 1940s.

NGÔ-TẤT-TỐ (1894-1954)

2096   Pham Nhu Oanh, trans. WHEN THE LIGHT IS OUT, A NOVEL. Hanoi: Foreign Languages Publishing House, 1960.

A documentary novel of the harsh life of villages under French rule.

NGUYEN-CONG-HOAN (1903-)

2097   CANTON CHIEF BA LOSES HIS SLIPPERS, SELECTED STORIES. Hanoi: Foreign Languages Publishing House, 1960.

2098   IMPASSE. Hanoi: Foreign Languages Publishing House, 1963.

First published in 1938. A novel of upper-class life under the French occupation.

NGUYÊN-NGOC

2099   THE VILLAGE THAT WOULD NOT DIE, A STORY OF VIETNAM'S
       RESISTANCE WAR. 2d ed. Hanoi: Foreign Languages Publishing
       House, 1961.

       A prize-winning novel of the war against the French, 1946-54.

NHAT LINH [NGUYÊN TUONG TAM] (1900-1963)

2100   O'Harrow, Stephen. "Some Background Notes on Nhat Linh (Nguyen
       Tuong Tam), 1906-1963." FRANCE ASIE, 22 (1968), 205-20.

       On a right-wing writer of the 1930s who represents an earlier
       twentieth-century tradition in fiction.

TÔ HÛU [TO HOAI] (1920-)

2101   Dang Thi Binh, trans. DIARY OF A CRICKET. Hanoi: Foreign Lan-
       guages Publishing House, 1963.

       A leading Communist writer whose subjects are social realism
       and the minority peoples of Vietnam.

2102   Palmer, Aileen, trans. POEMS. Hanoi: Foreign Languages Publishing
       House, 1959.

CENTRAL ASIA

Chapter 13
MONGOLIA

A. BIBLIOGRAPHY

2104 Sanders, Alan J.J. THE PEOPLE'S REPUBLIC OF MONGOLIA: A
GENERAL REFERENCE GUIDE. New York: Oxford Univ. Press, 1968.

A useful general guide. Literature and the arts, pp. 68-82.

B. REFERENCE

2105 Barthold, V.V. TURKISTAN DOWN TO THE MONGOL INVASION.
Trans. H.A.R. Gibb. 2d rev. ed. London: Luzac and Co., 1958.

By an authority on the Mongols of Central Asia. A general
historical work.

2106 Bawden, Charles R. THE MODERN HISTORY OF MONGOLIA. London: Weidenfeld and Nicholson, 1968.

An extensive history of the modern period. Illustrated.

2107 Bretschneider, E. MEDIAEVAL RESEARCHES FROM EASTERN ASIATIC
SOURCES. 2 vols. London: Kegan Paul, 1910.

Translations of Chinese sources for the history of Mongolia,
with notes.

2108 Howarth, Henry H. HISTORY OF THE MONGOLS FROM THE NINTH
TO THE NINETEENTH CENTURY. 5 vols. London: Longmans, Green,
1876-1927.

In need of some revision, but the standard reference work on
the Mongols.

2109 Poppe, Nicholas. MONGOLIAN LANGUAGE HANDBOOK. Washington, D.C.: Center for Applied Linguistics, 1970.

A very complete study of the nature of the language.

2110　Prawdin, Michael. THE MONGOL EMPIRE, ITS RISE AND LEGACY. Trans. Eden and Cedar Paul. London: Allen and Unwin, 1940.

　　　A very readable, reliable general account.

C. LITERARY HISTORY AND CRITICISM

2111　Bawden, C[harles] R. "Mongolian Literature." In GUIDE TO THE EASTERN LITERATURES, pp. 343-57. See entry no. 57.

　　　A good brief account, with a section on individual writers.

2112　_____. "Some Recent Work in Mongolian Studies." BULLETIN OF THE SCHOOL OF ORIENTAL AND AFRICAN STUDIES, 23 (1960), 530-43.

　　　Contains references to literary material, especially poetry and the chronicles.

2113　Bira, Sh. MONGOLIAN HISTORICAL LITERATURE OF THE XVII-XIX CENTURIES WRITTEN IN TIBETAN. Ed. T. Damdinsuren. Bloomington, Ind.: Mongolia Society and Tibetan Society, 1970.

　　　A brief account of some important sources for Mongol history.

2114　Bowden-Smith, A.G. "A Mongol Mystery Play." JOURNAL OF THE ROYAL CENTRAL ASIAN SOCIETY, 37 (1950), 293-97.

　　　Description of a temple festival play, performed annually.

2115　Damdinsüren, Tsendiin. "Ancient Mongolian Literature." INDO-ASIAN CULTURE, 8 (1959), 179-85.

　　　An excellent if brief survey of the earliest period.

2116　Kr[ueger], J[ohn] R. "Mongolian Literature." ENCYCLOPEDIA BRITANNICA. 1974 ed., pp. 1123-24.

　　　Brief account of the literature in the context of Central Asian arts.

2117　Montgomery, David G. "Mongolian Heroic Literature." MONGOLIA SOCIETY BULLETIN, 9 (1970), 30-36.

　　　General discussion of the nature of the epic in Central Asia down to recent times. Some analysis of structure.

2118　Žamcarano, C.Ž., ed. THE MONGOL CHRONICLES OF THE 17TH CENTURY. Trans. Rudolf Lowenthal. Wiesbaden: Harrassowitz, 1955.

　　　Description and translations of five major historical chronicles. First published in 1936.

D. ANTHOLOGIES AND MISCELLANEOUS TRANSLATIONS

2119   Bawden, C[harles] R. "Calling the Soul: a Mongolian Litany."
BULLETIN OF THE SCHOOL OF ORIENTAL AND AFRICAN STUDIES,
25 (1962), 81-103.

2120   _____. "Mongol Notes." CENTRAL ASIATIC JOURNAL, 8 (1963), 2
281-303.

2121   _____. "Mongol Notes: II. Some 'Shamanist' Hunting Rituals from
Mongolia." CENTRAL ASIATIC JOURNAL, 12 (1968), 101-34.

     Bawden's first three articles contain translations and full
analyses of verse rituals.

2122   _____, trans. TALES OF KING VIKRAMĀDITYA AND THE THIRTY-
TWO WOODEN MEN. 2 vols. New Delhi: International Academy
of Indian Culture, 1960-62.

     Translations of Mongol folk tales.

2123   Cleaves, Francis Woodman. "The Boy and his Elephant." HARVARD
JOURNAL OF ASIATIC STUDIES, 35 (1975), 14-59.

     Translation and study of a very obscure Mongolian inscription
found near Peking. Highly technical.

2124   Lohia, Sushana. THE MONGOL TALES OF THE 32 WOODEN MEN.
Wiesbaden: Harrassowitz, 1968.

     Another translation and study of the folk cycle noted in entry
no. 2122.

2125   MONGOLIAN FOLKTALES, STORIES, AND PROVERBS IN ENGLISH
TRANSLATION. Bloomington, Ind.: Mongolia Society, 1967.

     A small collection of typical folk tales.

E. EARLIER AUTHORS AND WORKS

Alexander Romance

2126   Cleaves, Francis Woodman, trans. "An Early Mongolian Version of the
Alexander Romance, Translated and Annotated." HARVARD JOURNAL
OF ASIATIC STUDIES, 22 (1959), 1-99.

     A Mongolian recension of the famous medieval romance of
Alexander the Great. A scholarly translation of a fragmentary
and difficult text, accompanied by plates.

Mongolia

Altan Tobči (seventeenth century)

2127   Bawden, Charles, trans. THE MONGOL CHRONICLE ALTAN TOBČI.
       TEXT, TRANSLATION AND CRITICAL NOTES. Wiesbaden: Harrasso-
       witz, 1955.

       A major historical chronicle recording events to 1604.

Arthasiddhi Avadana

2128   Kreuger, John R., trans. "The ARTHASIDDHI AVADĀNA TALE in
       Oirat-Mongolian, Provisionally Translated." MONGOLIA SOCIETY
       BULLETIN, 6 (1967), 29-33.

       Translation of an anonymous Buddhist poem entitled "Prince
       Attained-Merit of Middle-Earth."

Injannasi (1837-92)

2129   Hangin, John Gombojab. KÖKE SUDUR (THE BLUE CHRONICLE), A
       STUDY OF THE FIRST MONGOLIAN HISTORICAL NOVEL, BY
       INJANNASI. Wiesbaden: Harrassowitz, 1973.

       A full-length, specialized study of a novel of the Mongol
       Empire in the days of Genghis Khan.

2130   _____. "The Tümed Manuscript of Injannasi's KÖKE SUDUR."
       CENTRAL ASIATIC JOURNAL, 15 (1971), 192-201.

Jātakas

2131   Kreuger, John R., trans. "Manuhari Jātaka-Tale." In K'UEI HSING,
       pp. 137-66. See entry no. 32.

       Translation of an Oirat-Mongolian version of the famous col-
       lection of tales of the Buddha.

Kamālashrī-Rashīd al-Dīn

2132   Jahn, Karl. "Kamālashrī-Rashīd al-Dīn's 'Life and Teaching of the
       Buddha.'" CENTRAL ASIATIC JOURNAL, 2 (1956), 81-128.

       A study of a work which is an important source for Buddhism
       in Mongolia.

Lalitavistara

2133   Poppe, Nicholas, trans. THE TWELVE DEEDS OF THE BUDDHA: A

MONGOLIAN VERSION OF THE LALITAVISTARA MONGOLIAN TEXT. Seattle: Univ. of Washington Press, 1968.

Monggol-Un Niuca Tobca'an (Secret History of the Mongols) (thirteenth century)

TRANSLATIONS

2134 Rachewiltz, Igor de, trans. "THE SECRET HISTORY OF THE MON-GOLS." MONGOLIA SOCIETY BULLETIN, 9 (1970), 55-71.

> A translation of part of chapter 1 of the Mongolian version of this important history.

2135 Waley, Arthur, trans. THE SECRET HISTORY OF THE MONGOLS, AND OTHER PIECES. New York: Barnes and Noble, [1964].

> A translation (pp. 217-91) of that part of the HISTORY based on story tellers' tales from the mid-thirteenth century Chinese version.

STUDIES

2136 Ledyard, Gari. "The Mongol Campaign in Korea and the Dating of the SECRET HISTORY OF THE MONGOLS." CENTRAL ASIATIC JOURNAL, 9 (1964), 1-22.

> A highly technical study which establishes the date as after the mid-thirteenth century.

2137 Pao, Kuo-Yi. STUDIES ON "THE SECRET HISTORY OF THE MON-GOLS." Bloomington: Indiana Univ. Press, 1965.

> An analysis of chapter 9 with a translation.

2138 Rachewiltz, Igor de. "SECRET HISTORY OF THE MONGOLS." PAPERS ON FAR EASTERN HISTORY, 4 (1971), 115-63.

> Detailed general study of this important early work.

Rasipungsuy (early eighteenth century)

2139 Cleaves, Francis Woodman, trans. "The Colophon to the BOLOR ERIKE, Translated and Annotated." HARVARD JOURNAL OF ASIATIC STUDIES, 28 (1968), 5-37.

> Text, translation, notes, and plates. Highly technical.

Sa Skya Pandita (1185-1251)

2140   Bossom, James E., trans. A TREASURY OF APHORISTIC JEWELS:
THE "SUBHASITARATRANIDHI" OF SA SKYA PANDITA, IN TIBETAN
AND MONGOLIAN. Bloomington: Indiana Univ. Press, [1976].

Some 457 quatrains on religious subjects--texts and translations.

Ssanang Ssetsen, Chungtaidschi (Segang Secen or Sechen) (fl. 1662)

2141   Kreuger, John R., trans. THE BEJEWELLED SUMMARY OF THE
ORIGINS OF KHANS (QAD-UN ŬN-DŬSŬN-Ŭ ERDENI-YIN TOBČI).
A HISTORY OF THE EASTERN MONGOLS TO 1661 BY SAGANG
SECHEN, PRINCE OF THE ORDOS MONGOLS. 2d ed. Blooming-
ton, Ind.: Mongolia Society, 1967.

Translation of part 1, from the beginnings to the death of
Genghis Khan, of this important chronicle.

2142   _____. POETICAL PASSAGES IN THE "ERDENI-YIN-TOBČI." The
Hague: Mouton, 1961.

Valuable material on the nature of Mongolian poetry.

Vajracchedika Prajnaparamita (Diamond Sutra)

2143   Poppe, Nicholas, trans. THE DIAMOND SUTRA. THE MONGOLIAN
VERSION OF THE VAJRACCHEDIKĀ PRAJÑĀPARAMITĀ. Wiesbaden:
Harrassowitz, 1971.

Translation, text, and notes of the Mongolian version of the
famous Sanskrit Buddhist work.

F. MODERN LITERATURE

1. History and Criticism

2144   Aikman, David B.T. "Mongolian Poetry since the Revolution." MON-
GOLIA SOCIETY BULLETIN, 5 (1966), 11-21.

Valuable article on modern trends with some translated extracts.

2145   Bischoff, F.A. "In the Gobi with the Songsters." MONGOLIA
SOCIETY BULLETIN, 8 (1969), 63-66.

Notes on performances and songs done by a modern Mongolian
theatrical troupe in the Gobi Desert area.

2146   Gerasimovich, Liudmila K. HISTORY OF MODERN MONGOLIAN
       LITERATURE, 1921-1964. Bloomington, Ind.: Mongolia Society, 1970.

       Thorough, scholarly study of the considerable achievement of
       modern Mongolian writers and the press.

2147   Lusanvandan, S. "New Tasks of Language and Literature Studies."
       MONGOLIA SOCIETY NEWSLETTER, 4 (1965), 49-51.

       Translation of an article by the Secretary of Language and
       Literature of the Mongolian Academy on projected projects.

2. Authors and Works

DAMDINSÜREN, TSENDIIN (1908-)

2148   Luvsanvandan, S. "In Honor of Tsendiin Damdinsüren's Sixtieth Anni-
       versary." MONGOLIA SOCIETY BULLETIN, 8 (1969), 6-18.

2149   Raff, Thomas, trans. "How Soli was Changed for Another." MON-
       GOLIAN STUDIES, 1 (1974), 103-14.

       Translation of a fantasy by a modern writer (ca. 1944).

ERDENE, SENGIIN (1929-)

2150   Attangerel, D., trans. "The Dust of the Herds." MONGOLIAN
       STUDIES, 2 (1975), 157-63.

       Translation of a short story with a rural scene.

NATSAGDORJ, DASHDORJIIN (1906-37)

2151   Hangin, John Gombojab, trans. "Dashdorjiin Natsagdorj (1906-1937)."
       MONGOLIAN SOCIETY BULLETIN, 5 (1967), 15-22.

       A translation of two poems by a major poet, much persecuted
       by the Soviets.

Chapter 14
TIBET

A. BIBLIOGRAPHY

2152 Chaudhuri, Sibadas, comp. BIBLIOGRAPHY OF TIBETAN STUDIES. [Calcutta?]: Asiatic Society, 1971.

> Some two thousand items, mostly in European languages. Subject index.

2153 Hsu Ginn-Tze, comp. A BIBLIOGRAPHY OF THE TIBETAN HIGH-LAND AND ITS ADJACENT DISTRICTS. Peking: Science Press, 1958.

> A useful work: languages, pp. 110-14; literature, fine arts, and religion, pp. 115-26.

B. REFERENCE

2154 Haarth, Erik. THE YAR-LUNG DYNASTY. A STUDY WITH PARTIC-ULAR REGARD TO THE CONTRIBUTION BY MYTHS AND LEGEND TO THE HISTORY OF ANCIENT TIBET AND THE ORIGIN AND NATURE OF ITS KINGS. Copenhagen: C.E.C. Gad's Forlag, 1969.

> Lengthy scholarly study of the relation between early myth and history.

2155 Li Tieh-Tseng. THE HISTORICAL STATUS OF TIBET. New York: King's Crown Press, 1956.

> Reliable history of Tibet and its relation to China from early times.

2156 Richardson, Hugh Edward. TIBET AND ITS HISTORY. London: Oxford Univ. Press, 1962. As A SHORT HISTORY OF TIBET. New York: E.P. Dutton, 1967.

> A reliable brief history.

2157   Shen Tsung-Lien. TIBET AND THE TIBETANS. Stanford: Stanford
        Univ. Press, [1953].

        Contains much useful cultural material--social life, legends,
        religion,--on pre-Communist Tibet.

2158   Snellgrove, David, and Hugh Richardson. A CULTURAL HISTORY OF
        TIBET. London: Weidenfeld and Nicholson, 1968.

2159   Stein, R.A. TIBETAN CIVILIZATION. Trans. J.E. Stapleton Driver.
        London: Faber and Faber, 1972.

        This and the preceding entry are two excellent cultural his-
        tories. The Stein volume contains a chapter on arts and
        letters and illustrations.

C. LITERARY HISTORY AND CRITICISM

2160   Kolmas, Josef. "Tibetan Literature in China." ARCHIV ORIENTÁLNÍ,
        30 (1962), 638-44.

        An account of studies on and translations of Tibetan literature
        in modern China.

2161   Kun Chang. "On Tibetan Poetry." CENTRAL ASIATIC JOURNAL, 2
        (1956), 129-39.

        Useful summary of the poetic types with references to earlier
        authors. Translated excerpts.

2162   Lokesh, Chandra, ed. MATERIALS FOR A HISTORY OF TIBETAN
        LITERATURE. 3 vols. New Delhi: International Academy of Indian
        Culture, 1963.

        Religious texts with translations and annotations. The lengthy
        introduction is useful but technical.

2163   S[nellgrove], D.L. "Tibetan Literature." CASSELL'S ENCYCLOPAEDIA
        OF WORLD LITERATURE. 3 vols. London: Cassell, 1973, I, pp. 555-
        56.

2164   _____. "Tibetan Literature." ENCYCLOPAEDIA BRITANNICA.
        Chicago: Encyclopedia Brittanica, 1974. III, p. 1123.

2165   _____. "Tibetan Literature." In GUIDE TO THE EASTERN LITERA-
        TURES, pp. 323-39. See entry no. 57.

        Entry nos. 5059-61 provide three brief sketches of the litera-
        ture, each with a different enphasis, by an authority.

2166   Tucci, Giuseppe. TIBETAN PAINTED SCROLLS. 2 vols. Rome: Libreria dello Stato, 1949.

An elaborately produced work on the religious literature. Volume I, pp. 94-170, contains a historical sketch.

2167   Vostrikov, A[ndrei] I. TIBETAN HISTORICAL LITERATURE. Trans. Harish Chandra Gupta. [Calcutta]: Indian Studies Past and Present, [1970].

A thorough, often technical, scholarly description of the various historical works.

D. ANTHOLOGIES AND MISCELLANEOUS TRANSLATIONS

2168   Bryner, Edna, trans. THIRTEEN TIBETAN TANKAS. Boulder: Univ. of Colorado Press, 1956.

Poems on the Buddha's twenty-nine former incarnations.

2169   Chang Ch'êng-Chi, ed. and trans. TEACHINGS OF TIBETAN YOGA. New Hyde, N.Y.: University Books, [1963].

A brief, specialized collection.

2170   Dowman, Keith, trans. THE LEGEND OF THE GREAT STUPA AND THE LIFE STORY OF THE LOTUS BORN GURU. Berkeley: Nyingma Mediatation Center, 1973.

Translations of a text about the construction of the great stupa at the monastery of Samyeling and a biography of Guru Padma Sambhava, founder of the Nyingma sect.

2171   Duncan, Marion H., trans. HARVEST FESTIVAL DRAMAS OF TIBET. Hong Kong: Orient Publishing Co., [1955].

Translations of five historical and religious plays.

2172   _____. LOVE SONGS AND PROVERBS OF TIBET. London: Mitre Press, [1961].

A large collection of poems and 672 proverbs, with a brief introduction.

2173   Edgar, J.H. "Verse of the Tibetan Border." JOURNAL OF THE WEST CHINA BORDER RESEARCH SOCIETY, 8 (1936), 9-13.

Translations of four songs.

2174 Evans-Wentz, Walter Y., ed. TIBETAN YOGA AND SECRET DOC-
TRINES, OR SEVEN BOOKS OF WISDOM OF THE GREAT PATH.
2d ed. Oxford Univ. Press, 1967.

> Translations of works on yoga with introductions and annota-
> tions.

2175 Francke, A.H. "The Ancient Historical Songs from Western Tibet."
INDIAN ANTIQUARY, 38 (1909), 57-68.

> Texts and translations of ten songs.

2176 _____. "Ladakhi Songs." INDIAN ANTIQUARY, 31 (1902), 87-106,
304-11.

> Translations of thirty songs.

2177 Manen, Johan van, trans. MINOR TIBETAN TEXTS. Calcutta:
Asiatic Society, 1919.

> Translations of fourteen songs with introductions and notes.

2178 _____. "Three Tibetan Repartee Songs." JOURNAL OF THE ASIATIC
SOCIETY OF BENGAL, 17 (1921), 287-318.

2179 Nomun, Sang. "Two Tibetan Folk Tales." TIBETAN SOCIETY BULLE-
TIN, 6 (1973), 15-19.

2180 Thomas, F[rederick] W., comp. and trans. TIBETAN LITERARY TEXTS
AND DOCUMENTS CONCERNING CHINESE TURKESTAN. London:
Royal Asiatic Society, 1935.

> Translations of various religious texts of very early date
> (655 ff.) unearthed in Chinese Turkestan. With an index
> by E. Conye.

2181 THREE TIBETAN MYSTERIES: TCHRIMEKUNDAN, NANSAL,
DJROAZANMO, AS PERFORMED IN TIBETAN MONASTERIES. TRANS-
LATED FROM THE FRENCH VERSION OF JACQUES BACOT BY H.I.
WOOLF. London: Routledge and Sons, [1924].

> Ritual dramas retranslated from Bacot's TROIS MYSTERES
> TIBETAINES (Paris, 1921).

2182 Tucci, Giuseppe, trans. TIBETAN FOLKSONGS FROM THE DISTRICT
OF GYANTSE. Ascona: Artibus Asiae, 1949.

> Fifty-four short songs and one long marriage song with texts
> and English translations.

E. EARLIER AUTHORS AND WORKS

Bardo Thödol (Book of the Dead)

2183   Evans-Wentz, W[alter] Y., ed. THE TIBETAN BOOK OF THE DEAD,
       OR THE AFTER-DEATH EXPERIENCES ON THE BARDO PLANE, AC-
       CORDING TO LAMA KAZI DAWA-SAMDUP'S ENGLISH RENDERING.
       3d ed. Oxford: Oxford Univ. Press, 1957.

> An important Tibetan sacred book. This edition contains a
> psychological commentary by C.G. Jung.

Blue Annals

2184   Roerich, George N., trans. THE BLUE ANNALS. 3 vols. Calcutta:
       Royal Asiatic Society of Bengal, 1949-53, rpt. 1976, 3 vols. in 1.

> A religious chronicle and a major document for Mahayana
> Buddhism and the development of sects in Tibet.

Nāropa (twelfth century)

2185   Guenther, Herbert V., trans. THE LIFE AND TEACHING OF
       NĀROPA, TRANSLATED FROM THE ORIGINAL TIBETAN WITH COM-
       MENTARY. Oxford: Clarendon Press, 1963, rpt. 1971.

> The teachings of a great sage with a commentary based on
> the oral transmission of the text.

Sangay, Phadampa

2186   Evans-Wentz, W[alter] Y., ed. THE TIBETAN BOOK OF THE GREAT
       LIBERATION, OR THE METHOD OF REALIZING NIRVANA THROUGH
       KNOWING THE MIND. Oxford: Oxford Univ. Press, 1968.

> Various texts on Tantric and Buddhist yoga by a guru.

Chapter 15
TURKIC AND OTHER LITERATURES

(This section contains material on the Turkic literature of Central Asia, but not on the literature of Ottoman Turkey or the modern Republic of Turkey).

A. BIBLIOGRAPHY

2187   Hofman, H.F., comp. TURKISH LITERATURE: A BIO-BIBLIOGRAPHICAL SURVEY. SECTION III. MOSLEM CENTRAL ASIAN TURKISH LITERA-TURE. Utrecht: Library of the Univ. of Utrecht and Royal Asiatic Society of Great Britain, 1969.

2188   Loewenthal, Rudolf, comp. THE TURKIC LANGUAGES AND LITERA-TURES OF CENTRAL ASIA, A BIBLIOGRAPHY. Wiesbaden: Harrasso-witz, [1956]; The Hague: Mouton, [1957].

   Covers the entire area from the Caspian Sea to Siberia. About two thousand titles, very few in English.

B. REFERENCE

2189   Bellenitsky, Aleksandr. CENTRAL ASIA. Trans. from Russian by James Hogarth. Cleveland: World Publishing Co., [1968].

   A good general account of the cultures of the region.

2190   Clauson, Gerald. "The Diffusion of Writing in the Altaic World." In ASPECTS OF ALTAIC CIVILIZATION. Ed. Denis Sinor. Blooming-ton: Indiana Univ. Press, 1963, pp. 139-44.

   A useful brief sketch.

2191   Henze, Paul B. "Politics and Alphabets in Inner Asia." JOURNAL OF THE ROYAL CENTRAL ASIAN SOCIETY, 43 (1956), 29-51.

   An interesting study of the relations of language to the politi-cal scene.

Turkic and Other Literature

2192 Jyrkankallio, Paul. A SURVEY OF PRESENT-DAY TURKIC PEOPLES. Trans. John R. Krueger. 2d ed. Washington, D.C.: [Central Asian Collectaneal], 1961.

> Valuable brief survey of the languages and geographical distribution of the peoples.

2193 Kaushik, D. CENTRAL ASIA IN MODERN TIMES, A HISTORY FROM THE 19TH CENTURY. Ed. N. Khalfin. Moscow: Progress Publications, [1970].

> Useful sketch, mostly of the earlier period of Soviet influence.

2194 Krader, Lawrence. PEOPLES OF CENTRAL ASIA. Bloomington: Indiana Univ. Press, 1963.

> A general handbook on what is mostly Soviet Central Asia--people, languages, history, religion, and society.

2195 Menges, Karl H. THE TURKIC LANGUAGES AND PEOPLES: AN INTRODUCTION TO TURKIC STUDIES. Wiesbaden: Harrassowitz, 1968.

> The first fifty pages provide a description of the history and migrations of the people; the remainder is on the classification and structure of the languages.

2196 Rupen, Robert Arthur. MONGOLS OF THE TWENTIETH CENTURY. 2 vols. Bloomington: Indiana Univ. Press, 1964.

> A major reference work on the area. Part I is a survey of the history, part II a bibliography of some three thousand works.

C. LITERARY HISTORY AND CRITICISM

2197 Durrant, Stephen W. "Repetition in the Manchu Origin Myth as a Feature of Oral Narrative." CENTRAL ASIATIC JOURNAL, 22 (1978), 32-43.

> Compiled in 1782. A mythological account of the origin of the Manchu state which is close to the folk tradition.

2198 Eckmann, János. "The Mamluk-Kipchak Literature." CENTRAL ASIATIC JOURNAL, 8 (1963), 304-19.

> On the Mamluks who founded the Ayyudbid dynasty. A general survey of the literature with some material on poetry.

2199 Emmerick, R.E. "Khotanese Metrics." ASIA MAJOR, 14 (1968), 1-20.

> Highly technical scholarly study.

2200 Mansuroğlu, Mecdut. "Turkish Literature through the Ages (with Bibliography)." CENTRAL ASIATIC JOURNAL, 9 (1964), 81-112.

> Excellent outline of the Turkic literatures of Central and West Asia with bibliographical notes by periods.

2201 Mollendorf, P.G. von. "Essay on Manchu Literature." JOURNAL OF THE CHINA BRANCH OF THE ROYAL ASIATIC SOCIETY, 24 (1890), 1-45.

> Pioneering study of the material, but useful only to the specialist.

2202 Rofé, Husein. "Central Asian Turkish Literature." EASTERN HORIZON 7, No. 5 (September-October 1968), 60-64.

> Brief historical sketch.

2203 Sinor, Denis. "Some Remarks on Manchu Poetry." In STUDIES IN SOUTH EAST AND CENTRAL ASIA. Ed. Denis Sinor. New Delhi: International Academy of Indian Culture, 1968, pp. 105-14.

D. EARLIER AUTHORS AND WORKS

Ahmadi (early fifteenth century)

2204 Bodrogligeti, A. "Ahmad's BARAQ-NAMA: A Central Asia Islamic Work in Eastern Middle Turkic." CENTRAL ASIATIC JOURNAL, 18 (1974). 83-128.

> A popular Sufi poetical work, with notes, text, translation, and and facsimiles.

2205 Eckmann, János. "A Contest in Verse between Stringed Instruments from the Chagatay Literature of the 15th Century." In ASPECTS OF ALTAIC CIVILIZATION. Ed. Denis Sinor. Bloomington: Indiana Univ. Press, 1963, pp. 119-21.

> An amusing poem about a contest between a tanbura (lute) and other stringed instruments. Summary and commentary.

Jātakas

2206 Dresden, Mark J., trans. "The JĀTAKASTAVA or 'Praise of the Buddha's Former Births.'" TRANSACTIONS OF THE AMERICAN PHILOLOGICAL SOCIETY, 45 (1955), 395-508.

> An Indo-Scythian (Khotanese) version of the famous Indian stories. Text, translation, and notes.

Turkic and Other Literature

Kālacakra

2207   Hoffman, Helmut H.R. "KĀLACAKRA Studies I: Manichaeism, Christianity and Islam in the KĀLACAKRA TANTRA." CENTRAL ASIATIC JOURNAL, 13 (1969), 52–73.

Köz-Kaman

2208   Hatto, A.T. "Köz-Kaman." CENTRAL ASIATIC JOURNAL, 15 (1971), 81–101, 243–83.

   Study of a Kirghiz oral epic recited in 1862, with a translation.

Navā-ī

2209   Birnbaum, Eleazer. "The Ottoman and Chagatay Literature: An Early 16th Century Manuscript of Nava-i's DIVAN in Ottoman Orthography." CENTRAL ASIATIC JOURNAL, 20 (1976), 157–90.

   The poet Navā-ī was instrumental in creating the new literary Chagatay language, the vehicle for Muslim belles lettres in Central Asia. Historical background and summary of the work. Illustrated.

Rāmāyana

2210   Bailey, H.W. "Rāma." BULLETIN OF THE SCHOOL OF ORIENTAL AND AFRICAN STUDIES, 10 (1940–42), 365–76, 559–98.

   A Khotanese text of the famous Indian epic, with English translation and notes.

Shāhī (fifteenth century)

2211   Eckmann, János. "Shāhī, a hiterto unknown Chagatay Poet of the Fifteenth Century." CENTRAL ASIATIC JOURNAL, 13 (1969), 263–86.

   Literal prose translations of a number of ghazals with romanized text.

Book of Zambasta

2212   Emmerick, R.E., ed. and trans. THE BOOK OF ZAMBASTA, A KHOTANESE POEM ON BUDDHISM. London: Oxford Univ. Press, 1968.

   Parallel text and translation of a religious poem.

E. MODERN LITERATURE

1. History and Criticism

2213   Allworth, Edward. CENTRAL ASIAN PUBLISHING AND THE RISE OF NATIONALISM, AN ESSAY AND A LIST OF PUBLICATIONS IN THE NEW YORK PUBLIC LIBRARY. New York: New York Public Library, 1965.

2214   _____. "The Focus of Literature." In CENTRAL ASIA, A CENTURY OF RUSSIAN RULE. Ed. Edward Allworth. New York: Columbia Univ. Press, 1967, pp. 349-96.

   Allworth's first two essays are a good guide to the literary and publishing situation.

2215   _____. UZBEK LITERARY POLITICS. The Hague: Mouton, 1964.

   Careful study of nationalism and Soviet influence on literature.

2216   Laude-Cirtautas, Ilse. "On the Development of Literary Uzbek in the Last Fifty Years." CENTRAL ASIATIC JOURNAL, 21 (1977), 30-31.

   Mostly on politics and language reform in the new Uzbek (ca. 1920 ff.), as against Chagatay, the older form.

2. Authors and Works

CHOLPAN [ABDUL HAMID SULEYMAN] (1897-1938)

2217   Hayit, Baqmirza. "Two Outstanding Figures in Modern Uzbek Literature: Qadiri and Cholpan." JOURNAL OF THE ROYAL CENTRAL ASIAN SOCIETY, 52 (1965), 49-52.

   An account of a modern dramatist (Cholpan) and a novelist.

MUKHTOR, ASGAD (1920-)

2218   Battersby, Harold R. "Asgad Mukhtor, an Uzbek Writer and his Works." CENTRAL ASIATIC JOURNAL, 15 (1971), 55-74.

   Life and bibliographical sketch of a poet, prose writer, and translator who moved from traditional to working-class themes.

QADIRI (1897-1939)

2219   Hayit, Baqmirza. "Two Oustanding Figures in Modern Uzbek Literature." See entry no. 2217.

Chapter 16
CENTRAL ASIA—PERIODICALS

2220 CENTRAL ASIATIC JOURNAL. The Hague: Mouton, 1955-- .

2221 JOURNAL OF THE ROYAL CENTRAL ASIA SOCIETY. London: Royal Central Asia Society, 1914-- .

> The first two scholarly journals listed here cover all aspects of the various cultures.

2222 MONGOLIAN STUDIES. Bloomington, Ind.: Mongolia Society, 1974-- .

> Scholarly studies mostly devoted to literature and culture.

2223 MONGOLIA SOCIETY BULLETIN. Bloomington, Ind.: Mongolian Society, 1961-63.

> Superseded by MONGOLIAN STUDIES, above.

2224 TIBET SOCIETY BULLETIN. Bloomington, Ind.: Tibet Society, 1969-- .

INDEX

INDEX

The index lists the names of all authors, coauthors, editors, coeditors, and translators, whether of primary or secondary works. Corporate authors (e.g., Japan National Commission for UNESCO) are also listed. When no author or editor is indicated for a secondary work, it is indexed by the title. Asian authors are listed by the names which they are commonly given in literary histories, which are sometimes pseudonyms. Variants of these names are indexed, along with any other names the author may have, with a cross-reference to the main entry. For a discussion of Asian proper names, see the introduction. The titles of all primary works are indexed both in English and transcription, where the latter is useful. The titles of secondary works are not indexed. This index is alphabetized word by word and numbers indicate entry items.

Index

Index

Index

DOCTRINE OF THE MEAN, THE 389-92
Dofu, Shirai 1328
Doi, Kōchi 944, 1060
Dolby, William 263, 289
Dolezalova, Anna 778
Delezelová-Velingerová, Milena 493, 682
Donne, C.W. 1682
Dotson, Lillian Ota 1643
Dowman, Keith 2170
Downer, G.B. 237
DRAGON BEARD DITCH 691
DREAM OF THE RED CHAMBER, THE 549-56
Dresden, Mark J. 2206
Drew, G.W.J. 1916
DRIZZLE, THE 1598
DRUM SINGERS, THE 689
Dubs, Homer H. 443, 445, 525
Dudbridge, Glen 580
Duk Keam 1747
Duke, Michael S. 510
Duncan, Marion H. 2171-72
Dunn, Charles J. 893, 1000
Durrant, Stephen W. 2197
DUST OF THE HERDS, THE 2150
DUTCH IN PERAK, THE 1928
Duus, Louise 1279
Duyvendak, J.J.L. 331, 464
DWELLING OF PLAYFUL GODDESSES, The 353
Dye, Harriet 581

E

EARLY JAPANESE POETS 1037
EARLY MONGOLIAN VERSION OF THE ALEXANDER ROMANCE, AN 2126
EAST GOES WEST 1601
Eber, Irene 332-33
Eberhard, Wolfgang 110
Ebon, Martin 625
Echols, John M. 1664, 1771
Eckmann, János 2198, 2205, 2211
Edgar, J.H. 2173
Edogawa Alempo 1217
Edwards, Evangeline D. 286-87, 319
Egerod, Søren 156, 2014

Egerton, Clement 361
Ehwa Women's Univ., English Student Association 1469
Eichhorn, Werner 111
EIGHTEEN LAMENTS, THE 548
Elrod, Jefferson McRae 1370
Embree, Ainslie 51
Embree, John F. 1643
Emmerick, R.E. 2199, 2212
ENCOURAGEMENT OF LEARNING, AN 995
Endō, Shūsaku 1218-19
Engle, Hua-Ling 725
Engle, Paul 725
Englehart, E.T. 1318
English, Jane 370
Ennin 911-12
ENNIN'S DIARY 991
ENNIN'S TRAVELS IN T'ANG CHINA 992
Ensink, J. 1814
Erdene, Sangiin 2150
ERDENI YIN-TOBČI 2142-43
Erickson, Lois J. 1234-35
Erkes, Edward 472
Ernst, Earle 876, 894, 1105
Eschelbach, Claire John 1280
ESSAY ON LANDSCAPE PAINTING 457
ESSAY ON LITERATURE 500
ESSAYS IN IDLENESS 1112
ESSENCE OF THE NOVEL, THE 1355
ETHICAL AND POLITICAL WRITINGS OF MOTSE, THE 523
Evans-Wentz, Walter Y. 2174, 2183, 2186
EVOLUTION OF VIETNAMES LITERATURE, THE 2049
EX-EMPEROR GO-TOBA'S SECRET TEACHINGS 999
EXISTENCE AND DISCOVERY OF BEAUTY, THE 1237
EXOTIC JAPANESE STORIES 1205

F

Fa Hsien 424-25
FACE AT THE BOTTOM OF THE WORLD 1223
FACE OF ANOTHER, THE 1201

Index

Index

Hwang Sun-Wŏn 1597-98
HYAKU NIN ISSHU 1007-13
Hyech'o 1512
Hyŏn Chin-Gŏn 1599-1600
Hyŏn Ung. See Hyun, Peter
Hyun, Peter 1433, 1580

I

I AM A CAT 1326-27
I CHING 393-400
I CHING (THE BOOK OF
  CHANGES) 393
I CHING OR BOOK OF CHANGES,
  THE 395
I LA GALIGO 1799
I-LI 402
IBARA SAIKAKU'S NIPPON EITAI-
  GURA 1076
Ibuse, Masuji 1225-27
Ichikawa, Sanki 853
Ienaga, Saburo 795
IGNORANT AND FORGOTTEN, THE
  772
Ikeda, Hiroka 941
Ikimoto, Takashi 1338
IKKU JIPPENSHA 1014
Ikkyu Sōjun 1015
Ikuto, Atsumi 1172
Ilyŏn 1528
Im Pang 1474
IMPASSE 2098
IMPERIAL SONGS 1243
IN THE DEPTHS 1594
IN THE VINEYARD 1592
IN THIS EARTH AND IN THAT WIND
  1629
INCONSTANCY OF MADAME
  CHUANG, THE 358
INDEX TO ENGLISH PERIODICAL
  LITERATURE PUBLISHED IN KOREA
  1373
INEM 1848
Ingalls, Jeremy 1303
INHYŎN WANGHU CHŎN 1513
Injannasi 2129-30
INJUSTICE TO TOU O 452
INNER CHAPTERS 370
INNER ICE AGE 4, 1198
INNOCENT, THE 1606
Inoue, Jūkichi 1101

Inoue, Yasushi 1228
Inoura, Yohinobu 902
International P.E.N., Asian Writers
  Translation Bureau 1401-02
International P.E.N., Korean
  Centre 1538, 1553, 1574
INTRIGUES OF THE WARRING
  STATES 351
INTRIGUES: STUDIES OF THE
  CHAN KUO-T'SE 351
Irwin, Richard Gregg 537
Irwin, Vera R. 30
Iryŏn. See Ilyŏn
Isaacs, Harold Robert 643
ISE DAIJINGŪ SANKEIKI 1016
ISE MONOGATARI 1017-18
Ishibashi, Hiro 947
Ishikawa, Takuboku 1231-32
Ishikawa, Tatsuzō 1233
Ishizuka, Ryugaku 1006
Iskander, T. 1896, 1912
Ismail, Yahya 1941-42
Issa Kobayashi 1019-20
ITA SEXUSUARISU 1295
Itakura, Jūnji 1023
Itō, Aiko 1326, 1329
Iwasaki, Yōzan T. 1176, 1361
IZAYOI NIKKI 1239
IZO NO ODORIKO 1239
Izumi Shikubu 944, 1021
IZUMI SHIKUBU DIARY, THE 944,
  1021

J

Jackson, Barry 1113
Jackson, J.A. 534
Jacob, Judith 1755
Jahn, Karl 2132
Jan Yun-Hua 1512
Janeira, Armando Martins 948
Jansen, Marius B. 8
JAPAN: ITS LAND, PEOPLE, AND
  CULTURE 796
Japan National Commission for
  UNESCO 1179, 1330
Japan P.E.N. Club 790, 949
JAPAN THE BEAUTIFUL AND MY-
  SELF 1238
JAPANESE FAMILY STOREHOUSE,
  THE 1007

Index

Index

M

Index

Index

Index

Index

Index